"A gripping account of how the practical intellect of one person and the trail-blazing activities of an organization have been able to achieve something close to a miracle." — **Amartya Sen, Nobel Laureate in Economics**

Freedom
from Want

The Remarkable Success Story of BRAC, the Global Grassroots Organization That's Winning the Fight Against Poverty

Ian Smillie

Praise for *Freedom From Want*

"This is the inspiring story of a person and an organization that have expanded the boundaries of the possible. When BRAC began, no one could have dreamt of what it would become. Now we can appreciate as never before the astonishing scale, diversity, and spread of its activities and achievements in Bangladesh and other countries. This book has been crying out to be written. It is a powerful counterblast to cynics and pessimists. It challenges all of us working in development to raise our sights, aim high, and aspire to do the undoable."

—Robert Chambers,
Institute of Development Studies, Sussex,
Author of *Rural Development: Putting the Last First*

"BRAC is the most astounding social enterprise in the world. This story combines the raw excitement of how a huge business can spring from one man's acumen with the emotive charge that comes when poverty and oppression are routed. Business can be exhilarating, and reading why can be a pleasure."

—Paul Collier,
Author of *The Bottom Billion*

"This is a great international story about what I consider the world's most successful and unusual nongovernmental development organization, advancing the frontiers of health, education, and microfinance, with a particular focus on women. It truly is an astounding record."

—Allan Rosenfield, MD,
Dean Emeritus, Mailman School of Public Health, Columbia University

"We support BRAC because they invest in the 'girl effect' and are one of the world's most effective champions for poor women and their families. We've seen BRAC in action in Bangladesh and can attest that Smillie's book captures the magic of the organization and the transformation that happens person by person."

—Jennifer and Peter Buffett,
NoVo Foundation

"BRAC's entrepreneurial approach to creating decent work for poor people is sorely needed in the world today. BRAC has created 8.5 million opportunities for self-employment in Bangladesh and is now helping to create better livelihoods elsewhere in Asia and in Africa. Smillie reveals BRAC's success in organizing the most vulnerable, particularly poor women, for their own self-empowerment, rights, protection, work, and collective voice."

—Juan Somavia,
Director-General, International Labor Organization

"Smillie has managed to make one of the world's largest and most diverse NGOs come to life for his readers. So rarely does one find a tale of greatness that is so honest about failures and the exacting demands of a robust learning process. Ian Smillie's insights and wry humor make this a wonderful read that will inspire even the most doubtful."

—Jim Yong Kim,
Co-founder, Partners in Health

"If BRAC was a business, it would be the darling of Wall Street, but BRAC instead stands as one of the world's most important anti-poverty organizations. Day after day, BRAC shows how to be innovative, effective, and fast-growing in tough environments. *Freedom from Want* cuts through complexities to share BRAC's remarkable story with clarity and style."

—Jonathan Morduch,
Co-author of *Portfolios of the Poor: How the World's Poor Live on $2 a Day*

"Through an inclusive approach, engaging poor people and communities, BRAC is demonstrating how to help millions climb out of poverty and build better lives."

—Peggy Dulaney,
Founder and Chair, The Synergos Institute

"The story of BRAC is one of creativity and innovation in the face of immense political, economic, and logistical challenges. Through constant learning and evolution, BRAC has developed some of the most effective ways of reducing poverty that exist today."

—Pierre Omidyar,
Founder and Chairman of eBay, Co-founder of Omidyar Network

"In this beautifully written book, Smillie examines perhaps the most successful program in the world for empowering women and families and truly alleviating poverty in a sustainable way. It should help convince those who still doubt that empowering people is key to successful economic, social and personal development."

—James Wolfensohn,
Founder, Wolfensohn Center for Development, former President, World Bank

FREEDOM FROM WANT

FREEDOM FROM WANT

The Remarkable
Success Story of BRAC,
the Global Grassroots Organization
That's Winning
the Fight Against Poverty

Ian Smillie

Kumarian Press
An Imprint of Stylus Publishing

Freedom From Want

Published in 2009 in the United States of America by Kumarian Press
22883 Quicksilver Drive, Sterling, VA 20166-2012 USA

The text of this book is set in 10/12.5 New Baskerville
Proofread by Publication Services, Inc.

Index by Publication Services, Inc.

Production and design by Publication Services, Inc.

Printed in the United States of America by Thomson-Shore, Inc.
Text printed with vegetable oil-based ink.

∞ The paper used in this publication meets the minimum requirements of the American National Standard for Information Sciences-Permanence of Paper for printed Library Materials, ANSI Z39.48-1984

Cover Image: Jhonuka is twenty-one years old and has participated in several BRAC programs. She lives in the village of Ishwarpur, in Bangladesh's Gazipur District. Forced to leave school for want of funds, she obtained a loan to start a tailoring business, and is using the proceeds to put herself through Open University. She would like to be a teacher or work in a professional organization. She is married, but she still lives at home because her husband's job is located elsewhere. She helps support the family's living expenses, including the school fees of her younger sister. Because of Johonuka, the whole family—including her grandmother, who is resting on the bed behind her—has shifted their attitude about what is possible for girls. Ben Stirton, Getty Images.

Library of Congress Cataloging-in-Publication Data

Smillie, Ian.
    Freedom from want : the remarkable success story of BRAC, the global grassroots organization that's winning the fight against poverty/Ian Smillie.
       p. cm.

Includes bibliographical references and index.
    ISBN 978-1-56549-294-3 (pbk. : alk. paper)—ISBN 978-1-56549-285-1 (cloth : alk. paper)
1. BRAC (Organization) 2. Rural development—Bangladesh.
3. Non-governmental organizations—Bangladesh. I. Title.
    HN690.6.Z9C66453 2009
    361.7'7095491—dc22

                                                                                2008053520

For Morgan and Gavin

This is the farmer sowing his corn,
That kept the cock that crowed in the morn,
That waked the priest all shaven and shorn,
That married the man all tattered and torn,
That kissed the maiden all forlorn,
That milked the cow with the crumpled horn,
That tossed the dog,
That worried the cat,
That killed the rat,
That ate the malt
That lay in the house that Jack built.

—*The House that Jack Built,* popular British nursery rhyme

Table of Contents

Preface

In 1972, shortly after the Liberation War, I was sent by CARE to Bangladesh—"a thumbprint of a country in a vast continent," as Tahmima Anam has so eloquently described it. I was to work on a self-help housing cooperative project. We provided plans, material, and technical assistance to help people build their own low-cost, cyclone-resistant houses. We imported thousands of tons of cement and enough corrugated tin sheets to cover a dozen football fields. The project was massive, but it failed. The houses were constructed, but the cooperatives—which were arguably the most important component, because they aimed to generate funds for longer-term agricultural development and employment—failed miserably. We had a large office in Dhaka (then known as *Dacca*), lots of jeeps and trucks and speedboats, and many international staff with energy and commitment to spare. Our only problem was that we had almost no idea what we were doing.

While I was in Dhaka ordering freighters full of cement from Thailand, a tiny organization was forming on the other side of town and in the rural areas of faraway Sylhet to the north. I recall meeting Fazle Hasan Abed at least once in 1972 or 1973, and I remember people speaking about BRAC with a kind of awe. Their attitude did not flow from anything remarkable BRAC was doing at the time; everything was remarkable in those terrible postwar years. What caught people's attention was the fact that BRAC was a *Bangladeshi* development organization—something that few outsiders had ever heard of, much less conceived.

Over the years I have been privileged to return to Bangladesh many times, often to work with BRAC on a project design, an evaluation, or a report. I have never found the same organization twice. On each visit there is always something new: ten thousand more schools; a dairy; a university; a functional cure for tuberculosis. In 2007 BRAC's microfinance lending topped a billion dollars. A *billion*. The amazing thing about all of BRAC's achievements is that they have been accomplished in one of the most hostile climates in the world—hostile in every sense of the word:

meteorologically, economically, and politically. And now BRAC is taking its lessons to other Asian countries and Africa.

One's first overseas assignment often leaves the most lasting impression, although the first impression is not always the most accurate. My first assignment was not in Bangladesh; it was in Sierra Leone, where I taught high school in the country's wild-west diamond mining region. In the late 1960s, the idea of development seemed obvious: schools, roads, electricity, clinics. Sierra Leone was growing, and I could see firsthand the eagerness with which parents sent their children to school and the seriousness with which children studied. Nobody, least of all me, foresaw that Sierra Leone would descend into political mismanagement, corruption, and eventually a war that would last for a decade, killing tens of thousands of people and displacing more than half the population. Nobody, least of all those of us who taught at Koidu Secondary School, could foresee that the diamonds beneath our feet would fuel this war and others like it in Angola, the Congo, and Liberia.

Over the years my career took a variety of turns, and South Asia occupied a large part of my life. But in 1999 I had an opportunity to reacquaint myself with diamonds when a young Sierra Leonean friend opined that the war in Sierra Leone would not end until the diamonds were brought under control. With colleagues at Partnership Africa Canada, an Ottawa-based NGO, I worked on a campaign to halt the trade in "blood diamonds" and helped to design the Kimberley Process Certification Scheme, which now regulates the world's trade in uncut diamonds. In the course of that work, I served on a United Nations Security Council expert panel that studied the connection between diamonds and weapons, and I again traveled extensively in Africa. In West Africa, responsibility for the diamond wars could be laid primarily at the feet of Liberia's warlord president, Charles Taylor, a man who played a major role in destroying his own country and the lives of millions of people in others. In 2008 I had the honor of serving as the first witness at his war crimes trial in The Hague.

I mention all of this because, remarkably, BRAC has recently started to work in Sierra Leone and Liberia. It will, I'm sure, play an important part in the reconstruction of these two countries that have suffered so much in recent years. Perhaps BRAC can convey there the lessons it has learned in Bangladesh, lessons that remained to be learned in the 1960s and 1970s: that development is not about buildings; it is about what goes on inside the buildings, and inside the heads of the people in the buildings. It is about persistence, hard work, enterprise, optimism, common sense, and values. These things, when correctly applied in the right measure, can bring lasting development to very poor people in very poor countries.

This book owes a debt to the late Catherine Lovell, who wrote about BRAC as it was fifteen years ago. I am especially grateful to Marty Chen, who first wrote about BRAC twenty-five years ago, but whose experience of Bangladesh predates BRAC and whose most recent visit always seems to have been the day before yesterday. Many, many people in BRAC have helped me to understand the organization as it is, and as it was: Aminul Alam, Mushtaque Chowdhury, Salehuddin Ahmed, Safiqul Islam, Shabbir Chowdhury, Sheepa Hafiza, Sukhendra Sarkar, S.N. Kairy, Syeda Sarwat Abed. For their insights and assistance, I am grateful to Susan Davis, Imran Matin, Ron Grzywinski, Mary Houghton, and Steve Rasmussen. Several readers struggled with an early draft of the book: Rumee Ali, Cloudy Beltz, Faruq Choudhury, John Hailey, Syed Hashemi, Mahabub Hossain, Brian Rowe, and David Wright. And valuable advice on specific chapters came from Thomas Dichter, Wendy Quarry, and Rabiya Yasmin.

Unless a quotation is footnoted, you can assume that it comes from an interview I did myself, and there were dozens in Bangladesh, Africa, and elsewhere—too many people to name and thank except by way of including their names, their insights, and their experience in the story itself. I am especially grateful to Tamara and Shameran Abed for telling me things about their father that his own modesty prevents him from discussing. And to Abed—thank you for the opportunity to revisit and think about thirty-five years of truly stunning accomplishment. In a world beset by despair, cynicism, and mediocrity, you, your team, and your achievements stand out as a bright beacon of success and hope.

Ian Smillie
Ottawa, January 2009

The Age of Ambition

This book is about the triumph of optimism, enterprise, and common sense over despair. It is about development without borders. It is about one man and the incredible organization he created to deal with abject poverty in a broken country. But it is about far more than Bangladesh and what this organization has achieved. The borders that BRAC has crossed are not just political borders, although these are real enough. It has breached the borders of development orthodoxy, discovering the fallacies in standard approaches to community development and demonstrating that poverty can be pushed back dramatically if it is tackled directly. It has shown that poor, even completely destitute, women in a conservative Muslim society can learn, earn, and lead. It has shown that enterprise, sound business principles, and the market can be powerful allies in the fight against poverty. BRAC has demonstrated that a charitable organization need not be soft, small, or irrelevant. It has breached the borders of small, turning tiny experimental efforts into huge enterprises that are staffed almost exclusively by tens of thousands of villagers who once had nothing and whose own borders were once defined by ignorance, ill health, isolation, and fear.

The book is about social enterprise, not neat ideas like collecting used eyeglasses for the poor or pilot projects that can never be replicated. It is about inspired innovations in health, education, agriculture, and income generation that contribute to lasting change for tens and hundreds of thousands of people. It is about individuals who see challenge where others see only hopelessness. It is about people who see opportunity where others see peril. It is about an organization that has exposed the deepest roots of human degradation, challenging old nostrums about the limits to change and showing what can be done, not in one or two model villages, but in tens of thousands. Unlike Grameen Bank, BRAC is not well-known outside Bangladesh, but that will change because BRAC is undoubtedly the largest and most variegated social experiment in the developing world. The spread of its work dwarfs any other private,

1

government, or nonprofit enterprise in its impact on development, women, children, and thousands of communities in Bangladesh, other Asian countries, and Africa.

Four million children, 70 percent of them girls, have graduated from BRAC's 68,000 primary and preprimary schools. Millions benefit from the work of BRAC's health centers, its diagnostic laboratories, its health workers, and the 70,000 community health volunteers who have joined the effort. BRAC's microfinance operations loaned more than US$1 billion to poor people in 2008, achieving a repayment rate of more than 95 percent. Microcredit, however, much vaunted as a solution to all development problems, even held by some to be a basic human right, can be little more than a one-way ticket to the kiosk economy if meaningful opportunities for investment and growth are absent. BRAC has demonstrated that opportunities for sustainable productive enterprise do exist in the villages of developing countries, but, where the physical and economic infrastructure is weak or distorted, credit alone is not enough.

BRAC research, accompanied by rigorous testing and evaluation, has discarded many seemingly good ideas, but it has turned others into multimillion-dollar enterprises for the poor. Village chickens, for example, produce only 40 to 60 eggs a year, while high-yielding varieties can produce five times that number. Introducing new breeds and even marketing more eggs, however, is easier said than done. BRAC had to develop a system for poultry vaccination, chick rearing, feed production, and chains of feed sellers and egg collectors, all village women working at jobs financed by microcredit. Today, there are more than 20,000 poultry vaccinators alone, giving a sense of the scale of achievement.

In the dairy sector, BRAC has improved cattle breeds through the establishment of 1,100 artificial insemination centers, education on cattle rearing, loans for the purchase of a million cows, 67 chilling plants, and a central dairy that processes 90,000 liters of milk a day. There are other stories like this in social forestry, silk production, fisheries, and prawn cultivation. BRAC operates a bank, a university, a housing finance corporation, tea companies, and feed mills. BRACNet, its Internet service provider, is installing a new wireless broadband technology, WiMAX, which can transmit wireless data over long distances, revolutionizing education and communication. All of these enterprises contribute directly or indirectly to the aims and objectives of the organization and its financial sustainability. In 1980, BRAC's US$780,000 budget was covered entirely by donors. By 2006, its income, not counting its microfinance operations, was US$495 million, only 20 percent provided by donor organizations.

The numbers only tell part of the story. BRAC's founder, Fazle Hasan Abed, gave up a senior management job at Shell Oil to undertake what he thought would be a temporary effort to supply emergency relief to cyclone and war victims in 1972. He was wrong on the temporary, but not on much else, gradually gathering an impressive team of dedicated men and women who understand, but are not daunted by, the challenges facing the poor. This book examines the nature of the leadership provided by Abed and his colleagues, looking at the place in BRAC of risk, innovation, quality control, and learning. And it examines the context in which they have worked, a country with great needs that was beset by political turbulence, economic uncertainty, and recurrent natural disaster.

BRAC began as an acronym, standing for Bangladesh Rehabilitation Assistance Committee. When its relief work turned to development, the name changed to Bangladesh Rural Advancement Committee. By the 1990s, it was tackling the problems of urban slums as well as rural poverty. It had extended well beyond Bangladesh, and the word "committee" hardly described its management structure. BRAC ceased then to be an acronym, and it became a motto instead, "Building resources across communities."

In part, the BRAC story is told through people: a young Marxist radical who discovered the true meaning of struggle; a kid who liked statistics and wound up as a dean of public health; a young woman who walked out of the black smoke of New York's financial district on September 11 and into a multimillion-dollar operation and a dream job in Bangladesh. There is also a former American president; the chairman of Microsoft; a woman with thirteen sheep and plans for 100; and many more very much like her.

The book also examines what BRAC has achieved in other countries, where the organization is disproving the idea that its success must have been location- or culture-specific. Today, BRAC is the largest NGO in Afghanistan, operating not just in the safe northern areas, but in the embattled provinces of the south. In Tanzania, Uganda, and the Sudan, it is demonstrating that the apparent limits to African development have been artificial, constrained as much by limited ambition as anything else. Fresh vision, determination, and an ability to learn are turning BRAC from a newcomer in Africa into something of a prodigy.

The book challenges the idea that NGOs must be small and that civil society has inherent limits. It turns standard notions about development, business, poverty alleviation, and management on their head. And it confronts the idea that the drivers of development in poor countries must inevitably come from abroad, above, or some other place than the midst of the people who are to be developed. In that sense, the book is not just about BRAC and Bangladesh. It is about the entire development enterprise and what it must learn if it is to end poverty.

In 1941, addressing the United States Congress, Franklin D. Roosevelt spoke of four freedoms. The first two were freedom of speech and freedom of religion; the fourth was freedom from fear:

> The third is freedom from want, which, translated into world terms, means economic understandings which will secure to every nation a healthy peacetime life for its inhabitants—everywhere in the world.

He was wrong when he said that this was "no vision of a distant millennium," but BRAC is demonstrating that what Roosevelt described in 1941 is possible today. "It is a definite basis for a kind of world attainable in our own time and generation."

CHAPTER 1

Sonar Bangla

Rivers often describe the boundaries between nations, but, in Bangladesh, rivers are the country's substance. They are the force that has shaped the land, its history, and its people. On a clear day, it is possible to see Kanchenjunga, the third-highest mountain in the world, from Bangladesh. But, with the exception of the Chittagong Hill Tracts and the rolling hills of Sylhet and Mymensingh, Bangladesh is a flat land, a vast delta through which two of the great rivers of the world flow. The Ganges enters Bangladesh from the west, while the Brahmaputra, here known as the Jamuna, enters from the north, draining the melting snows of the high Himalayas. They meet near Faridpur; take on a new name, Padma; and wash as much as 2.5 million tons of rich sediment across the country side when they are in full spate, reinvigorating the land each year for the next season's crops.

Other rivers join them: the Tista in Rangpur, the Karotoya, the Gumti, and the Karnafuli. The Surma, flowing out of Sylhet, joins with the old Brahmaputra at Bhairabbazar, where it becomes the Meghna. At Chandpur, the Meghna and Padma finally join forces, flowing out into the warm waters of the Bay of Bengal. These rivers have been the country's highway since time immemorial, transporting goods and travelers, traders, explorers, and invaders. The rivers feed the crops and nurture the country's bounteous fishery. They are its lifeline and, at times, its greatest peril. Each summer and autumn, Bangladesh is lashed by cyclones and tornadoes, sometimes accompanied by tidal surges that sweep up from the bay, wiping out everything on newly formed *char* land. Farmers with short memories often settle this area because the land is new and free—and as fertile as it is dangerous.

But there is another Bangladesh, the Bangladesh of late autumn, winter, and spring. This is when the floods recede and the sun shines. This is when evenings are cool and the days are warm and bright. A hundred years ago, the great Bengali poet, Tagore, wrote about his Bengal of gold, perhaps describing rice awaiting the harvest or vast carpets of blooming mustard. Perhaps it was the brilliant fire of a hundred sunsets, unchallenged for weeks on end by a single cloud. He wrote so lyrically about the fragrance of the mango groves in spring, the full-blossomed paddy fields in autumn, and the quilt of shades spread at the feet of the banyan trees and along the rivers that, when they were at last free, Bangladeshis made his poem, "*Amar Sonar Bangla** (My Bengal of Gold)" their national anthem.

In the earliest days of recorded history, the area in which Bangla came to be spoken was a series of principalities with frequently changing borders and allegiances. The oldest archeological remains in Bangladesh date from 700 BC. The Gupta Empire, one of the largest in ancient India, annexed most of the area, bringing it under a single political system some time after 550 AD. But the territory was not fully unified until the advent of a Buddhist Empire that was established in 750. The Pala brought relative peace and stability to the region for almost 400 years. The early Muslim rulers in Delhi overran Bengal in the twelfth century, although it was not until a period of independence under Ilyas Shahi rule between 1342 and 1487 that the country became known as Bangalah. Some time after 1332, the great Moroccan traveler, Ibn Battuta, visited Bengal on his way to China, stopping at Kamrup, Sylhet, and Sonargaon, the Ilyas capital. He wrote:

> This is a country of great extent, and one in which rice is extremely abundant. Indeed, I have seen no region of the earth in which provisions are so plentiful.[1]

During this time, the Bengali language and culture began to coalesce around a new literature fostered by the Sultans of Bangalah.

Other dynasties followed the Ilyas until the Afghans overran the Bengal in 1538. Afghan rule lasted less than 50 years, but, during that brief period, a great highway was constructed, the Grand Trunk Road, linking Peshawar in the west to Delhi and then pushing east to Sonargaon. The Mughals used the highway for their conquest, arriving in 1576 and making their new capital at Dhaka, not far from Sonargaon, on the banks of the Meghna. They raised a grand red sandstone fortress in the style of those at Delhi and Agra, ushering in a new period of peace and stability, one accompanied by a flourishing of the arts. With the death of the Mughal Emperor Aurangzeb, Bengal again broke away from Delhi, and a series of independent Nawabs ruled until the Battle of Plassey in 1757. Power over the region then passed to new invaders, the British East India Company.

---

*Although invariably spelled this way when transliterated, "sonar" is pronounced *shonar*.

Arab traders had reached Bengal long before the Muslim conquest of 1199, and the first Portuguese arrived in the fifteenth century. The Dutch, French, and English all came as well in the sixteenth and seventeenth centuries, establishing factories where they traded what they had for cotton goods and legendary Dhaka muslin. The first Portuguese factory was established at Dhaka in 1616, and its factors built a church in 1677, which still stands in a crowded part of Tejgaon. The Dutch, French, and Greeks were not far behind. Unlikely as it may seem, an Armenian colony was founded in Dhaka in the early part of the eighteenth century. The Armenians pioneered the jute trade. In 1781, they erected the Church of the Holy Resurrection, which stands today in a part of the city still known as Armanitola.

The Mughal collapse and arrival of the British East India Company heralded a general economic decline, made more precipitous by the introduction of British yarn in the 1780s. Until then, growing cotton, spinning, weaving muslins, and creating fine embroideries had accounted for a large part of the economy and huge volumes of exports to Europe. But this was not to last. The British Industrial Revolution, founded on steam and the manufacture of ever-cheaper cloth and supported by a 75 percent duty on imported cotton, ended the Bengal muslin trade in less than three decades. The export of muslin to England, which had been valued at 3 million rupees in 1787, fell to 850,000 rupees in 1807. By 1817, cotton exports had ceased altogether.[2]

In 1824, Reginald Heber, Anglican Bishop of Calcutta, visited Dhaka and found "a wreck of its ancient grandeur."

> Its trade is reduced to the sixtieth part of what it was, and all its splendid buildings, the castle of its founder Shahjehanguire, the noble mosque he built, the palaces of the ancient Nawabs, the factories and churches of the Dutch, French and Portuguese nations, are all sunk into ruin and overgrown with jungle.[3]

It would be another three decades before the economy would begin to revive, revitalized by the growing fortunes of jute, indigo, and tea plantations and then by the end of East India Company rule and its trade monopolies in 1858.

The British unwittingly laid the foundations of modern-day Bangladesh in 1905. The presidency of Bengal, which included Assam as well as East and West Bengal, had become politically unwieldy. Calcutta, the capital of India, drew political and economic attention away from the surrounding districts, and there was unhappiness in the largely Muslim eastern areas about the absence of growth and development. In February 1904, during a visit to Dhaka, the viceroy, Lord Curzon, announced the creation of a new province of Eastern Bengal and Assam with its own lieutenant governor and capital at Dhaka. He said:

> One of the principal results of the adoption of this enlarged scheme is that the interest of the transferred districts should obtain greater attention than they have received in the past, obtain that is to say, the attention they require and deserve.

It happened as he said it would, but it did not last. The partition of Bengal did bring major advantages to East Bengal. The Port of Chittagong was expanded, railway lines were laid, and bridges were built. New schools and colleges were opened, waterways were dredged, and Dhaka obtained a new lease on life, experiencing a building boom with the arrival of the provincial political apparatus. The division of Bengal, however, became a rallying cry for Indian nationalists, who saw it as a divide-and-rule tactic, pitting Hindu against Muslim. In 1911, the capital of India was moved to Delhi. At the same time, the two provinces were reunited, shorn of Orissa, Bihar, and Assam. The reunification, however, sowed even greater seeds of discord between Hindu and Muslim as the largely Muslim East Bengal disappeared from the map and Dhaka was once again reduced to a district town.

For the next 60 years, the treatment of East Bengal as a political, economic, and social backwater, first of British India and then of Pakistan, was flint for the spark that would lead to the creation of Bangladesh in 1970. The nationalist Indian National Congress, founded in 1885, tried to speak for all Indians, but this did not prevent the formation of the All India Muslim League, founded in Dhaka in 1906. The Muslim League was spurred in part by a British decision to make Hindi the official language of the United Provinces in place of Persian. This, in effect, favored a language spoken mainly by Hindus, at the expense of one perceived to be a Muslim tongue. Affront was taken where none may have been intended, and the decision fuelled the fortunes of the All India Muslim League, which, apart from a desire for independence, had little in common with the Indian National Congress.

In 1940, Mohammed Ali Jinnah, president of the All India Muslim League, articulated the sentiments behind what became known at the Pakistan Declaration:

> Hindus and the Muslims belong to two different religions, philosophies, social customs, and literature . . . It is quite clear that Hindus and Muslims derive their inspiration from different sources of history. They have different epics, different

heroes, and different episodes . . . To yoke together two such nations under a single state, one as a numerical minority and the other as a majority, must lead to growing discontent and final destruction of any fabric that may be so built up for the government of such a state.[4]

Ironically, the same would later be said of East and West Pakistan.

British policies, combined with a competitive struggle between the two nationalist movements and the towering egos of their leaders, led inexorably to the partition of India and the creation of Pakistan. The new country was divided into two parts with East Bengal (now East Pakistan) separated from West Pakistan by 1,000 miles of Indian territory. Pakistan's birth was cataclysmic. It began with the division of Punjab, where communal rioting soon spiraled out of control and spread across the entire country. Massacres and atrocities were widespread with convoys and trains full of refugees attacked at random. Soon huge segments of the population were on the move. Hindus were leaving the new Pakistan; Muslims were flowing toward it. Conservative estimates place the number of dead at 500,000. An estimated 5.5 million people moved each way between East and West Punjab, 400,000 Hindus left Sindh, and more than 1 million left East Pakistan for West Bengal.[5]

With independence, East Pakistan found itself once again relegated to the political, economic, and social wilderness. Within months of partition, Urdu, spoken by less than 8 percent of the population of the new country and by almost nobody in the East, was declared the national language, a symbol of the arrogance that was to follow from the West. The West Pakistani elite, dominated by Punjabis, monopolized the civil service, business, industry, and armed forces. In the East, the language issue became a rallying cry of student leaders, Bengali nationalists, and the homegrown political parties that soon eclipsed the All India Muslim League.

The grievances went beyond language, however. Although the small stock of medium- and large-scale manufacturing was more or less evenly distributed between the two wings of the new country at independence, this soon changed. With only 43 percent of the population, West Pakistan soon came to dominate the economy as it did all aspects of government. In the first 23 years of independence, East Pakistan's share of the GNP declined to 41.2 percent while income disparities grew. Between 1949 and 1970, per capita income remained stagnant in East Pakistan while it grew by 55 percent in the West. Revenue spending in the West over this troubled period was more than triple what it was in the East. Despite the poverty in the East, 75 percent of all foreign aid between 1947 and 1970 was spent in the West.[6]

Political instability and a military coup marred Pakistan's first decade.

During the 1960s, as a return to civilian rule became likely, proposals from the East for a federal political system that would allow each wing greater economic autonomy became more strident. These were resisted in West Pakistan, and Bengali nationalists were harassed and jailed. In 1967, the leader of the Bengali nationalist Awami League, Sheikh Mujibur Rahman, was arrested with a large number of his colleagues and charged with conspiracy against the state. The case became a *cause celèbre,* raising Mujib's status and fuelling nationalist sentiments, until it was finally withdrawn in 1968. Before that, Mujib could draw a crowd of thousands. The day after his release from prison, he drew a million people, all cheering his demands for democracy and regional autonomy.

The final straw was perhaps the government's desultory response to one of the greatest natural calamities of the century. On November 12, 1970, a cyclone of unparalleled intensity roared northward out of the Bay of Bengal, pushing a massive wall of water ahead of it. Everything in its path was washed away. A survivor in Chittagong, which missed the worst of it, said:

> Sleep was impossible throughout the night. The frightful wind screamed, shutters banged, glass shattered, branches cracked, and even resilient palm trees snapped like matchsticks.[7]

When it was over, animals, crops, and houses were gone. As many as 500,000 people died. A newspaper headline read, "Do Not Send Children's Clothing to Cyclone Affected Area. No Children Remain."[8]

In the aftermath of the disaster, Sheikh Mujib spoke to the throngs he now drew of Pakistan's criminal neglect. Ill-timed national elections three weeks later became, in a sense, a plebiscite on greater provincial autonomy. The elections certainly demonstrated Bengali unity in the face of a generation of Pakistani-imposed adversity. The elections were, in fact, intended to herald a return to civilian government after a decade-and-a-half of military rule. When the ballots were counted, Sheikh Mujib's Awami League won 167 out of the 169 seats in East Pakistan, representing an absolute majority in the full National Assembly. The runner-up, the Pakistan Peoples Party led by Zulfikar Ali Bhutto, won only 81 seats in West Pakistan. But the prospect of a nationalist Bengali prime minister was too much for Pakistan's military and Bhutto. In March, the martial law authorities announced an indefinite postponement in convening the National Assembly.

The reaction in East Pakistan was swift. Strikes crippled the country, and student leaders issued calls for independence. Riots, arson, and looting ensued. To counteract the growing disorder, the Pakistan army initiated one of the most brutal acts of political repression ever unleashed on a civilian population. Ostensibly aimed at apprehending an insurrection, the first targets were not rioters, but the East Bengal Regiment, the East

Pakistan Rifles, border guards, and police, which were all judged to be untrustworthy. Soon the Pakistan army, manned and officered by West Pakistanis, was out of control, turning its wrath on the civilian population and a hastily formed army of freedom fighters.

A *Newsweek* article in April said:

> All in all, the bitter campaign seemed to suggest that the West Pakistanis had more than purely military objectives in mind. In city after city, in fact, the soldiers were apparently determined to shatter the economic base of East Pakistan in order to crush the independence movement. On orders from the Islamabad high command, troops systematically gunned down students, engineers, doctors, and any other persons with a potential for leadership, whether they were nationalist or not.[9]

The number of people killed has been estimated conservatively at 1 million, and it may have been as high as 3 million. Hundreds of thousands of women are said to have been raped, a singular way of humiliating and defiling an individual and her entire family. By late summer, a long war of attrition between the army and freedom fighters loomed, and refugees poured across the borders into India. At the height of the exodus, 10 million refugees, almost 20 percent of the population, had flooded into refugee camps in West Bengal and Assam, placing a monstrous burden on India and turning the situation into the worst humanitarian crisis of all time. The Security Council debated but did nothing, in part because the United States, then working on its détente with China, had been using Pakistan as a go-between. In July, National Security Advisor Henry Kissinger had secretly visited Beijing after flying on a Pakistani military aircraft, and plans were in the works for President Nixon's groundbreaking trip to Beijing in February the following year. While the United States tilted toward Pakistan, a strong ally of China, East Pakistan burned.

In the end, the brutality of the crackdown accomplished the precise opposite of what was intended. It made the independence of Bangladesh a certainty. In December, the Indian army intervened. Within two weeks, it was over. Bangla Desh (land of Bengalis) had finally become an independent nation.

Notes

1. Betsy Hartman and James Boyce, *A Quiet Violence: View From a Bangladesh Village,* (London: Zed Press, 1983), 11.

2. Ahmed Hasan Dani, *Dacca,* (Dacca: Asiatic Press, 1962), 110.

3. Dani, *Dacca,* 103.

4. Michael Edwardes, *The Last Years of British India* (London: NEL Mentor, 1961), 81.

5. Percival Spear, *A History of India,* Vol. 2 (Harmondsworth: Penguin, 1965), 238.

6. A.M.A. Muhith, *Bangladesh: Emergence of a Nation* (Dacca: Bangladesh Books, 1978), 101–104.

7. Viggo Olsen, *Daktar: Diplomat in Bangladesh* (Old Tappan, N.J.: Spire Books, 1973), 320.

8. Olsen, *Daktar,* 321.

9. *Newsweek,* April 26, 1971.

CHAPTER 2

Arms and the Man

Abed

In *Twelfth Night,* Shakespeare writes, "Be not afraid of greatness: some are born great, some achieve greatness, and some have greatness thrust upon them." Fazle Hasan Abed, a Shakespeare aficionado, was not born great, and he did not have greatness thrust upon him. And there was little in his background to suggest he would achieve greatness. There was certainly nothing in his background to suggest, on a November evening in 1970 as he made his way to the Chittagong Club for a drink, that the life he had led until then was coming to an end and that, from the next morning on, everything would be changed forever.

Abed's family name is Hasan. Abed, a nickname his parents bestowed upon him at birth, stuck. To family and friends, he is Abed, not Fazle. His passport and other official documents also give his surname as Abed. The nickname then did double duty as the surname, which eventually became the surname of his children as well.

Family legend has it that Emperor Jehangir sent an early Hasan ancestor to Bengal, probably some time before 1627. The family then migrated from Murshidabad to East Bengal, and the earliest name in the genealogy is of one Anisul Hasan from Kishorganj, whose son married into a family in the Sylhet village of Baniya Chong. Baniya Chong would become the family seat for the next seven generations. The young Hasan who moved to Baniya Chong died early, and his son, Obaidul, went off in search of fortune, eventually landing in Calcutta. There he became a Persian scholar of high standing. This, and perhaps the family's earlier history, made him known to the Nawab of Murshidabad, a city on the Ganges north of Calcutta that was the capital of Bengal for many years. This was probably around 1750, just as the British East India Company was beginning to assert itself in the region. The Nizam of Hyderabad learned of Obaidul Hasan, who had become author of books in Persian, and engaged him as a tutor for his two children. In those days, when an Indian king died, his surviving sons often decided the succession by force of arms or murder. But, in this case, Obaidul had so endeared himself to the family that he was asked to arbitrate the decision.

The grateful incoming Nizam bestowed great riches on Obaidul, who returned to Baniya Chong in 1760. He bought large tracts of land, settling down as a scholar *zamindar*. The grand house he built, Abed's paternal home, still stands. Obaidul's son, Mofizul Hasan, was different. He is remembered as a profligate who chased women, selling off much of his father's property. Mofizul's son (Abed's great-grandfather), Moyeedul was different again, a pious, saintly man who, through a family marriage, caused Abed's paternal and maternal grandfathers to be first cousins.

In those days, Calcutta was the only place where one could obtain a good high school and college education, and several of the family's young men made the pilgrimage. Calcutta University was established in 1857, but only the very best gained entry. One of the first to enroll was Abed's maternal great-grandfather, who became the first Muslim graduate in 1861. His son, Abed's maternal grandfather, also graduated from Calcutta University, starting his working career as a magistrate. He retired early and went into politics, becoming Bengal's minister of agriculture in 1943 and minister of education between 1945 and 1947. Abed's paternal grandfather took work with the revenue department in land transfers, a job that allowed men of the landed gentry to live and work from the family seat. So the ties to Baniya Chong remained strong.

It was a family of leaders and professionals. Syed Shamsul Huda, one of Abed's great-uncles, was a lawyer, publisher, and professor of law who also promoted the spread of education for young Muslims. He became involved in politics and served as a member of the Imperial Legislative Council. Huda was the first Bengali to sit on the Governor's Executive Council, a rare distinction at the time. He was honored with the title of Nawab in 1913. In 1916, he was knighted by the crown.

Syed Shamsul Huda had no children, so he adopted all of his sister's children—Abed's father and his three uncles. The four boys thus lived a privileged life in Calcutta, living in the Nawab's mansion, attending St. Xavier's school and college, and mingling with the political elite of India's great capital city. Abed's father eventually settled down in Baniya Chong, taking up his grandfather's role as subregistrar of lands. One uncle became a dentist; another became a lawyer and later a judge. A third uncle, Saidul, could recite Tagore poetry for hours, and he passed on his love of literature to his nephew.

Abed says:

> When we were children, he would select for us a particular
> poem of either Nazrul or Rabindranath to memorize in the

shortest possible time. I always used to come first in this contest. Tagore's poems and songs first awakened in me a love of
poetry, great chunks of which I could recite from memory.[1]

In 1950, Saidul went to London as Pakistan's trade commissioner, and
it was not long before he sent for Abed's older brother. In 1954, Abed
followed. He had completed his primary and secondary education in
district schools. In 1952, he was admitted to a two-year intermediate
science course at Dhaka University. But, for an 18-year-old from a good
family, the world beckoned. Traditional ideas about going into government service seemed outdated in the new postcolonial world, and Abed
wanted to do something out of the ordinary. He still cannot explain very
well what drew him to naval architecture, except for the fact that it was,
well, out of the ordinary. Soon he found himself in Glasgow. The naval
architecture course was a four-year program with alternating six-month
periods in the classroom and the shipyard, where students learned
through hands-on experience. After six months of basic physics and
mathematics, he went to the Yarrow & Company shipyard as an appren-
tice draftsman, an experience he describes today as "not that lovely." The
second year, he skipped the shipyard and began to think ahead. He was
beginning to realize that, as a naval architect, he could well be obliged to
spend the rest of his life in Glasgow, Belfast, or Norway. He visited Norway
in 1955 to take a look, and he was not impressed. He wrote to his uncle
in London, saying he had concluded that naval architecture was "not my
line" after all.

His father objected to him quitting, but Saidul welcomed him to London,
where he now concluded that his options lay between law and accounting.
He thought there were already too many lawyers in the family, and he
needed money. In those days, accounting students worked for companies as
they studied, and this presented the agreeable prospect of immediate, if not
munificent, financial gratification. He would find the accounting boring,
and it would take him seven years to complete his studies, but these years
provided him with opportunities he might not otherwise have had.

He began to read. He studied Shakespeare and consumed books
voraciously, including Homer, Virgil, Dante, Goethe, and Rilke. He read
English and American nineteenth- and twentieth-century novels, and he
worked his way through Tolstoy, Dostoyevsky, Flaubert, Hugo, and Proust.
"My love affair with English and European literature continued for almost
a decade," he said. He also developed a taste for Western classical music
such as Bach, Mozart, and Beethoven. A week before one of his annual
exams, he started reading Joyce's *Ulysses*. He said, "I was told it was a
difficult book to read. But when I started it, I couldn't put it down." The
book consumed four days, and the exam was a bust.

Fazle Hasan Abed, 1968 (Photo by BRAC)

His growing love of music and literature was augmented by a deepening relationship with a young woman named Marietta, an opera enthusiast. He said:

> She and I would not miss any opera performed at Covent Garden in London. She was also a connoisseur of European art, of early renaissance painters and of the French impressionists.

We frequently visited art galleries in London, and we went to Rome, Florence, Venice, Milan, Padua, Verona, Paris, Madrid, and Amsterdam. Music, art, and literature left little time for accountancy for me.

In 1962, he took out British citizenship. It was much easier to travel with a British passport than with a Pakistani one. He and Marietta bought a four-story Edwardian house in London, and he dabbled on the fringes of radical politics. Most of his friends were Marxists, and he attended regular Sunday study meetings with them. One friend ran for Parliament as a Communist, and Abed campaigned for him, although he knew there was no chance a Communist would ever come anything but last in Hampstead. He recalls them as "a very marginalized lot," attending boring, if idealistic, meetings when they were not busy with opera, literature, and travel. He always dressed well. He took to smoking cigars, and his friends called him the "Lord of Camden."

He liked to cook. His mother had been an excellent cook, and he thought he had inherited a latent talent for it from her. He thought his *rezala,* a curry made with lamb or beef, was one of the best.

"I remember cooking *rezala* for the great novelist E.M. Forster at his Kings College Cambridge flat," he said.

Abed had friends in Cambridge, and the elderly professor often held court with young people from Asia. Forster loved the *rezala,* and he said it reminded him of the days, decades earlier, when he had lived and worked in India, gaining inspiration for his masterwork, *A Passage to India.*

Abed says:

> I have not the slightest regret for the delay of a few years in starting a traditional professional career. Those carefree, wonderful years shaped me as a person and made me aware of the human condition around me. I would like to think of myself as a free thinker—not having much faith in the rituals of religion but a strong mooring in the core ethical and human values.

But carefree, wonderful years have a way of ending. Marietta wanted them to be married. Knowing Abed would want to go home someday, she and her brother visited Dhaka in 1965 to see what it was like. It was not a positive experience, and she decided she could not live there. They decided to take a break from each other. Marietta went to study philosophy at Oxford; Abed went to McMaster University in Canada to do a diploma course for financial executives on the IBM 360 computer. When it was over, he decided to go home.

In January 1969, he landed a job with Shell Oil, and he was posted to Chittagong. Over the next two years, he had two promotions. He headed the company's accounting staff; he lived in a large house with servants. He had a car, and he joined the Chittagong Club, where businessmen and senior government officials could network, play tennis and snooker, and have the occasional drink.

On the evening of November 12, 1970, he was at the club with friends, aware of the impending cyclone. He thought to himself, "My God, tomorrow so many people will be dead."

Swept Away

On November 5, as Tropical Storm Nora abated, it moved west from the South China Sea across the Malay Peninsula and into the Bay of Bengal. There, it gathered into a tropical depression with all of the ingredients for a great storm. As the growing depression started to move north, the Indian Meteorological Department upgraded it to a cyclonic storm. It slowed on the evening of November 9, but then began to move north again, gaining speed on November 10. By the next day, a clear eye had formed, and the storm turned toward the northeast, intensifying as it approached land. On the night of November 12, it made landfall 95 kilometers west of Chittagong, sweeping across the flat islands of the delta with winds that were recorded in Chittagong at 144 kilometers per hour until the weather station was blown away. It was, in a sense, a perfect storm because it coincided with a full moon and a high tide, causing a tsunami-like surge 10 meters (33 feet) high to wash over the farms, villages, and towns that stood in its way.

It was the most deadly tropical cyclone in history. Because recordkeeping was poor and the official relief effort was so slow to begin, the actual death toll will never be known, but estimates range from 300,000 to 500,000, half of them children. To put this number into perspective, the estimated death toll from the 2004 Asian tsunami was 230,000. The Asian tsunami was well-documented, most of the affected areas were reachable within hours, and the world responded generously.

In Bangladesh, the story in 1970 was different. There were no foreign tourists, there was no film, relief agencies were slow to mobilize, and the government was even slower. More than 3.6 million people were affected. Thirteen offshore islands were wiped clear of animals, trees, and any structure not made of concrete. As terrible as the immediate situation was, the aftermath was in many ways worse. Drinking water was in short supply because wells, like farmland, had been inundated with saltwater. Food supplies, warehouses, and shops had been swept away. Standing crops had been destroyed. Livestock and poultry were drowned. Houses had vanished.

The official response was slow, but many ordinary people were quick to act. Several professionals at the Pakistan-SEATO Cholera Research Laboratory in Dhaka headed for Chittagong, among them Candy Rohde and her husband Jon, a Harvard-trained pediatrician; Lincoln Chen, another Harvard-trained American doctor, and his wife Marty, who was working on a PhD dissertation; and Richard Cash, a young doctor from Wisconsin. Joining them was Father Dick Timm, an American Holy Cross priest.

It was the Muslim fasting month of Ramadan, and Father Timm, acting principal of Dhaka's prestigious Notre Dame College, put together a small group of vacationing students and set off on the train for Chittagong to see what could be done. Timm, who had lived in Bangladesh for 18 years, was an accomplished biologist who had discovered over 250 nematodes (parasitic roundworms). In fact, one, the *timmia parva,* discovered in 1952, was named after him. Timm and the others would soon discover what havoc intestinal parasites could create among a traumatized populace without access to clean water.

When the people from Dhaka began arriving in Chittagong, they needed somewhere to stay. Abed, shocked by the magnitude of what had happened, opened his house on the Shell Oil compound to them. His cook began preparing meals for 50 people instead of one, and the rooms started filling up with relief supplies. Shell gave him two speedboats, and friends in other oil companies provided kerosene and petrol. Father Timm was one of the first to reach the ruined islands, arriving at Hatiya on November 25. He and his students slept under the stairs and on concrete benches in the ferry terminal. The following day, he was able to get to Manpura Island on a speedboat. Manpura, a narrow, low-lying island about 2 kilometers wide and 10 kilometers in length, had borne the full brunt of the cyclone and the tidal bore. Abed had reached Manpura five days after the cyclone, and what he and Timm saw would stay with them the rest of their lives. Dead and bloated bodies of people, goats, and cattle were floating in the water. They had washed up on the shore, unburied after days in the sun. Of the island's 36,000 people, only 13,000 survived, and the destruction was almost complete. An 80-foot steamer, the *Manpura,* had been torn from its moorings in Hatiya and had wound up 100 meters inland on the western shore of Manpura, dragging its anchor all the way.

As relief materials began to arrive, Marty Chen and Candy Rohde realized they needed to formalize what they were doing. Back in Dhaka, the Chen's next-door neighbor was an American consultant to the Water and Power Development Authority.

"He came over one night," Marty recalled.

"You gals are just nickel-and-diming this operation," he said. "What do you need?"

He had a blank pad of yellow paper, and he made a chart of how many cows, ploughs, and whatever else was needed on this island. He pulled together a proposal for a million rupees.

They incorporated the organization. Abed became the chair. Marty, Candy, and a lawyer, Vikarul Chowdhury, were board members. Abed persuaded Akbar Kabir, a retired deputy secretary to the government of Pakistan, to become the coordinator. They called the new organization Heartland Emergency Lifesaving Project (HELP). "Moen," the word from which Manpura had taken its name, meant "heart." The German relief organization, Bread for the World, arrived and asked what they needed, and Marty Chen was able to produce the plan that had been scribbled out so quickly. Among other things, they had calculated that Manpura would require 5,000 houses, cyclone shelters, and other forms of assistance. Marty asked for a million rupees (about US$140,000) and got US$1 million instead. In Abed's recollection, they requested 3 million Deutschemarks (about US$750,000). Whatever the amount, it was a lot at the time. Perhaps because there was so much to do, they were not especially surprised when it was approved.

All of them were amateurs where relief work was concerned, but they were all professionals in their own fields. If the chief accountant of Shell Oil was running HELP, and if American doctors and a priest were involved, the organization must be trustworthy.

Abed recalled, "There was nothing else one could give money to." Abed persuaded a colleague at Shell Oil, Kaiser Zaman, to act as number two to Akbar Kabir, and he asked Father Timm if he would serve as HELP's field coordinator on Manpura, writing to the board at Notre Dame College to ask for his release. For coordination purposes, they set up an informal office in Dhaka, staffed by volunteers. One of them was Akbar Kabir's daughter, Khushi, who assisted on a part-time basis while holding down a day job in the design department of an advertising agency.

Meanwhile, Timm was having problems on Manpura. The army, led entirely by officers from West Pakistan, had finally arrived, and it was using a heavy hand in its attempt to take over relief distribution. People were being threatened and beaten. Hordes of reporters arrived as well, pointing cameras in the faces of desperate victims. Timm exploded at a group of them:

> You take all the places on the helicopters, which could be bringing relief supplies and personnel. Yet you criticize how little is being done, even though you never lift a hand to help. You interview only foreigners because they can speak good English. Then you rush back to Dhaka to give an authentic

firsthand account of the way things really were in the most devastated area.[2]

HELP distributed saris, lungis, blankets, and food. It brought in engineers to survey ponds for desalinization. Soil samples were sent out for testing to determine levels of salinity in farmland. Vegetable seeds for winter cultivation were distributed, along with hoes and other agricultural implements. They started to form cooperatives and build hope among those who had survived. The relief workers lived in tents, and their own rations were meager. On Christmas Day, Father Timm was on Sakuchia, an island south of Manpura, where he celebrated mass for five visiting relief workers. For Christmas dinner, they splurged on tins of tomato soup and Franco-American spaghetti that Timm had been saving for the occasion. The feast of tinned spaghetti delayed the visitors' departure, and they missed the tide. On the way back to Manpura, their motorboat grounded on a sandbank, and they spent the night singing Christmas carols in the dark.

HELP and the work on Manpura changed everyone involved. Although he did not know it at the time, for Abed, it was the beginning of a new life. Father Timm would go on to work for a Catholic relief and development organization that became, for a time, one of the largest in Bangladesh. In 1995, he published his memoirs, *Forty Years in Bangladesh*. Today, halfway through his ninth decade, he still teaches at Notre Dame College in Dhaka. Lincoln Chen would go on to Harvard, the Ford and Rockefeller Foundations, and an eminent career of public service. His wife Marty would become an author and a leader in the international women's movement. Kaiser Zaman never went back to Shell Oil. He would work with many NGOs over the years and the United Nations High Commissioner for Refugees, serving in settings as diverse as Geneva, New York, Somalia, Hong Kong, Thailand, and Azerbaijan. Jon Rohde went on to a distinguished career in health, working in Indonesia and Haiti and serving as head of UNICEF in India. All, however, would be drawn back to Bangladesh repeatedly over the years, and all would contribute, some of them in very profound ways, to the creation and evolution of BRAC.

But in those desperate days on Manpura, all of this lay in the future. And the cyclone, as it turned out, was not the worst of their problems. Less than a month after the storm, on December 7, Pakistan's most important general elections were held, a prelude to ending military rule. The elections were not just a test of the army's willingness to hand over power. They were a test of the strained relationship that had festered between the country's eastern and western wings since independence. When the votes were counted, Zulfikar Ali Bhutto, Benazir's father, had won 81 of the seats, all of them in the West. Small parties and independents won 59 seats. Sheikh

Mujibur Rahman's Awami League won 167 out of the 313 seats. It was a clear and undeniable majority, but it revealed the giant chasm that had opened between the country's two wings. The results were not surprising, given the history of East Bengal and the government's halfhearted response to the cyclone. The election was, in fact, little short of a referendum—if not for greater autonomy, then for complete independence. Neither Bhutto nor the West Pakistan-dominated army, however, was willing to cede power to the Awami League or a Bengali prime minister.

Intense negotiations on possible power-sharing arrangements were held over the following weeks, but no deal could be reached. On March 7, Sheikh Mujib addressed a massive crowd in Dhaka's racecourse. "Our struggle this time," he said, "is a struggle for independence." And he used the phrase on everyone's lips. "*Joi Bangla!* (Victory to Bengal!)"

Even then, it was not clear that complete independence was the objective. But the strikes and civil disobedience intensified. The government effectively ceased to function, and the economy began to slide. Yahya Khan flew to Dhaka for discussions with Mujib while simultaneously reinforcing the army with fresh troops. PIA commercial aircraft and military C130s began flying in troops around the clock to bolster forces already on the ground. On the night of March 25, they acted. Sheikh Mujib was arrested, and the crackdown began.

The first target was the East Pakistan Rifles, whose barracks were attacked by troops from the West with tanks, bazookas, and automatic rifles. Next were newspaper offices and the university, where hundreds of students were massacred in a frenzied bloodbath. The army had lists, and the violence spread out like a stain across the country. Hindus were special targets, seen to be agents of India. Saidul Hasan, who had sponsored Abed's trip to Britain years before, went to the army to plead on behalf of Hindu friends who had been arrested. He was never seen again. Across the land, killings, rape, and destruction became the order of the day. Resistance began to form, but each act of defiance was met with a fierce rejoinder, and a human disaster of unimaginable proportions loomed. Indian journalist Anthony Mascarenas visited the 16th Division Headquarters at Comilla and was told:

> We are determined to cleanse East Pakistan once and for all of the threat of secession, even if it means killing off 2 million people and ruling the province as a colony for 30 years.[3]

Within days of the crackdown, most foreign missions and agencies pulled their international staff out. The Chens, Rohdes, and others from the Cholera Laboratory left. Father Timm stayed on Manpura and witnessed firsthand the army's genocidal hunt for Hindus. But HELP was quickly losing the plot, providing relief for cyclone victims in the midst of a new and fast-growing man-made humanitarian crisis. With three members of his four-member board of directors gone, Abed brought Father Timm and Akbar Kabir onto the board. Then he was forced to leave Chittagong as well.

The chairman of Shell Oil was a retired general with a list of his own. The military plucked Abed from his Chittagong retreat and took him to Dhaka, setting him up in the cantonment and making him their liaison for the oil companies, a strategically important function to the army in what was fast becoming a state of civil war. Abed knew he had to get out. Because he had a martial law pass, he had permission to buy plane tickets, but there was a problem. The only flights out of East Pakistan were to Karachi and Islamabad in the West. To escape, he would have to fly into the belly of the beast.

Taking a vacation after two weeks in the cantonment, he made it to Karachi, where he waited ten days and put together a plan. His idea was to fly to Kabul because flights to neighboring countries would not be as carefully watched as those heading for Europe. From Kabul, he could buy a ticket to London. While he was in Karachi, however, he happened to meet a Shell Oil employee who betrayed him, informing the chairman that Abed was in town "on vacation." The chairman quickly informed the Pakistani secret police, the Inter-Service Intelligence (ISI), that Abed was AWOL and demanded his arrest.

Unaware of all this, Abed made his way north to Islamabad. In a good-natured way, he dropped in on the Shell office to greet friends. Within minutes, two ISI colonels arrived and arrested him. Police fetched his luggage, and a search was conducted. Although the danger was now grave, Abed's strongest memory is of the silliness of the moment. In his suitcase, the only thing of interest to the colonels was his salary slip. When they saw how much he was earning, one of them said, "You must be the most eligible bachelor in East Pakistan!"

The interrogation took place at military headquarters, where Abed stuck to his story about being on vacation, refusing to be pinned down on anything that might incriminate him or his family. He said he had been appointed as military liaison for the oil companies. He said the work was not demanding, so he was on holiday. If ordered to return, he would do so. He had cleverly bought a return ticket when he left Dhaka, and he showed it to them. The ticket and his British passport probably saved his life.

As soon as he was released, he wasted no time. He hired a taxi and drove to Peshawar in the North-West Frontier Province, taking a room in the best hotel he could find. Friends told him that a gentleman in a good hotel would be less suspect than others. They were right. The next day, he boarded a crowded bus for the winding journey that would take him up through the Khyber Pass and on to Kabul. There, he learned the weekly flights to London were fully booked, but, after two weeks, he obtained a ticket to Istanbul. From there, he finally flew to London, where he had spent so many happy and carefree days.

BRAC

In London, Abed went immediately to Shell's headquarters, tendered his resignation, and denounced the company's Pakistan chairman for causing him to be used as a pawn in the midst of a civil war. It made him feel good, but it accomplished little. Many assumed the liberation struggle would be a long one. Abed's own view was that it might take between five and seven years. Now jobless, he had to face the fact that he was little more than a refugee himself. In order to survive, he sold his share in the house he had bought years earlier to Marietta, realizing £7000 in the sale (about US$17,500 at the prevailing exchange rate). In today's money, that represents about $95,000, not a bad nest egg for a refugee. He figured he would need about £200 a month to live, so he would be able to manage without work for at least three years if nothing else transpired.

He and others began raising funds for war victims, creating Action Bangladesh in support of the liberation struggle and Help Bangladesh for victims of the conflict. They demonstrated in front of embassies, talking to any reporter who would listen and campaigning on behalf of the beleaguered country. Back home, remnants of the East Pakistan Rifles and others had taken to the forests, fighting a guerilla insurgency. But, by the middle of 1970, the so-called crackdown was looking more and more like a genocidal war against an entire people. Millions streamed across the borders into Calcutta in the west, Meghalaya in the north, and Assam and Tripura in the east. If the cyclone had been the most deadly natural disaster, this was surely the worst man-made disaster of all time. For months, Abed shuttled between London and Calcutta, delivering relief supplies and funding for the refugee camps. In the end, the struggle for independence took only nine months. India declared war on Pakistan on December 3. On December 16, less than two weeks later, the Pakistan army surrendered.

Abed returned in January. He had consumed only £1,000 during his seven months in London, so he had £5,800 to devote to a new reconstruction idea. He found that, although it still existed, HELP was suffering from management and financial problems and Father Timm had left to do other things. Rather than take on the problems that had developed in HELP, he gathered together some of his old friends and created a new organization, calling it the Bangladesh Rehabilitation Assistance Committee (BRAC). During the first four months, they lived mainly off Abed's savings, using the car he had purchased from Shell for their transportation and working from the office of his lawyer friend, Vikarul Chowdhury.

Abed wasted little time. He knew that, for returning refugees and victims of the war, the situation was as urgent as it was grim. January could be cold in Bangladesh with nighttime temperatures dipping not far above the freezing mark. Clothing, shelter, and renewed livelihoods were the priority. He chose an area he knew, not far from Baniya Chong, a predominantly Hindu area of Sylhet known as Sulla. He traveled there on January 17, only days after his return from England, to get an idea of the need. After his return to Dhaka, he organized six students from the university to carry out a full survey of the area, including the number of people, houses destroyed, nutritional and medical needs, land use, and livelihoods. He then traveled to Calcutta to buy tools and agricultural implements for farmers and nylon twine for fishermen. From there, he flew to the Indian city of Shillong on the northeastern border of Bangladesh, where he met the chief minister of the state and appealed for timber and bamboo for house reconstruction. He bought 3 million bamboo poles that were soon lashed together into rafts and floated down the Khushiara River to Sulla.

Using Vikar's office in Dhaka, he wrote BRAC's first funding proposal. Khushi Kabir left her job in the advertising agency and joined as his assistant, secretary, and general factotum, helping with the proposal and everything else. Abed said she was employee number one, but, even if he was still living off his savings, Khushi gave him that honor. "I was only employee number two," she said. At £189,000, the proposal they wrote was large by the standards of the day, and it was especially large for an organization with no track record, few assets, and fewer than 10 employees.

But foreign relief agencies were now pouring into the newly liberated country. The needs were enormous, and many of the newcomers had no track record themselves. Few knew about East Bengal. In those early days, few had any way to reach people beyond the main cities. Although this new BRAC did not have the Americans that had added to the credibility of HELP, one international organization was willing to take a chance. Oxfam had recently opened an office in Dhaka, operated by Raymond Cournoyer, a Canadian who had taught school in Bangladesh for many years as a Catholic Brother. Here was someone who did know Bangladesh and who was an astute judge of character. In March, Cournoyer took Oxfam's visiting director of overseas operations, Michael Harris, to meet Abed. Two weeks later, the project was approved.

In October, Abed wrote a report on what had been achieved with the money over BRAC's first nine months, from the start of February to the end of October 1972. They had planned to build 10,500 houses, but, in the end, they built more than 14,000. The overachievement, something that would become a BRAC hallmark over the years, had happened for several reasons. The bamboo from India had been made available at a fraction of the regular price. The new government gave them 200 tons of corrugated iron sheeting, adding to the 800 tons they bought with project funds. And they had divided recipients of the housing into four categories. Depending on their income potential, some families made token payments for the houses, allowing BRAC to build more. They distributed 25 tons of rice seed, hired power tillers where bullocks were in short supply, distributed 4,500 pounds of nylon twine to fishermen, and constructed 200 boats for fishermen who had lost theirs during the war. They provided tools for carpenters and boat-builders, and they bought 125 handlooms for weavers. They formed 52 agricultural cooperatives, and they organized four medical teams that treated 200 patients a day. Paramedics provided basic health education, including information on how to deal with the country's number one child killer, diarrhea, in all of the 187 villages in the project area.

When the project was finished, Abed did two things. First, he reported to Oxfam that there was Tk 500,000 remaining (about £16,500 at the time), and he asked if they wanted the money back. Oxfam staff had so rarely experienced a recipient offering to repay leftover funds that they hardly knew what to say. They told Abed to apply it to the next project.

The next project was the second thing. Abed had seen BRAC as a temporary phenomenon, something that might last a year or so. After the emergency had passed, it would disband, and he would start to look for a job. He asked the people who had worked with him in Sulla what they thought. All had seen the area's deep-seated poverty, and all knew their relief and reconstruction efforts had only touched the surface of the need. All had begun to see that there were real opportunities for an organization like BRAC to make a lasting difference, but it would require more time and more money.

In October, Abed sat down to write a new funding proposal, one that would take the organization through to 1974, seeing the name change to Bangladesh Rural Advancement Committee. In the proposal, he said, "The struggle for liberation has brought about a new climate, a new awareness, and a desire for change." He wrote about ending corrupt, exploitative rural control systems and the potential for a new kind of leadership, eager and ready for a new future. He wrote about how "people, so long groping in ignorance and mistrust" were now receptive to new ideas and new institutions that could help them break with their centuries-old subsistence economy.[4]

For Abed, an avocation was being transformed into a vocation; an intermission was becoming the main event. The old life of operas, museums, and radical study circles was gone for good. He was the product of a privileged life and a family of professionals for whom challenge and service were natural, so he had never felt any innate limit on what he might do with his own life. Here at last was something with meaning. Here at last was the something out of the ordinary he had sought in Glasgow 18 years before. The poverty on Manpura and in Sulla had deeply affected him. It had been there all along, and he had never really noticed it. After nine months, he knew that poverty and injustice were not things that could or would be eradicated easily, but the BRAC idea and the plans that were gathering in his mind could be a start.

His financial skills would serve him well in the years ahead, as would a growing ability to bring others to the cause and persuade them that change was possible and small ideas could be transformed into meaningful action. He did not know that, in the years ahead, he would confront and surmount some of the greatest development challenges on the planet and everything he knew about economics, health, and education would be turned on its head. He could not foresee that some day he would walk with presidents and kings. Nor could he know that, had he returned to the corporate world, even if he had become president of Shell Oil, he could never achieve half as much as he would with BRAC.

Notes

1. Several of the Abed quotes regarding his years as a student and in England are taken from an interview in *The New Age,* Dhaka, Aug. 27, 2004. Others are from interviews conducted by the author in 2007 and 2008.

2. Richard Timm, *Forty Years in Bangladesh: Memoirs of Father Timm* (Dhaka, Bangladesh: Caritas, 1995), 144.

3. Anthony Mascarenhas, *The Rape of Bangla Desh* (New Delhi: Vikas Publications, 1972), 117.

4. Quotations and figures in the preceding paragraphs are from BRAC, "Sulla Project: An Integrated Programme for Development, 1972–73," Dhaka, October 1972.

CHAPTER 3

The Plan

BRAC's relief effort in Sulla had been exemplary. Abed and the team had accomplished huge feats in a short space of time. They had reached villages and people in a remote part of the country, and they had been innovative. They lived under rough conditions, and they worked long hours, sitting at night with kerosene lanterns to review the day's work and make plans for the future. Their ingenuity was second only to their fortitude. BRAC workers had spent two—and sometimes three—weeks floating down the Khushiara River aboard rafts, some of which were two miles long, made of the bamboo poles that would be used for housing. They had introduced new ideas about health care, and they had recovered some of their costs from those who could afford to pay, a harbinger of things to come.

In October 1972, Abed sat down with his team and started drafting a new proposal for Oxfam. This would be Sulla: Phase II. The relief effort was over, and now long-term development could begin.

The plan was ambitious, but it was not complicated. The idea was to build 125 community centers (*gonokendras*) for meetings of cooperative members and adult literacy programs. In the plan, BRAC noted that 80 percent of the adult population was illiterate, and, without education, development efforts were doomed from the start. Abed wrote:

> We believe that an adult literacy program is critical to the success of all development efforts and that it must be functionally related to the improvement of the occupational skills of the people so that literacy can directly contribute to higher productivity.

Without literacy, he wrote, "the sum total of achievement in all rural development programs so far launched . . . in Bangladesh is insignificant."[1] BRAC planned to reach the entire illiterate adult population of the region (84,000 people), and it planned a campaign to get all children between the ages of five and eleven into primary schools.

29

It aimed to create 220 primary cooperative societies for fishermen and farmers, and it would link these to the government's new Integrated Rural Development Programme, which planned to create cooperatives across the entire country. In Sulla, BRAC would implement the program, working hand in hand with the new government. It would work with farmers on the provision of better seeds, fertilizer, and farming techniques. Abed wrote:

> If the other BRAC programs—cooperatives and functional literacy—make their due contribution, the target of three times the pitifully meager present yield [of rice] should not be too difficult to achieve.

"Not too difficult to achieve." Their confidence was boundless. Not only did they expect to succeed, they thought their efforts at an integrated, concentrated program blanketing an area of 160 square miles might become a model for others.

> It is hoped that the results of the concentrated attention being given to the area will not be confined within its boundaries, but will have a rippling effect, gradually making itself felt all over Bangladesh.*

Seventeen months later, they submitted a sober report to Oxfam. Things had not worked out exactly as planned. For a time, the law-and-order situation had deteriorated badly with armed gangs roaming the countryside in search of plunder. The Bangladesh economy was in deep trouble, and the inflation rate had soared over the previous 18 months to 70 percent. Many of BRAC's field assistants had been "found wanting in leadership qualities and mental discipline."[2] Twenty had to be sacked in the middle of 1973. Because communications were so problematic, BRAC had to reorganize and decentralize the field staff. The teachers they had engaged for their functional literacy program were a disappointment.

> We were generally dissatisfied with the results. Most teachers are unable to impart functional education to the learners and are concentrating more on alphabetization.

---

*Abed chuckled when the Sulla plan was compared to the Millennium Villages of today. Promoted by Jeffrey Sachs and the Earth Institute at Columbia University, they aim to demonstrate that a concerted, integrated approach to development in 79 African villages can end poverty and meet the United Nations Millennium Development Goals. Abed laughed, not at the idea of development in 79 villages, but at the thought that the world would gasp with wonder at the brilliance of it all, change its ways, and start at last to do everything right. "We tried that in Sulla," he said. "It didn't work."

Class attendance fell, and new approaches had to be adopted. They realized that, without trained staff, none of their programs would work, so they were forced to establish a training center with an evaluation process that could deal with staff qualifications before all other issues.

The medical centers established during the relief period had been phased out, and BRAC had turned to the idea of paramedics who could diagnose and treat common ailments such as dysentery, worms, tetanus, scabies, and malaria. But even that had been less successful than hoped. Seventy-two candidates had been whittled down to 21 trainees after field testing during a scabies eradication campaign, but only 11 had been able to complete the course.

There were achievements. They had started a journal, *Gonokendra,* for use in the literacy classes, and they were printing 3,000 copies a month. UNICEF liked it and started paying for print runs of 50,000 so it could be distributed to every primary school in the country. They had established rice and vegetable demonstration plots, and they were distributing seed on half credit. They had formed 85 cooperatives, holding weekly meetings with each of them to impart training and encourage savings. They had provided hundreds of hours of extension services to farmers and livestock owners.

But there were problems with the cooperatives. They were part of the government co-op system, and the government had purchased huge numbers of irrigation pumps. In order to encourage more food production, the government was renting the pumps out at rates that did not even cover maintenance costs or depreciation. This undercut any idea of cost recovery and turned the whole effort into little more than a giveaway, an approach that would be completely unsustainable over time.

BRAC had imported nylon twine for fishermen's nets, but the organization was again faced with the dilemma of real-world prices. The cost of twine in Bangladesh was almost five times more than what BRAC had paid for the Korean variety. Even Korean prices were skyrocketing, however, because nylon was derived from petroleum, and the world had just been thrust into its first dramatic oil crisis. Between October 1973 and March 1974, oil prices had risen from less than US$3.00 a barrel to US$12.00, creating economic havoc in industrialized countries and something close to ruin in the developing world.

BRAC sold the nylon twine to its fishing cooperatives at cost because it understood that fishermen, as a group, were "one of the most exploited communities in Bangladesh, with moneylenders and local landlords claiming astronomical rates of interest," along with a share of the catch. But BRAC was dismayed to discover that "the fishermen, in their turn, exploit their womenfolk by paying them a pittance for net making and for curing and drying fish." In the report to Oxfam, they said, "BRAC feels strongly about exploitation of any kind; exploitation by an exploited group cannot be condoned." In response, they formed women's cooperatives for net making, and they established four vocational centers for training destitute women in tailoring, embroidery, and vegetable gardening.

BRAC asked Oxfam for an 18-month extension on the project.

> The wider and deeper experience of the development process now convinces us that the time we allowed ourselves is too short for the far-reaching changes in ideas, attitudes, and priorities we hoped to bring about in the project area.

The experience had been wider and deeper in other ways. The Chens had been reposted to Bangladesh, and Marty recalled meeting Abed for the first time after a two-year absence. Years later, she said:

> I went home and wept because here was a totally different man. Before, he had worn smoking jackets and ascots, and he would listen to Beethoven and smoke a pipe. He was British, very British—sort of effete, if you will. And now he was different. I knew the person, and I knew something fundamental had changed. After the cyclone, he had been bemused by these ladies running around trying to do relief . . . now he was on a completely different path.

In April 1974, BRAC was barely two years old, but some of the future could be discerned in what they wrote. First, they were brutally honest about what had been achieved and about what they had learned. They also demonstrated a clear ability to roll with the punches, adapting to new circumstances and better understanding. The average aid recipient would shrink from the idea of describing so many setbacks to its primary donor. But this kind of report would be typical of the BRAC approach over time. The idea was not to prove that they had all the answers before they started, but to find out what worked and apply the lessons.

Second, they had learned the critical importance of competent staff. Many who were not so good had been let go, and a training center was established for those who remained. Training and the constant upgrading of staff would become a permanent feature in BRAC. Third, the economics of their approach to poverty comes through loud and clear, most notably in the concern about heavily subsidized irrigation pumps and the usury of moneylenders. Subsidies might never be a sustainable way forward, but there was certainly room to lower the costs of production.

Fourth, they had begun to see that women represented a special problematique in Bangladesh society. This would become more obvious in the months ahead, but the recognition was there at an early stage. Finally, at the end of the report to Oxfam, BRAC talked about donor funding.

"Well-conceived development programs achieving their stated objectives can always attract funding," the report said, but other ideas were already percolating. "In order not to continue to be totally dependent on foreign funding, BRAC is presently developing schemes for the generation of substantial funds locally."

There are a few important things missing from the report, however. There is, as yet, no appreciation of the generalized injustice and the deep schisms in the social makeup of the average Bangladesh village. Missing is an understanding of poverty as anything more than a simple economic equation. Poverty is viewed primarily as a lack of income, to be remedied with training and credit for better seeds and fertilizer. Also missing is any understanding that "community" is not congruent with "village" and that community development, as described in standard textbooks, would never work.

If its efforts were going to succeed, BRAC would require a radical reinterpretation of the problem.

Notes

1. Quotations regarding the development plans are from BRAC, "Sulla Project: An Integrated Plan for Development, 1972–1973," Dhaka, October 1972.

2. Quotations on problems and achievements are from BRAC, "Sulla Project: Phase II Interim Report," Dhaka, April 1974.

CHAPTER 4

The Problem

Beginning at the Beginning

In January 1972, Sheikh Mujibur Rahman was released from prison in what had been, until the month before, West Pakistan. He returned to a rapturous welcome from compatriots in the country whose independence he had helped to win. But the Bangladesh he found was a broken country. Average annual per capita income before independence had been in the neighborhood of US$70, the lowest in the world. It meant that the average Bangladeshi had few resources to fall back on in times of calamity. Independently, the cyclone and the war had been disasters of major proportion; together, they were cataclysmic. In addition to the hundreds of thousands of deaths, there was the problem of 10 million refugees in India. Infrastructure had been destroyed, and several planting seasons had been disrupted.

Damage estimates in 1972 dollars were placed at US$1.2 billion. Housing, bridges, railways, and public utilities were all seriously damaged. The transport, communications, and power transmission sectors were broken. The damage was compounded by the fact that there had been so little infrastructure in the first place. To give a sense of the state of development in a country with more people than there were in France, Austria, and Switzerland combined, one could look at things that are taken for granted elsewhere. In the newly independent Bangladesh, there were only 300 gasoline pumps, 20,000 private cars, and 5,000 buses. There were fewer than 50,000 telephones, only 300,000 radios, and barely 10,000 television sets.[1] Televisions and cars, however, were the farthest things from the minds of most Bangladeshis, whose first priority in those days was survival. Most people lived in villages, 68,000 or more of them scattered across the country. And most lived in houses made of mud and bamboo with thatch roofs. Water and sanitation conditions were generally abysmal, education and health facilities were rudimentary or nonexistent, and 80 percent of the population was illiterate.

Most of East Pakistan's exports, primarily jute and tea, had gone to West Pakistan, and subsidies had protected them. With independence, all of that collapsed immediately. The price of rice had doubled by mid-1973 and did so again the following year, a result of dislocation, bad harvests, an oil crisis, and the new government's inability to revive a wrecked economy. For development experts, the food/population nexus was the most worrying issue. Seventy million people living in a country the size of Maine had turned Bangladesh into the most densely populated land on earth, one that was far from self-sufficient in food. Although food production had increased during the 1960s, it had not kept pace with population growth. By the end of the 1960s, East Pakistan was importing 1.3 million tons of grain every year.

The Harvard University Center for Population Studies made projections, looking forward to the turn of the century. If family planning was pushed with determination, the population might be limited to 153 million by 2000. If not, it could rise to as much as 229 million at the 1972 growth rate.[2] Either way, there would be food problems. Even with the most intensive efforts to improve rice production, including new varieties; more fertilizer, pesticide, and irrigation; and better drainage, the very best estimate of milled rice production by 2003 was 27 million tons, an unbelievable number that was three times pre-independence levels.

Multilateral and bilateral aid agencies were generous to the new Bangladesh, as were NGOs. George Harrison and Ravi Shankar organized the world's first big charity rock concert, "The Concert for Bangladesh," raising $250,000 for relief and reconstruction. But, among experts, the prognosis was dire. In December 1971, as Bangladeshis struggled for their independence, Alexis Johnson, a United States Undersecretary of State, said in a meeting of the National Security Council that Bangladesh was likely to become an "international basket case." Henry Kissinger was said to have replied that it would not necessarily become "our basket case."[3] The offhand remark, often quoted and misquoted and much resented in Bangladesh, was not without prescience. Few experts could see in 1972 how Bangladesh could possibly survive.

But, like Sheikh Mujib, many would ignore the harsh reality in the statistics, exhorting a poverty-stricken, ill-equipped populace to pull itself up by its own bootstraps. One prominent study tried to be optimistic, but, like others, it fell back in the end on exhortation:

> Social change is necessary in Bangladesh—to reduce birth rates, improve the status of women and mobilize communal efforts in the villages . . . There is a need to build up a momentum towards development from within the village itself . . . too much is expected from the government.[4]

Sometimes the experts, perhaps foreseeing disaster in the numbers and embarrassed by their own hortatory nonsense, would drift off into dreamland. "Bangladesh's luck might turn," said one book. "There are hopes that the search for oil might succeed."[5]

At independence, Bangladesh was one of the poorest countries on earth. The average per capita income in 1972 was about US$0.17 per day, the equivalent of about US$0.83 cents in today's dollar. Per capita averages conceal many things, however, and a more instructive number relates to the poorest 20 percent, who, at the time, were living on one-third of the national average, the equivalent of US$0.06 per person per day, or US$0.30 in 2009 dollars.[6] Numbers like these do not mean a great deal because the average Bangladeshi would not see much cash from one day to the next, and the poorest in those years lived a hand-to-mouth existence that focused almost entirely on food. In the rural areas, almost three-fourths of the income of a rural family was devoted to food, and the poorer the family, the greater the level of effort required to obtain it.

Food intake, therefore, became a more common way of defining poverty, and a science has grown up—more aggressively in Bangladesh than almost anywhere else—around the measurement of the number of calories needed to sustain a healthy life. The average individual requirement in Bangladesh has been estimated at something between 2,020 and 2,150 calories per day[7] while the actual consumption at independence was slightly less. For the poorest, however, the situation was much worse. A definition of absolute poverty in 1977 referred to people whose average intake was less than 90 percent of the minimum requirement, and the extremely poor were those consuming less than 80 percent of the daily requirement. By those standards, 78 percent of the population lived in absolute poverty in 1974, and 42 percent lived in extreme poverty.[8]

These reductionist averages, which condense life into a single-ingredient recipe for survival, conceal many things. Seasonal changes may mean inadequate food supplies during some months and starvation in others. People who do not eat properly cannot work properly, and they are more prone to illness. For the poor, clean drinking water may be unavailable, and health facilities are largely beyond reach. Recovery from illness is less certain for the malnourished, and it takes longer. Life expectancy is abridged. Women will generally be less well fed than men, and children may suffer the most. Studies during the 1980s found that 94 percent of children in Bangladesh suffered from some degree of malnutrition.[9] The worse the malnutrition, the greater the likelihood of permanently impaired physical and cognitive development, contributing to a vicious cycle of ups and downs, all well below what is required to sustain the basic requirements of life, let alone a decent life.

Seen by outsiders and from the perspective of statistics, solutions to some of these problems might seem rather simple, as they did to BRAC in Sulla. And certainly some of the techniques employed over the years have been simplistic, if not simple, including more and better education; health facilities; access to the pumps, seeds, and fertilizer needed to produce more food; relief operations; and food-for-work schemes during the hungry seasons and emergencies, in order to tide the poorest over from one good period to the next.

All of these things and more were initiated in Bangladesh by the army of foreign aid agencies, charities, and experts who arrived in the first years after independence. As it moved from relief to development, BRAC also took a conventional approach to problem-solving. Three years after independence, however, Bangladesh suffered a famine that, in its human devastation, rivaled any in history. The causes were manifold, a combination of bad weather, bad harvests, aid cutbacks, government ineptitude, and corruption. The poorest suffered most. Hundreds of thousands of people died of hunger in 1974. BRAC, by then in its third year, was beginning to see that changing the status quo would not be as simple as a wave of a checkbook and some investments in agriculture, no matter how small or large the scale and no matter how intense the effort. The logic of development theory was simply not surviving the translation into reality. The poor remained poor, exceedingly vulnerable, seemingly ignorant, untrusting, and fatalistic.

Ending poverty was not going to be a matter of more, and development was not going to be about growth alone. There was a reason. As former World Bank economist Herman Daly famously observed, "When something grows, it gets bigger; when it develops, it gets different."[10] What was missing in much of the effort to deal with poverty was an understanding of how to make things different, that is, how to change patterns of distribution and power and status. To reach that kind of understanding, it would be necessary, as the king told Alice, to begin at the beginning, that is, to reach an understanding of how things actually were on the ground, in the rural areas of Bangladesh where more than 90 percent of the population lived.

Deeper Combinations: We See Nothing but Darkness in Front

Since the first development efforts in Sulla, BRAC hallmarks have been the quality and the depth of its research, its acknowledgement of failure as part of the learning process, its ability to listen to village voices, and the adaptive approach it takes to development. While planning has always been a strong suit, BRAC learned early that no large-scale plan of any kind should be initiated until there is enough solid evidence, that is, evidence derived from research, testing, and small-scale efforts and pilots, to show that replication is actually feasible. Dennis Rondinelli might have been describing BRAC when he wrote that effective development:

> [I]s unlikely to emerge from conventional principles which emphasize comprehensive, detailed, and control-oriented planning and management. In an uncertain and complex world, planning must be participatory, and administration must be adaptive.[11]

While the wisdom in these words may seem self-evident, even today, it gets more lip service than real attention, and it was far from evident in the development world of the 1970s. Bangladesh is littered with the ruins of a hundred or more massive rural development projects initiated by the government and donors and planned to the last detail except one, an understanding of how things really work in the lives and in the minds of those whom the projects sought to assist.

Who Gets What and Why: Resource Allocation in a Bangladesh Village, a 200-page report on life, work, and poverty, was one of BRAC's first efforts to understand and write down how things really work in the rural areas.[12] Adaptive learning did not come easily, however. During the 1970s, all of BRAC's senior staff and field workers came from the educated urban elite. Although most had an image and perhaps some experience of rural Bangladesh when they began, it was mostly an idyllic view, possibly remembered and shaped by holiday visits to grandparents and cousins who themselves were undoubtedly among the rural upper crust. The rural Bangladesh that BRAC thought it knew in the early 1970s was beginning to shed its veil by the middle of the decade, and the idea of treating the various causes and symptoms of poverty in isolation from one another was beginning to look rather foolish.

Robert Chambers wrote extensively about the way outsiders understand a poor rural society. "Poor people on disaster courses may not be recognized," he wrote in his now-famous *Rural Development: Putting the Last First.*

> A nutritionist may see malnutrition but not the seasonal indebtedness, the high cost of medical treatment, the distress sales of land, and the local power structure which generate it. A doctor may see infant mortality but not the declining real wages which drive mothers to desperation, still less the causes of those declining real wages. Visibility and specialization

combine to show simple surface symptoms rather than deeper combinations of causes. The poor are little seen, and even less is the nature of their poverty understood.[13]

Some of what Chambers wrote in 1983 was based on what he had seen and learned from visits to BRAC, which, by then, had produced a series of reports based on what it was seeing and learning.

Another early BRAC study, entitled "Famine," examined what Chambers had called "the deeper combination of causes" in relation to food shortages. This study, undertaken at the end of a drought in mid-1979, began with a statement of the commonly held view of famine, that is, an event preceded by a natural calamity, for example, a delay in the arrival of rains, a low crop yield, or floods. To a fatalistic people, destiny through blind misfortune must seem both unchangeable and preordained. What BRAC researchers found, however, when they dug into the reality of the lives of villagers in Rangpur, Jamalpur, Jessore, and Comilla, was something else entirely. People actually had a very sophisticated understanding of the determinants of their plight. While they had few resources with which to change them, they could certainly explain their situation to people who were willing to listen.

Villagers explained how, as food shortages begin to appear, landowners would inevitably begin to stockpile, awaiting a rise in prices. By then, the poor, for whom day labor is often the only source of employment, would already have been hurt by a reduced demand for weeding and harvesting. And because there would now be many more people than jobs, wages would fall. The only recourse for the most desperate under these circumstances is to begin selling what few possessions and household utensils they have. People told the BRAC researchers stories of being pressed in by almost every conceivable obstacle.

> The sheer desperation of acquiring some cash with which to feed the household combines with the fact that the only people who have enough wealth to make any purchases are the big landlords. Thus another avenue of exploitation opens up.[14]

The first inclination is to pawn anything of value, but the amount of the loan will usually be low in relation to the value of the item, and the rate of interest will be high. In the end, the transaction typically turns out to be little more than a sale at bargain prices.

Many transactions are made worse by the historical relationship between borrower and lender. A man in Rowmari spoke of an elder cousin who pawned some earrings to a wealthier relative. Although he eventually repaid the loan, he felt unable to ask for the return of the earrings because this might have upset the delicate balance in their relationship.

> He genuinely dreaded the day when he might have to return
> to this relative for another loan, and thus did not want to jeop-
> ardize his future chances by appearing too sure of himself.[15]

Land remains the most important asset for anyone living in the Bangladesh countryside. Land is a productive asset, and the life of every village revolves around agriculture. At independence, more than 90 percent of the population lived in the rural areas, and over 80 percent of all employment was in agriculture. Sixty percent of the GNP was derived from farming, and 90 percent of the country's exports were agricultural or farm-related.

For the villager, land is also the most prominent form of capital accumulation. It is a hedge against bad economic times and can serve as collateral for survival loans and loans for other productive enterprise. It is also the most important indicator of status. Those with land are not just better off; they are important. Those without it are nothing. Unlike Pakistan, where it is not uncommon for a rich farmer to own 100 acres or more, landholdings in Bangladesh are relatively small. The average at independence was about three acres, and fewer than 3 percent of all farms were larger than 12 acres.[16] But, as always, the averages conceal many things. In rural Bangladesh, more than half of all households owned no land at all— except, perhaps, for the land underneath the house.

In rural Bangladesh, those with land always keep an eye open for new acquisitions, and periods of distress offer a real opportunity. For the desperate marginal landholder, the road to complete landlessness may start with a small loan with land serving as collateral. But where the loan is used to buy food for survival, it may not be long before the land changes hands permanently, driving people from the edge of poverty into deep and permanent misery. The social fabric of the community and families begins to come apart at the seams. Men leave, hoping for work in towns and cities and aim to send money home. But many simply disappear into the urban vortex, leaving their wives and the elderly to manage the family as best they can. Quarrels over property become acute, violence erupts, and crime grows. A cobbler in Jamalpur, unable to buy hides, began to systematically poison cows in the area. A woman, unable to stand the cries of her hungry children, hung herself, leaving them orphaned. Another woman, having sold her four children, turned to begging; yet another turned to prostitution. One man told BRAC researchers, "The boat was floating. Now it has sunk. We see an unending sea all around." Another said, "We see nothing but darkness in front."

In the late 1970s, BRAC examined relationships in the rural village. Its researchers learned that poverty "is not just a fortuitous condition."

> Rural poverty is a result of some of the processes that are at work within the society. These processes tend to confer a built-in disadvantage to a particular set of households, while conferring an operational advantage to the wealthy.[17]

These processes are economic in nature, but they also relate to social and cognitive processes that confer value, prestige, credibility, authority, and freedom of choice and association. The BRAC researchers identified three dominant themes in the economic relationships among villagers: discontinuity, dependency, and disadvantage.

In discontinuity, they referred to the clusters of families that are common in Bangladeshi villages. These factions may be based on kinship or the location of homesteads. Or they may be less formal, especially where the poorest are concerned. But a faction would create for those in it a higher degree of cooperation and interaction than for those outside. It might also provide opportunities for casual borrowing and lending, shared information, and mutual assistance on projects requiring physical labor. For the poorest, association with a particular faction might help during bad times, but bad times would inevitably increase the rivalry between factions, perhaps creating greater advantage for those within a faction that are already better off, but not for the rest.

The researchers found that discontinuity leads to dependency. The poorest in a village depend on those with land to provide them with day labor, sharecropping opportunities, and credit. The wealthy, therefore, have enormous influence over the poor, who can ill-afford to do anything that might upset the balance, no matter how lopsided it may be. It is almost inevitable that such relationships will be exploitative, whether in wages or in the terms of the loan a poor family may need to survive.

> Even in terms of the exchange involved in political support, the loss of independence and self-determination for the landless peasant seems to far outweigh, if such things were measurable, the cost to the landlord of providing protective patronage.[18]

So the poor are at a significant disadvantage in virtually all of their relationships with the better-off parts of the village, a disadvantage that shows up in the countless little services that villagers will render to their patron and the thousand small humiliations they must endure.

In a play on the now-threadbare idea of integrated rural development, Chambers wrote about integrated rural poverty and how combinations of factors conspire to keep the poor in a disadvantaged state. Physical weakness is part of it, that is, the physical weakness of individuals who are inadequately fed and clothed as well as the weakness of the entire household, which may have several dependents, including children, the elderly, and the infirm. Isolation is also a factor. The household may be on peripheral land at the edge of the village, but it is isolated in many other ways. Illiteracy prevents people from reading. Lack of schooling inhibits understanding. Poverty ensures that radio is an unreachable luxury. Lack of status guarantees that the poorest will be last on anyone's information list, and they will rarely be consulted on anything. This adds to more obvious forms of vulnerability, including a lack of assets to sell or borrow against and little or no surplus agricultural production. And the poor have little resistance to easily remedied illnesses that for them become killers: infections, respiratory ailments, and diarrhea

All of this contributes to powerlessness in the face of adversity, powerlessness in the face of abuse, and powerlessness in the face of criminality.

Perhaps the worst examples of powerlessness among the poor and of the abuse and criminality they endure take place around emergency relief efforts that are intended to assist them and save lives. During a 1979 drought, BRAC once again became involved in emergency activities, but some of their workers questioned the need for BRAC's involvement when so much government assistance was available. They soon discovered, however, that small groups of powerful men were siphoning off large amounts of relief food. In order to better understand what was happening, BRAC field workers undertook a five-month study of 10 villages. The first part of their work, the researchers wrote, "was to record carefully all the examples of oppressive, exploitative, and illegal activities we could find."[19] They did not have to go far. In fact, villagers "gave us pens and paper and insisted we record everything." They later said it was "like shining a torch into a dark room." They called it the "gossip methodology."

In each village, they first identified the different factions, then the leaders, their landholdings, and something about their background. For example, "Matin Master," age 35, came to one of the villages from a nearby *thana* and bought four acres of land from desperate refugees. He taught at the primary school, and he was secretary of the union branch of one of the political parties. He had good connections with the local member of parliament, the union chairman, the secretary of the local teachers' association, and the central teachers' association in Dhaka. Matin Master worked his contacts to excellent advantage, and he had made a substantial amount of money with assistance from the MP, mainly by planting and harvesting crops on disputed land.

Kadir, age 50, had eight acres of illegally occupied land. His main activity was cattle rustling, which he managed by obtaining false sales receipts from the clerk of the union, through someone named Alim Master. Alim Master, age 50, was so named because he was a music master. He had two wives and many mistresses. The previous year, he had paid taxes on nine acres but exercised rights over nearly 30 through his connections with the clerks in the district revenue office who helped legitimize his titles. Before 1971, he had been clerk to the union council member, a man who had the power to allocate abandoned land to refugees. When the member was killed during the war, Alim Master and a crony took his papers and used them to acquire even more land.

"The Net: Power Structure in Ten Villages" laid out the relationships between men like these and then examined how the connections came into play during the drought when government relief supplies arrived to assist the starving. Food, often donated by the UN and foreign aid agencies, is commonly used in food-for-work schemes. People are paid in food for their work on rural infrastructure projects. Basically, this involves moving earth by hand to build or repair roads, canals, embankments, and ponds. The local union council administers the allocation of work and payment in food. Without the need for a great deal of investigation, BRAC discovered that a large proportion of the food simply vanished. During a four-month period, 26 schemes in one area had been sanctioned with 86.4 tons of food allocated to pay for the work. In the end, less than 24 percent of the food was distributed for the work. The rest went to local worthies, elected officials, and government officers at several levels in the hierarchy. The methodology was simple. Some projects were sanctioned twice. Work done halfway was reported as complete. Phantom projects and phantom workers were created where none existed.

In addition to food-for-work, the government operated a ration system for the poorest. Under this countrywide system, a registered dealer sells food at low, fixed prices to government-approved ration cardholders under the supervision of the elected union council. BRAC discovered this was going wrong in a variety of ways. In some cases, the wrong people had ration cards, often many. In others, the dealer was simply selling the food at full market prices and bribing the inspectors. In yet other cases, local politicos were buying up the food at ration prices, paying off the dealers and inspectors at various levels of government, and pocketing the proceeds from resale. Again, 75 percent of the food was misused. Even when it did go to the poor, it was controlled by men who would eventually be asked for favors from those who were dependent on their factions.

The BRAC findings were far from unique, and they were easy enough to discover by those who took the trouble. In 1974 and 1975, two Americans, Betsy Hartman and Jim Boyce, lived for nine months in a small village called Katni in Rajshahi Division, eventually writing about what they saw in *A Quiet Violence: View from a Bangladesh Village*. They described in detail how the most powerful man in the village diverted relief assistance to his own ends as a matter of course. By Bangladesh standards, Nafis was an extremely wealthy man with several businesses and 70 acres of land, much of it obtained illegally during the independence struggle. Yet he was not above stealing relief blankets and corrugated tin sheets and diverting funds intended for road repairs to his own lands.

> Nafis's biggest patronage plum, however, was a deep tubewell for irrigation, one of 3,000 installed in northwestern Bangladesh under a World Bank project at a cost of about $12,000 each. Nafis acquired the tubewell by virtue of his political connections, paying less than $300 for it. On paper, the tubewell is to be used by a cooperative irrigation group, of which Nafis is the manager, but, in practice, it is his personal property. The tubewell will irrigate 30 acres of his land, allowing him to grow a profitable extra rice crop in the dry winter season.[20]

Given their dependency, vulnerability, and isolation, it is not surprising that poor people watch this kind of theft and take this kind of abuse almost as a given. But the BRAC researchers said "it would be wrong to think that they are merely passive victims or observers." Occasionally, someone goes too far. Occasionally, an honest official steps in. Occasionally, people are able to organize and resist. There were several violent peasant revolts in Bengal during the nineteenth century. And, during the twentieth century, before partition, there were repeated risings against powerful landlords. At the end of World War II, an organized Tebhaga sharecroppers movement demanded a two-thirds share of their crops instead of half, but this movement, like others before it, was violently suppressed. Bangladeshis understood injustice and, when roused, would fight against it. In due course, Sheikh Mujib would also use force to quell a restive population, demonstrating at once his own weakness and the strength of his people.

Hunger Pushed Away Their Veil

Community development, as it was understood in Bangladesh at independence, derived almost exclusively from experiments that had been carried out over the previous decade by the Academy for Rural Development at Comilla, a district town some 90 kilometers east of Dhaka. The Academy was blessed with three important assets.

The first was the size and scope of its laboratory. The government allocated the entire Comilla *thana*, an area of 100 square miles with some 300 villages, for the use of the Academy. Academy programs would supersede those of government where agriculture, irrigation, and cooperatives were concerned.

The second asset was the amount of interest devoted to the Comilla experiment by external donors. The Ford Foundation became its patron, and Michigan State University, Harvard, and others supplied highly qualified instructors and researchers. Although somewhat disdained by government officials, Comilla rarely wanted for money or the best international expertise that money could buy.

The Academy's third asset was its first director, a man who served in the position until the independence of Bangladesh. Akhtar Hameed Khan was not a typical administrator or teacher. A graduate of Cambridge and a scholar of Persian, Arabic, and Pali, he had studied Islamic and Buddhist classics in their original languages. In 1937, he had become a member of the august Indian Civil Service, an elite body of administrators in the higher echelons of the British raj. After almost a decade, however, he did the unthinkable, resigning from the ICS, which he had come to see as part of a dying system. "After nine years," he wrote, "I left the imperial service. There was nothing more to learn from British teachers. I needed a different kind of apprenticeship."[21] He returned to philosophy and religion and, for a time, worked as a laborer and locksmith in Aligarh. He later taught in Delhi, eventually moving on to East Bengal where he became principal of Victoria College in Comilla. In 1958, he was asked to take the helm of the new academy, an institution he would build with distinction over the next decade.

Khan was a teacher, but he believed that, to teach, one had to learn. As principal of Victoria College, he had seen recurrent floods destroy the rural economy, leading to famine. Despite heavy investments in flood control by government, little changed. Khan argued that the flooding resulted not from rain, but from a breakdown in the feudal systems of control and management that had ensured the maintenance of drainage systems. The government could not operate a feudal system, and Khan argued that the only solution lay in new organizations where rural people organized into new institutions. "God made me contemplative," he once said. "but I insist on action, not just contemplation."[22]

Much of the Comilla experiment was founded on rural works, for example, the reconstruction of *khals, bundhs,* and roads. Local project committees were formed to do the work without contractors, saving large amounts of money. Controlled irrigation became a cornerstone of the effort, pumping surface water for irrigation and sinking tubewells for drinking water. Management of the tubewells and pumps was given not to government or elected councils, but to beneficiary groups to help make them self-supporting. Rural works rebuilt the infrastructure, and regular maintenance provided employment for the poor.

The Academy's second objective was to improve the productivity of small farmers. To this end, two institutions were created. The first was a training and development center where people could meet government officials, religious leaders, and each other. The second was a set of farmers' cooperatives. The model did not come easily. As Khan put it in 1963:

> Our training activities have been formulated around these rules: that training should be supported by research; that training should be supported by experimental efforts to test theories and find workable procedures . . . When we began work, the first serious problem was that the instructors had no experience in rural development. Whatever knowledge they had was academic in nature. The instructor in rural business management had only the experience of having managed to get himself out of the village! Our ignorance could not be removed by reading books. The number of surveys in this part of the world is very small and most of these are about India. But even these only describe things as they exist. We were here to discover things as they should be and then plan the training accordingly.[23]

When BRAC began to turn its attention from emergency assistance to rural development in Sulla, the approach was conventional and not unlike initiatives found today in many parts of the world, including Bangladesh. The community in community development meant the entire community. The model was Comilla, where the Academy had showed the potential that might lie in new types of organization, improved farming technologies, and better access to seeds, fertilizer, and other inputs. BRAC's plan in Sulla had been similar to the Comilla idea, but in a relatively manageable area of about 200 villages and 120,000 people. The plan was to introduce improved agriculture and horticulture, fisheries, adult education, health and family planning, and vocational training. BRAC introduced the two-tier cooperative system developed at Comilla in parallel with an ambitious government plan, the Integrated Rural Development Program (IRDP), which aimed to do the same thing nationally.

BRAC worked on the assumptions that education and training would change attitudes and behavior, and that village communities, although far from homogenous, could be induced, if not persuaded, to pool their resources and work cooperatively. It identified two subgroups in the village as deserving of special attention. It saw potential in the large number of educated, but unemployed, youth, who might be mobilized into community social action. And it identified women as another vulnerable group in need of special attention. The special attention, as envisaged in 1973, would focus on adult literacy and vocational training in tailoring and handicrafts.

By that time in the West, the women's liberation movement was in full spate. Betty Friedan's *The Feminine Mystique* was almost a decade old, and writers like Gloria Steinem, Germaine Greer, and Kate Millet had recently added to a widening feminist discourse. Theirs was a new kind of feminism, one that went far beyond the correction of tangible manifestations of gender discrimination in law and the workplace. They delved deeply into more abstract ideas about gender relationships, women's reproductive rights, and male-dominated models of society and politics.

These ideas, radical as they were even in the West, would eventually become the bedrock of BRAC's entire modus operandi. But, in 1973, to an organization thinking about tailoring and handicrafts for women, they might as well have originated on another planet. Just as it would take time for BRAC to understand the dynamics of rural poverty, it would take time to develop a deeper understanding of the lives of rural women. But that understanding would be essential before there would be any meaningful change.

In fact, until the early 1970s, there had been very little research done by anyone into the lives of rural women in Bangladesh. The change began in part with independence from Pakistan and the phalanx of international NGOs and aid agencies that arrived to assist the fledgling nation. Many of the newcomers, however, saw women almost exclusively as the centerpiece in debates about population. Food remained the country's number one priority in those years. Starvation had accompanied the country's birth, and famine again stalked the land in 1974. Questions about national food security invariably turned to population growth and frightening scenarios that projected as many as 229 million Bangladeshis by the turn of the century.[24] For a country that could not feed 70 million, the prospects were terrifying. Family planning, therefore, became a major focus of attention with wide-ranging plans, pilots, and projects aimed at educating and motivating both women and men.

What programmers began to discover, however, was that, if they knew little about the poor, they knew next to nothing about the lives of women, their attitudes, problems, skills, or their contribution to the family and society. Hitherto the subject of little study, most Bangladeshi women and their lives were hidden from view by *purdah*. One woman who did understand was Taherunnesa Abdullah. She had worked at Comilla on literacy, nutrition, and cooperatives for women. In 1974, not yet 40, she was appointed joint director of the government's IRDP, where her special concern was the creation of women's cooperatives and family planning. By 1978, she had created 180 rural women's cooperative societies, one in every district, demonstrating what could be done. While the IRDP went on to less than stellar success, the influence of Taherunnesa Abdullah on thinking about women was profound.* As other studies began to emerge, they described something very different from the bucolic ideal described in the rich legacy of Bangla ballads and poetry. They unveiled a dark world in which the lives of women, especially poor women, were nasty, brutish, and short. Bangladesh was the only country on earth where men outlived women.

In most families, boys were viewed as assets and girls were liabilities. There was often no call for prayer (*azan*) when a girl was born. From her earliest years, she was trained for her primary role in life as a mother and caregiver. By the age of five or six, she was looking after younger children in the family. If she were lucky enough to go to school, she would invariably drop out after a year or so. This effectively meant that the primary caregiver, the family's chief nutritionist, and primary role model for young children was illiterate, uneducated, and disconnected in almost every way from the wider world beyond the home. Apart from what her own mother had told her, she was unschooled in anything relating to her human rights, her legal rights or, for that matter, her reproductive rights. By the age of 12 or 13, with the onset of puberty, she was forced to observe *purdah,* rarely venturing beyond the family homestead. Although deeply religious, she would never enter a mosque. She would never go to the market, town, or city. Soon she would be married, usually to a man ten years her senior, someone she may never have seen before. During her lifetime, she could expect to have 10 or 12 pregnancies with perhaps five or six live births. Only three or four of her children would survive beyond the age of five.

In addition to cooking, cleaning, sewing, and bearing and raising children, village women played an essential role in the agricultural life of the family and the village. They cleaned, parboiled, dried, and husked rice. They tended family vegetable plots, made sugar from cane, wove mats, sewed blankets, and even produced the mud stove on which they cooked the family's meals. If their husbands worked in jute farming, they would be involved in the latter stages of processing. If there was wheat, women would do the threshing, processing, and storing. If there was livestock, women would feed any goats or cattle and conserve the droppings for fuel and fertilizer. Women would manage chickens and ducks. Women would

---

*Taherunnesa Abdullah is today a member of BRAC's board of directors.

gather firewood and fetch water for the family's cooking and drinking needs. They would often eat last. In times of shortage, they would eat less than their husbands and their sons.

Women were absent from most aspects of national public life. The 1972 Bangladesh constitution provided 15 reserved seats for women in the new parliament, and two women had been appointed as ministers of state, but these were in the traditional women's portfolios of social welfare and education. Because women could vote, it was important that there be women's wings in the national political parties, but their role and their structures mirrored the dictates of *purdah* at all levels. A few women's organizations dated from Pakistan times, but these were mostly urban and mostly organized around education and welfare.

Under *Sharia* law, Muslim women have clear rights regarding marriage, divorce, and property. In Islam, or at least under Muslim personal law, as it is practiced in Bangladesh, marriage is a social contract between two individuals. Provision is made for *mehr* (money payable to the bride). Half is to be paid after the wedding; the other half is reserved (to be paid later) on demand or in the case of divorce. If the man initiates a divorce, he must pay the remaining part of the *mehr.* If the woman initiates the divorce, she must repay the first half. Where property is concerned, a widow inherits one-eighth of her husband's property when he dies—one-fourth if the couple was childless. Daughters inherit half of what their brothers do.

In practice, however, few of these second-class legal provisions meant anything among the rural poor of Bangladesh. Instead of *mehr,* dowries became a way of making a bride more saleable. Divorce was common, but women rarely initiated it. The result of a divorce was seldom positive for the wife, who would often be shunned by her own family and forced into a life of destitution. A study at the time spoke of a common sight in rural Bangladesh:

> [G]roups of women proceeding from house to house begging, with little bundles of rice they have collected along the way. These are mostly widows who have produced no surviving children to support them in their old age or only daughters in whose husbands' homes the husbands' widowed mothers live and are supported, but in which there is no place for a wife's widowed mother.[25]

But things were changing. As a BRAC worker put it at the time, "The pain of hunger pushed away their veil."[26] Simplistic ideas about tailoring and handicrafts were not likely to have much impact on situations like these. In fact, as BRAC delved deeper into the problems of women,

Marty Chen with son Greg and villagers, 1970s
(Photo by Marty Chen)

the organization began to distinguish between levels of poverty, identifying ways in which wealthy villagers influenced the village economy and controlled its societal norms. Women spoke not just about how the wealthy controlled all paid labor opportunities in the village, but about how they influenced what women could do if they dared to venture beyond the village.

Marty and Lincoln Chen and several of the doctors who had worked with Abed and HELP on Manupura after the cyclone had campaigned for Bangladesh in the United States during the war, and some had returned. Marty Chen began to work with BRAC. On an old organization chart, she is described as an executive assistant to Abed, but her growing passion paralleled BRAC's emerging understanding of the country's gender problems. Soon she was devoting all of her time and attention to programs for women. Where *purdah* was concerned, she wanted to understand why some activities were regarded as falling within the acceptable bounds of *purdah* and why others were *bepurdah* (beyond the pale). She observed that, when women from wealthy families had to go to town to appear in court for days at a time in connection with a property dispute, this was sanctioned as *purdah*. But when poor women asked about going to town for a day to attend a training session, this was *bepurdah*. It seemed the norms of *purdah* could be relaxed and constricted at will.

"How," Chen asked, "can the rich or elders dictate these norms? Don't the *mullahs* have a say in what is *purdah* or *bepurdah?*" The answer she received was a lesson not so much in religion, but in economics. It turned out that a small-town *mullah* was not unlike a small-town American church minister in days gone by, dependent in many ways upon church elders and bill-paying parishioners and mindful of their views. The *mullahs* did invoke the norm, but often at the behest of the rich and the village elders.

> The elders sit on the local mosque committee which elects the local *mullah,* sets his tenure, and determines his stipend. The *mullahs* have some say about religious norms, but the elders have the final say.[27]

In fact, *purdah* has been described as a middle-class concept that does not much apply to the rich or very poor. Few *mullahs* would criticize a destitute woman for taking a job breaking bricks on the roadside, a common enough sight in Bangladesh.

Chen later described the lessons BRAC learned in those early days about women and poverty.

> The first lesson the women taught us about poverty is that poverty is not static. The reality is not simply that some are rich and some poor. The reality is that poverty has a dynamic in which the rich and poor interact.

And the interaction is seldom to the benefit of the poor. Those living on the edge of survival are exploited ruthlessly and repeatedly. Women at a BRAC workshop described the downward spiral of poverty:

> During a drought [or] a flood . . . when the poor have no work, they have to go to the rich for loans which are given at a very exorbitant rate. Afterwards, they can only repay such loans by selling their homesteads and whatever household articles they possess. If they do not repay . . . they are forced to work in the homes of the rich throughout the year, for which they do not get fair wages. In addition, they have to go to the rich for money in the event of illness, death of a family member, or during the marriage of their daughters. The rich take advantage of these opportunities to cheat the poor and make fortunes for themselves.[28]

A second lesson BRAC learned was that:

> [P]overty erodes the traditional family support systems. As families get poorer, traditional family obligations begin to break down. The first victim is extended family ties. The second victim is immediate family ties.

Sons and brothers are unwilling or unable to look after a divorced or widowed family member. This breakdown in the family structure and self-esteem of human beings would prove to be a larger problem than BRAC initially understood, one that would return in discussions about the ultra poor 25 years later.

A third lesson in those early years, one that would provide BRAC with an important window of opportunity, was the lesson about poverty and the veil.

> Poverty forces women to work outside their homes. As households get poorer, all family members try as best they can to find work, to help eke out an existence. Women will seek employment from other women in wealthier households. They will care for animals, fetch water, weed the gardens, husk the grain, cook the food for more wealthy families.[29]

An overarching lesson, however, was the realization that community was a relative term with little currency in the lives of the poorest, most especially in the lives of the poorest women. If BRAC was going to make a difference, it would have to target its efforts more specifically at them. It had learned that poverty could trump *purdah*. But learning how to surmount the power dynamics of rural Bangladesh would take longer.

Notes

1. Just Faaland and J.R. Parkinson, *Bangladesh: The Test Case of Development* (London: Hurst & Co., 1976), 2.

2. Faaland and Parkinson, *Bangladesh*, 98.

3. Betsy Hartmann and James Boyce, *A Quiet Violence: View from a Bangladesh Village* (London: Zed, 1983), 22.

4. Faaland and Parkinson, *Bangladesh*, 194.

5. Faaland and Parkinson, *Bangladesh*, 193.

6. Azizur Rahman Khan, *The Economy of Bangladesh* (London: Macmillan Press, 1972), 23.

7. Khan, *The Economy of Bangladesh*, 5.

8. A.R. Khan, *Poverty and Landlessness in Rural Asia* (Geneva: ILO, 1977), quoted in Hasnat Abdul Hye, *Below the Line: Rural Poverty in Bangladesh* (Dhaka: University Press, 1996), 6.

9. Khan, *The Economy of Bangladesh*, 5.

10. Herman E. Daly and Kenneth N. Townsend, *Valuing the Earth: Economics, Ecology, Ethics* (Cambridge, MA: MIT Press, 1993), 267.

11. Dennis A. Rondinelli, *Development Projects as Policy Experiments* (London: Routledge, 1993), 187.

12. BRAC, *Who Gets What and Why: Resource Allocation in a Bangladesh Village* (Dhaka: BRAC, 1983). The original version, based on field work that began in 1977, was produced in 1979.

13. Robert Chambers, *Rural Development: Putting the Last First* (Burnt Mill, Essex: Longman Scientific & Technical, 1983), 25.

14. BRAC, *Peasant Perceptions: Famine; Credit Needs; Sanitation* (Dhaka: BRAC, 1984), 6.

15. BRAC, *Peasant Perceptions*, 7.

16. Khan, *The Economy of Bangladesh*, 39.

17. BRAC, *Peasant Perceptions*, 7.

18. BRAC, *Peasant Perceptions*, 7.

19. Quotations and descriptions in this section are taken from BRAC, *The Net: Power Structure in Ten Villages* (Dhaka: BRAC, 1983), originally published in February 1980.

20. Hartman and Boyce, *A Quiet Violence*, 132.

21. Akhtar Hameed Khan, *Orangi Pilot Project: Reminiscences and Reflections* (Karachi: Oxford University Press, 1996), xv.

22. Adele Freedman, "Dr. Akhtar Hameed Khan," *MIMAR 34: Architecture in Development* (1990): 27.

23. Akhtar Hameed Khan, "A New Rural Cooperative System for Comilla Thana," *Third Annual Report*, Pakistan Academy for Rural Development, Comilla, 1963.

24. The Harvard University Center for Population Studies projected numbers ranging between 153 and 229 million by 2000. (Faaland and Parkinson, *Bangladesh*, 98). The actual population in 2006 was 147 million.

25. Jean Ellickson, "Rural Women," in *Women for Women* (Dhaka: University Press, 1975), 82.

26. Quoted in Martha Alter Chen, *A Quiet Revolution: Women in Transition in Rural Bangladesh*, (Cambridge, Mass.: Schenkman Publishing, 1983), 60.

27. Chen, *A Quiet Revolution*, 73.

28. Chen, *A Quiet Revolution*, 62.

29. Chen, *A Quiet Revolution*, 62.

CHAPTER 5

Learning and Unlearning

Jamalpur

Some parts of BRAC's new understanding about poverty and the place of women in Bangladesh developed quickly during that first development effort in Sulla. Others took longer. After the first 20 months, Abed knew that Sulla was not going to be a two- or three-year effort and that, if they were to succeed, their investments would have to probe deeper into the societal problems that were beginning to reveal themselves.

They decided to take on new geographic areas. They feared their first emergency programs in Sulla might have contributed to a relief mentality among villagers with negative effects on the self-help ethic BRAC was promoting, so they looked for places where they could start afresh, trying different approaches in areas uncontaminated by early setbacks.

UNICEF, impressed with BRAC's education work in Sulla, asked if they would undertake a special program for women in Jamalpur, an area 120 miles north of Dhaka. It was a stop-gap effort to help 840 women who had been engaged in a UNICEF food-for-work project, and the idea was to give them something more before they returned to their previous lives. It was to be a limited project, beginning in June 1975 and winding up before the end of the year. As it concluded, however, BRAC saw an opportunity to widen and deepen the program and make it their own. Here they would have a program that dealt exclusively with women, and it would be targeted directly at the poor.

The plan was to provide functional education to the poorest women they could find in 28 villages. There would be literacy training, but, in discussions, they would also try to make women aware of the wider causes of their problems and help them with some real-life solutions. Many women had nobody who could offer advice on questions as simple as, "Should I marry my daughter to so-and-so at this age?" BRAC would work with them on health, hygiene, and family planning. It would encourage joint savings and cooperative economic activities, promoting poultry and horticulture. The number of women they sought to reach was not great. Gone was the idea of making tens of thousands of people literate. Here, the plan was for 320 students, no more than 280 cooperative members, and the total budget for a year was Tk 150,000 (US$10,000 at the prevailing exchange rate).

BRAC refined its approach to staff recruitment, hiring women under 30 from the immediate project area. Nobody would be parachuted in. They looked for people with at least an eighth-grade education, and they trained them. Few had any idea what they were getting into. Sajeda Begum was typical of those who joined. Married at 15, she had been widowed at 19 when her husband was killed during the war. She had two children. Because of her penury she had been forced to send the girl to her husband's family and she lived with her son in her father's house. At 24, she remarried, but, at home, she said she was doing "nothing except household work because my education is not enough to get a job."[1] Sajeda joined BRAC for a simple reason. It was not to save the world. "It was to save my children." Although she hoped to train others, she had her own problems in thinking beyond tradition. She said she believed there should be equality between husband and wife in the marriage relationship, but "our society does not believe in it. Men think equality humiliates their mastership."

Before it could challenge society, BRAC would have to build self-confidence and self-esteem among its own employees. Gradually, as trainees began their jobs, it started to work. Each woman would cover two villages, and the best would become team leaders, often chosen by their counterparts. A volunteer, or *shebika*, would be selected in each village as well, and she would be given training in family planning, hygiene, and functional education in order to provide continuity between visits from BRAC staff.

In a 1976 report, BRAC said, "Things worked out more or less as planned." Of those who enrolled in the literacy program, 143 passed a basic letter-writing test and were judged literate. There was a great deal of interest in family planning despite (or perhaps because of) a nationwide government program that had distributed birth control pills. The pills had caused a myriad of complications, and BRAC workers spent weeks in door-to-door discussions, explaining how the pills should be used and what should be done in the case of side effects and complications.

But they discovered something else about the targets of donor-inspired national family planning efforts. Mothers were not foolish. They did not go through an endless series of pregnancies simply because there were no pills or condoms. Quite apart from the natural desire for a family, children were an integral part of the family economic unit, and they were an insurance policy for the future. Because so many children died at birth and in their first five years, parents had to hedge their bets and make more babies than they needed. Mothers, therefore, worried about the health of their living children, and women who had undergone tubal ligations to escape the pregnancy trap were deeply concerned that their living children would survive. In the rush for family planning (pills, condoms, and camps for vasectomies and tubal ligations), the government and donor agencies had made the mistake of assuming that a reduction in population growth could be achieved by exhortation. The lesson BRAC was beginning to learn was that ignorant was not the same as stupid and that real changes in a family's attitude toward the number of children it wanted went far beyond access to family planning techniques. It was intimately related to health and child survival and the family's economic well-being.

One hundred and sixteen of the women BRAC worked with in the Jamalpur project were introduced to small income-generating schemes, including goats, rice husking, and potato farming. In one village, BRAC tried an experimental poultry project, persuading women to castrate all of the local cocks and introducing 20 sturdy White Leghorns to replace them. Women without chickens were given hens on loan. Within a few weeks, the village was abuzz with news of the newly hatched "white babies," which, as hens, would produce significantly more eggs. Volunteers, the *shebikas*, were trained in vaccination, and they discussed improved feed and shelter for their new breed.

BRAC abandoned the government's cooperative scheme and started to form its own co-ops, made up entirely of its target group of poor women. There would be no more hijacking by the village elite. Although it was difficult for poor women to save much money, BRAC insisted a cooperative had to accumulate at least Tk 100 if it were to receive any loan money from BRAC.

One of the lessons of microcredit is that, if it is done well, poor women can borrow money without collateral, and they can repay the principal with interest and on time. In those days, however, the term "microcredit" did not exist. Grameen Bank did not exist. BRAC had to pioneer the idea of targeted lending to poor women alone and without models. Microcredit will be discussed in greater detail in chapter 6, but, in 1976, BRAC was beginning to identify the fundamental challenge in lending money to poor women. The challenge had something to do with organization, collateral, and savings. These considerations were important, but they were not enough. Held back by ignorance, tradition, and sometimes malice, women were severely constrained in their investment opportunities.

As a BRAC report put it at the time:

> To identify and design viable economic projects which can ensure a reasonable return to each member of the cooperative is extremely difficult. But this identification and design is

crucial to all else. Much can be done to involve women in health, family planning, education, and other social development efforts, both as beneficiaries and as staff. However, it is economic development activities [that are most important] for rural poor women.

This would soon become a major preoccupation for BRAC, and it would set the organization apart from others, whose focus was more on the loan and the repayments, than what the loan might be used for.

When vegetable seeds introduced by BRAC failed to germinate and when the new white babies began to die, BRAC also realized that good intentions pave a very dangerous roadstead for the poor. Outsiders may well be able to persuade poor women to change their behavior and invest their time differently, but, if the outsiders don't know what they are doing, the opportunity cost for the poor can be more than high. It can be fatal.

Manikganj: "I liked Mao Tse-tung"

Not long after BRAC began its Jamalpur women's project in 1975, it also started to work in Manikganj, an area 45 miles west of Dhaka. Although it was close to the capital, Manikganj *thana* was exceedingly poor. The area was prone to flooding, agricultural yields were low, and the population density was about 10 times that of California. A huge proportion of the 163,000 people who lived in the *thana* were landless.

BRAC was drawn to the area by a famine. At the end of 1975, it ran a food-for-work project, transferring some of its Sulla staff and hiring others. One of the newcomers was a young man named Mohammed Aminul Alam, Amin. As a student at Dhaka University, Amin had been embroiled not only in the politics of the Bangladesh struggle for liberation, but in what he quaintly called "left politics."

> I liked Mao Tse-tung and others like him at that time. I was involved in communist politics, and my education suffered for that reason. I did an honors degree in physics, and I was good in mathematics, but I was not too much involved with studies.

Like other radical students thinking about a new kind of country, he went often to the rural areas to "talk to the people, the poor people."

"Not too much involved with studies" probably overstates Amin's dedication to his education during those turbulent years. His degree took six years because the university and most other institutions were closed during the liberation war; half the urban population fled to the countryside,

Aminul Alam (Amin), about 1975 (Photo by Marty Chen)

and millions crossed the Indian border to escape the marauding Pakistan army. By the end of 1974, Amin's school days were at last over, and a family friend told him that there might be a job in a relief organization called BRAC. Amin knew little of relief organizations beyond the fact that they all seemed to have big cars, so, putting his radicalism somewhere behind him, he set off for an interview with Abed.

Amin must have been an argumentative young man. When Abed offered him a job at Rowmari in Rangpur District, he argued (in vain) to be sent instead to Sylhet because he thought (wrongly) that it was close to Dhaka. Rowmari was BRAC's first venture beyond Sulla. There, over a six-month period, they returned to emergency assistance, feeding 15,000 children two meals a day. When Abed offered Amin a salary of Tk 500 a month (about US$60 in those days), he asked for more, and he was eventually able to squeeze another Tk 80 for a travel allowance. Laughing about it today, he says it was the first and last time he ever argued with Abed about his salary. But he was in for a shock when he got to his posting.

> It was the first time in my life I had seen really poor people. As students, we went to the villages and spoke to poor people, but they were not the really poor people. As someone from the urban higher middle class, when I saw people living in a house with a tin roof, I thought they were poor. But they were not. They were actually the better-off. In Rowmari, I changed my view . . . all of that communist talk. They were not working with the poor people at all; now I was seeing poor people for the first time.

Within a few months, he was transferred to the Manikganj food-for-work project where thousands of desperately poor women and men were doing road repairs, hauling headload after headload of earth up from ditches to fill potholes. In return, they were paid with meager allocations of wheat supplied by relief organizations. Stunned by what he was seeing, Amin thought and probably hoped that Manikganj would be a short-term assignment. As it turned out, he would stay there for eight years. It would change his view of the world forever, and he would eventually rise through the BRAC ranks to become one of its most effective and knowledgeable leaders.

With the lessons of Sulla under its belt, BRAC moved quickly from emergency food assistance in Manikganj to development projects. It focused entirely on the poor, setting up functional education centers as a prelude to other activities. It organized village health workers and paramedics who surveyed all of the villages in the area for health problems that could be handled without recourse to doctors and hospitals. It formed cooperatives, began savings programs, and made loans that would allow borrowers to engage in income-generation activities. In the first year, nine groups borrowed money to invest in rice husking, four took agricultural loans, and three took loans for weaving or pottery production. The following year, 35 groups borrowed money. In 1978, the number rose to 54.

The biggest challenge, however, was not group formation or educating people. As in Jamalpur, it was viable investment opportunities. Rice husking and cattle fattening were all very well. They were activities that had been going on in Bangladeshi villages for hundreds of years and required little training or innovation. If a poverty-stricken women used a loan to buy some paddy (unhusked rice) and a *dheki* to pound it, she might well earn extra income for her family. But paddy husking had always taken place in the village, as had cattle fattening and poultry-raising. By giving these opportunities to the poorest in the village, BRAC was only shifting work away from those who had been doing it before. In itself, this was no bad thing if it helped the poorest. But it did not create any new economic activity in the village. Some borrowed money to engage in petty trading, but that also had limited possibilities. Buying some fruit and a few vegetables and setting up a stall in the bazaar was not what one might call new, productive, or vibrant enterprise. It just added more people to an already crowded kiosk economy.

The challenge at Manikganj, once the motivation and the lending systems had been developed, was clearly the need to find new, productive enterprises for the landless poor, enterprises that would make enough money to repay the principal and interest on a loan and still leave something for the borrower. This, in fact, is the biggest challenge of microfinance worldwide. (And it is something the next chapter deals with in greater depth.) So BRAC staff kept experimenting with poultry, determined to find a way to produce larger, healthier chickens that could produce more eggs and survive under village conditions. Hand-dug ponds are common in Bangladeshi villages as a means of storing water over the dry winter months. Ponds could also be stocked with fish, and BRAC began organizing people for pond excavation, training others in pisciculture (fish farming). New varieties of fast-growing fish fries and fingerlings were introduced. They began to examine the silk business, discovering that a local variety of silkworm could be raised on castor leaves, a plant that grew well on marginal land that was unfit for rice or vegetable farming. Here was something a woman could do at home, rearing cocoons and spinning the silk.

All of this required testing and retesting and ever-larger numbers of villagers who required training. In 1977, BRAC established a training and research center (TARC) at Savar, halfway between Manikganj and Dhaka. Accessible enough for specialized trainers from Dhaka, it provided a convenient residential setting for as many as 90 Manikganj villagers at a time and BRAC's own staff, who were in constant need of upgrading and refresher courses. In time, the TARC would prove to be one of the best investments BRAC ever made because it institutionalized the organization's commitment to training and it became a permanent asset for ongoing education. Paulo Freire, a Brazilian educator we shall encounter in chapter 14, became Abed's bedtime reading, and he recommended Freire to everyone he met.

One of those who became deeply involved with the efforts at Manikganj was a young woman named Bahar, who had a master's degree in English. "Bahar" was the name her friends used. Before she married, her name was Ayesha Chowdhury. By 1973, Abed was 37 years old, and he still had no wife. This was an unusual situation for a Bangladeshi, and his family had been increasing the pressure on him for years. Given his procrastination, they finally decided a marriage had to be arranged. Abed relented, but only if he could nominate the candidate. Bahar was the sister of an old friend, so he knew her. But her three sisters were all married to up-and-comers, and her parents looked dubiously at Abed, wondering, at his age, what he might ever make of this thing called BRAC. But the two families had known each other for almost a half-century. In the end, as Bahar put it, "We satisfied everybody."[2] They were married in April 1973, and their first child, Tamara, was born a year later.

Abed, Tamara, and Bahar (Photo by BRAC)

Bahar quickly learned she would have to become involved in BRAC if she wanted to spend any time with her husband. Within months of their marriage, she told Khushi Kabir that she was already jealous, having to share Abed with Paulo Freire. But his passion became hers, and she would eventually make a name for herself, not as Abed's executive assistant, a position he gave her in 1975, but as a real source of inspiration and leadership in BRAC's efforts to improve the lives of poor women.

Struggle

There was a debate within BRAC during the late 1970s on how best to do this, especially where the issue of credit was concerned. There were some who believed that external injections of cash, regardless of the terms, simply extended the dependency of the poor. Any economic activities should and could be financed strictly from their own savings. More important than economic upliftment was the need for social organization, education, training, and a tough version of what Freire called "conscientization." Abed felt the approach was worth a try, so BRAC created the Outreach Program. In this experiment, landless villagers would be organized into groups, as in other BRAC programs. They would go through BRAC's functional training, and they would be organized around health activities and savings. But, if there were to be loans, they would come entirely from the villagers' own savings. BRAC's role would be catalytic, organizational, and educational, but external funding would not drive the program.

As a student of Shakespeare, Abed undoubtedly knew the famous lines from Hamlet:

> Neither a borrower nor a lender be;
> For loan oft loses both itself and friend,
> And borrowing dulls the edge of husbandry.

Perhaps that is why he sanctioned the Outreach Program as a parallel to the efforts in Sulla, Jamalpur, and Manikganj. Shorn of detail, the approach makes sense. The devil, however, is always in the detail. The Outreach Program was driven by anger that "all the beautiful promises of liberation had done little to alter the situation of the poor." And it was fuelled by a strong ideological zeal that saw organizations of the landless and the oppressed demanding their rights and perhaps sometimes even taking matters into their own hands. The Outreach Program was a struggle, one that would take place in the mind, the community, government offices, and courts of law. It would create peoples' institutions. The poor would be organized for power. As one report put it, "Efforts to make them nonapathetic to serious situations and class-conscious continuously takes place in all Outreach programmes."[3]

The Outreach Program was initiated in 41 unions in five different districts of the country, so it was no small effort. And by 1982, 427 village organizations had been formed, 164 of them for women. Group leaders and volunteers (the *sheboks* and *shebikas* of other BRAC programs) were called "cadres," as in historical revolutionary parties of the left. According to a report at the time, these cadres

> should possess the ability to identify burning issues and blazing problems which the poor confront in their near surroundings. They should be capable of galvanizing distressed minds and stirring the passive people into action.

This action might well eventually turn to confrontation in demanding basic services from government or in the occupation of fallow, government-owned *khas* land.

The Outreach Program fostered the development of savings among the poor, something BRAC had done in its other programs. But here, economic activities were limited by the amounts that very poor people could actually mobilize themselves. By 1982, 21,558 people in 427 village organizations had managed to save Tk 270,368 (US$18,000). This is not a small amount in total, but it represented an average of only Tk 12.54 (US$0.84) per member, the equivalent of a single day's pay for a landless laborer. This hardly represented a great pool of funding for economic activities. And there were additional constraints on the money. Before any investment could be approved, it would have to be discussed by the group as a whole, and "schemes which do not appear to be viable are rejected by a consensus of the people."

It is hardly surprising that, by 1982, fewer than 10 percent of those organized into the Outreach Program were involved in any BRAC-inspired economic activity. The BRAC Outreach staff was dismayed at the high dropout rate from their functional education classes when participants discovered there was no foreseeable economic benefit. And they had difficulty in identifying cadres who could lead the poor to the barricades. As though quoting a training pamphlet from the Paris Commune, they reported that the "social action strategy of the Outreach Program generally takes the form of hard collective bargaining, creation of pressures, and finally the strike." They took heart in the fact that they had been able to force the wages of day laborers up by as much as 50 percent in some project areas.

But, in a land of boundless labor, where flood and famine were as common as the changing seasons and where the poor had to husband long-term relationships within the village power structure, flag-waving, short-term victories, and strikes could prove very risky to long-term survival. In theory, it was sound or at least sounded good. Villagers had to be mobilized to demand their rights. Income-generation programs that might improve their economic lot would only dull their potential for what might become a real revolution. In this view of development, people had to be equipped primarily to fight against the establishment.

Amin, the erstwhile armchair communist, watched it all unfold from his post in Manikganj. It was a debate that harkened back to his radical student days.

> I had seen the people that the communist party worked with, but these were not the real poor; Lenin worked with labor— labor is not that poor, not landless like these . . . I saw Mao's revolution; his people were not as poor as these. Ho Chi Minh? He could not have mobilized Vietnam if he did not have America to fight against.

Amin was beginning to see that, for the truly poor, life was very different, and sustainable empowerment would require more than sloganeering and exhortation.

By 1983 or so, it was clear that the Outreach Program was not enough. People and savings could be mobilized, but, without adequate resources and viable investment opportunities, organization, education, and militancy alone would not hold a group together. The Outreach Program was quietly subsumed into what had become a more integrated approach by then, and external funding was added to the savings of group members for more substantial credit programs. Several key staff left BRAC during this period, convinced that credit weakened people's struggle and simply divided them. One was Khushi Kabir, employee number two. She joined a struggling NGO called Nijera Kori, and she would eventually become one of Bangladesh's most outspoken advocates for human rights and the landless poor. Nijera Kori, which means "doing it ourselves," still argues against microfinance. To make the point, in 2002, the organization published a book about its work entitled *We Don't Do Credit.*[4]

The late 1970s and early 1980s were the most important years in the formation of BRAC's management culture and its understanding of development. In these years, it learned about the deep and pervasive nature of rural poverty in ways that few outsiders could. It understood that external resources, if properly applied, could accelerate development among the poorest, but only if the poorest were directly engaged and treated as adults rather than children. It understood that women occupied a special place in the hierarchy of rural servitude and this had to be given priority attention. It learned about the importance of experimentation and learning and the application of lessons to new endeavors. This point cannot be emphasized enough in a world where cooperatives, microcredit, and community development are still too often applied by rote. Rote learning fails in schools, and it fails just as badly in the world of development assistance.

BRAC was also learning that new economic livelihood opportunities were central to any village development and credit alone was not enough. New opportunities had to be devised, but they had to be effective. Good ideas could be very destructive if they failed in their application. BRAC was also learning about the role that volunteers could play in village development. The *shebikas* were volunteers in the sense that they were not on the BRAC payroll, but they could earn real income by selling services based on skills learned from BRAC and by selling health and veterinary supplies provided to them at cost by BRAC. And BRAC was beginning to invest in its own infrastructure. The first Training and Resource Centre (TARC) was built during this period, the start of a training infrastructure that would become essential as the organization grew.

In Jamalpur, Marty Chen was coming to her own conclusions. In June 1976, she wrote in her journal:

> *Functional Education:* The problem here is supply, not demand. They have started the 124 village centers planned. But the staff worry about the graduates who, having been motivated, need further encouragement and support.
>
> *Family Planning:* A major constraint to family planning acceptance is the concern of mothers for their living children. The health care of living children is of more immediate concern and stands in the way of planning for future children. The staff decided in light of that and other constraints to cut the family planning target for the year in half: from 1500 to 750 acceptors.[5]

Chen realized that BRAC had to be more discerning still about which women it wanted to assist and how. They had learned that all women do not necessarily work well together and success would be based on the particular needs and interests of the women in a given group. They had learned that women had little interest in programs that did not offer concrete solutions to their problems. There was a very specific issue in this:

> Would we be able to identify and design viable economic projects to ensure each member of the group reasonable income in a subsistence economy with extremely limited demand for commercial goods and services?

"Our experimental year was over," Chen wrote, "and, on that pink and grey evening in Anandpur, I was to marvel how far we had come and how much farther we had to go."

Notes

1. Unless otherwise noted, quotations relating to Jamalpur are taken from BRAC, "Report on Jamalpur Women's Programme, January to December 1976," Dhaka, 1976.

2. Ramon Magsaysay Award for Community Leadership, "Biography of F.H. Abed," http://www.rmaf.org.ph/Awardees/Biography/BiographyAbedFaz.htm.

3. Unless otherwise noted, direct quotes dealing with the Outreach Program are taken from BRAC, "Outreach Annual Report 1982," Dhaka, 1982.

4. Naila Kabir, *We Don't Do Credit: Nijera Kori Social Mobilization and the Collective Capabilities of the Rural Poor in Bangladesh* (Dhaka: Nijera Kori, 2002).

5. Chen quotations from Martha Alter Chen, *A Quiet Revolution: Women in Transition in Rural Bangladesh* (Cambridge, Mass.: Schenkman Publishing, 1983), 42–43.

CHAPTER 6

Dulling the Edge of Husbandry?

A Modest Proposal

Where the invention of microcredit is concerned, macrocredit is usually given to Grameen Bank, which has made a worldwide name for itself through its promotion of small-scale lending to the poor. In a 1996 book about Grameen Bank, David Bornstein told the story of Muhammad Yunus, the Bank's founder, walking one day in 1976 in a village near Chittagong University, where he taught economics. There, he met a woman trying to earn a living by constructing bamboo stools.

> The woman had no money to purchase materials and so she barely earned enough to feed herself. Yunus related the story to his graduate students, and, together, they designed an experimental credit program to assist her and others.[1]

By the end of 1976, BRAC was already five years old. It had formed more than 75 cooperatives and smaller experimental groups of borrowers in Sulla, Manikganj, and Jamalpur. It had provided loan funds of more than a Tk 1 million. It was starting to get an idea about what worked and what did not. This is not to suggest that BRAC, rather than Grameen Bank, invented microcredit. All inventions are a combination of knowledge, techniques, and concepts. They involve people, both as individuals— creators, inventors, and entrepreneurs—and as a society. The cultural, historical, and organizational context in which an idea is developed and applied is always a factor in its success or failure. Successful invention is the science and the art of getting things done through the application of skills and knowledge. It is, according to historian Edwin Layton, "a spectrum, with ideas at one end and techniques and things at the other, with design as a middle term."[2]

Over the centuries, ideas have been transferred through trade and migration, art, and religion. They have been fostered and held back by commerce, governments, and educational institutions. New ways of doing things have been bought, copied, stolen, and occasionally developed through independent invention. Often, invention is stimulated by something very small. Sometimes, the stimulus, as with the invention of a successful steam engine or commercially viable electricity, has been enormous and of readily apparent import to a wide range of applications. Marconi is known as the inventor of radio, but he stood on the shoulders of earlier inventors, including the Serbian-born Nikola Tesla, a Russian named Alexander Stepanovich Popov, and a man born in what is today Bangladesh, Jagadish Chandra Bose. Although Marconi won the 1909 Nobel Prize in Physics, most of his patents were overturned in 1943 in favor of Tesla, while the unfairness of history has allowed the names of Popov and Bose to slip into obscurity.

The story of microcredit may very well begin with a well-off, educated man who, deploring the poverty around him, took money from his own pocket to make loans to the poor, requiring no collateral beyond a guarantee from neighbors. In the Bornstein version, the man is Muhammad Yunus, the year is 1976, the borrowers are women, and the loan amount is US$27.[3] But the idea of loans for the poor without financial security did not begin in Chittagong in 1976. Nor did it begin with BRAC. And, although much credit for the modern microfinance movement must go to these two organizations, historically, the concept had proven many times over to be far from impossible.

Two hundred and seventy-five years earlier, Jonathan Swift, Irish cleric, nationalist, and author of *Gulliver's Travels*, had done in Ireland precisely what Yunus did. Swift, whose 1729 satirical essay, "A Modest Proposal," remains one of the most scathing attacks on a society's apathy toward the poor, deplored the inability of impoverished tradesmen to obtain credit in Dublin. In response, he set up a revolving loan fund with £500 from his own pocket, lending money to those who had fallen on difficult times. He demanded no collateral, requiring only a guarantee as to the borrower's industry from two neighbors. According to his biographer, Thomas Sheridan:

> It was a maxim with him that any one known by his neighbors to be an honest, sober, and industrious man, would readily find such security; while the idle and dissolute would by this means be excluded.[4]

Here was social capital serving as a guarantee for financial capital.

Although Swift's scheme did not outlive him, it was, in many ways, a progenitor of the Irish Loan Funds, which began in the late 1700s and proved to be the most important source of credit in that country during the first half of the nineteenth century, a period when poverty in Ireland was as widespread and as deep as any place on earth. By the 1840s, the Irish Loan Funds were making 500,000 loans each year, mainly to the poorest two-thirds of the population.[5] Loans, averaging about £4, were repaid in weekly installments, and they were intended for productive purposes, that is, they were to finance an asset that would generate enough income to repay the loan, plus interest and a degree of profit. Some 300 Loan Funds across Ireland made an average of 1,650 loans a year with each borrower providing, as in Swift's scheme, two guarantors rather than collateral.

The Irish Loan Funds operated at a time when fewer than 1 percent of the borrowers could sign their names, when women in Ireland had few rights, and a married woman could not own property. Nevertheless, by the 1840s, unmarried women (spinsters and widows) represented a significant proportion of borrowers, with one estimate showing that an amazing 13 percent of all unmarried Irish women were taking loans.[6] The Great Famine of 1846–1848 intervened, ringing a death knell for the Irish Loan Funds. Out of a population of 8.5 million people, a million died and a million more emigrated, devastating the economy for generations to come. By the time it had recovered, the formal banking system had taken the place of the Irish Loan Funds.

But listen to this story of a woman who may not have been atypical of borrowers in the 1840s. With only minor changes, her tale could be transposed to one of the microfinance institutions of Bangladesh 175 years later:

> A widow holding two acres of land and having three children to support, incapable of affording her the slightest assistance, was accommodated with the Loan of £5; she bought a cow and readily paid the 5s a week from the proceeds of her milk and butter. From this cow, she has reared two calves, one of which is now an excellent milch cow, the other just ready for the butcher. A week or two since she sold her first purchase for £9 and states that, but for the assistance of the Society, she should have been a beggar.[7]

Ironically, it was the failed European harvests and the famines of 1846 that led to the beginning of another large credit operation for poor people, this time in Germany. Working independently of one another, Friedrich Wilhelm Raiffeisen and Hermann Schulze-Delitzsch formed a variety of programs aimed at assisting farmers and craftsmen who had fallen on hard times. Schulze-Delitzsch was an economist and politician who created the first peoples' bank, Vorschussverein, in 1850. By 1858, there were 25 of them, and, over the next few years, Schulze devoted himself to the formation of local centers, the establishment of the Deutsche Genossenschafts-Bank, and creation of laws of association that would regulate and protect the movement. Raiffeisen, who served as mayor of several German rural communities over the years, gradually concluded that self-help rather than charity was more likely to bring about lasting change. In 1864, he transformed his charitable organization into the world's first agricultural cooperative bank. Courtesy of these two men, by 1905, there were 13,000 credit unions or "popular banks" in Germany, reaching more than 2 million rural farmers.

A similar idea, growing from the same kind of concerns, began in Quebec at the beginning of the twentieth century. There, Alphonse Desjardins and his wife, Dorimène, began the *caisse populaire* movement out of a deep concern for the inability of the poor to obtain credit at reasonable rates of interest. The Quebec credit unions, like those in Germany, were often sponsored by parish priests. Unlike the Irish Loan Funds, the German and Canadian credit unions have survived and flourished. Today, there are 16.6 million members of German credit unions. Desjardins's credit unions in Canada have 5.4 million members.

Rabindranath Tagore, winner of the 1913 Nobel Prize in Literature, is less well-known for having pioneered the concept of collateral-free micro-credit in what is today Bangladesh. Early in the twentieth century, Tagore founded the Kaligram Krishi Bank in Patisar village in the subdistrict of Naogaon with the objective of assisting the poorest tenants on some of his family's vast estates. Akhtar Hameed Khan, widely regarded as one of the most important leaders in thinking about rural development in East Pakistan prior to the independence of Bangladesh (chapter 4), probably knew of Tagore's experiment, and he was heavily influenced by the German experiments in his development of a two-tier cooperative system for small farmers.[8]

There were other influences as well. In the 1950s and 1960s, there was growing recognition of informal rotating credit associations.[9] And where credit is concerned, the other traditional source of money is—and always has been—the moneylender. Chased from the temple by Jesus, money-lenders have been a source of scorn from time immemorial. But, as long-time credit-watcher Malcolm Harper has explained, moneylenders are simply micro-entrepreneurs.

> [A]nd, like any other business, their survival depends on their
> ability to satisfy the needs of their customers. They offer fast,
> convenient, and informal service, repayments can be flexible,
> and they are willing to lend for so-called consumption as well
> as productive purposes. Unlike many bankers, they are aware

that their customers' need to spend money on food, education, house repairs, health care, and clothing in order to be
able to earn money, so they are willing to make loans for these
purposes as well as for business and farming.[10]

The problem with moneylending has been its often usurious nature.
"Usury," from the medieval Latin *usuria,* means lending money at
interest, but, more commonly, it means at excessive rates of interest. The
charging of disproportionate rates of interest gave moneylending a bad
name in the Bible and caused the charging of any interest to be forbidden in Islam. It is why interest rates in formal banking systems today are
regulated, and it is why most countries have specific laws against usury
and loan sharking. The problem in countries such as Bangladesh,
especially Bangladesh in the 1970s, is that the formal banking system does
not reach the rural areas where most of the population lives. Even where
it does reach, banks have no interest in making unsecured small loans to
the very poor. So where microlending in Bangladesh was concerned in
the 1970s, moneylenders prevailed, interest rates were unregulated,
and borrowers paid the going rate, which was almost always in excess of
100 percent and, in some cases, triple that. The result was an unending
cycle of indebtedness, bonded labor, and poverty.

Small loans at reasonable rates became an answer to these problems.
Before long, small loans became known as microcredit. Together with
savings, loans, and other financial services, microcredit became microfinance. And, although microcredit has a history that is as broad as it is
long, the modern microfinance movement was certainly pioneered by
BRAC, Grameen, and other Bangladeshi organizations. The idea of
microcredit was not new in the 1970s. The innovation lay in the design,
the techniques that followed, and the results.

The Critique

Because microfinance has become so well-known and because it has now
been introduced to so many developing countries, it is worth considering
some of what its detractors say before returning to the BRAC story. In
Bangladesh, for example, there are those who decry lending as a soporific
for the poor, a sleeping potion that saps potential for social action and
social reform. That was the original justification for BRAC's Outreach
Program, which slipped beneath the waves in the early 1980s. Some of the
most strident critiques of microfinance today are based on an entirely
different set of premises, however. These critiques are clustered not so
much around what microfinance is, as on what some of its practitioners
claim it is, often with a kind of religious, almost fundamentalist, zeal. As

Thomas Dichter, a thoughtful critic of foreign aid has stated, "Microcredit is an almost perfect case of a phenomenon that has come to characterize much of development assistance, a widening gap between reality and propaganda."[11]

Muhammad Yunus has spoken of unleashing the energy and creativity of the poor through microcredit, "Once the poor can unleash their energy and creativity, poverty will disappear very quickly." In this case he was speaking to the appreciative audience that gathered to hear his Nobel Peace Prize lecture, and he explained how US$12 interest-free loans to beggars with vague repayment schedules have lifted 5,000 out of begging completely, with 80,000 more in the program.[12] He speaks frequently about credit being a "human right."[13]

Ariful Islam, BRAC's country director in Uganda, has a different take on it, having worked for BRAC in Bangladesh and Afghanistan and now Africa. Grameen, BRAC, and others offer specific loan products that they have created with specific parameters, terms, and rates of interest, designed to make the lender self-sufficient, not the borrower. This is not the stuff of rights that poor people can demand or even shape very much. He said:

> We are selling, and villagers are buying. If they aren't inter-
> ested, they won't buy. So how is that a right? If it's a right, the
> borrower should be able to ask, 'Why are you offering me Tk
> 10,000 and not the Tk 20,000 I need?'

In fact, Arif said, microfinance creates an opportunity, and, if it is well-used, it can become the vehicle for things that truly are basic human rights, including shelter, food, a livelihood, and choice.

Microcredit is frequently offered as a wonder cure for poverty. Because it appears to have been so successful, it has been taken up by more and more NGOs, bilateral and multilateral donors, and, more recently, the private sector. Blue Orchard, for example, a Geneva-based company, specializes in linking capital markets and companies like Compagnie Financière Edmond de Rothschild Banque, and Dexia Banque Interna-tionale à Luxembourg, to microfinance operations in developing countries. Invariably, microfinanciers explain their work with a vignette. The home page of Blue Orchard carried the following story in November 2008:

> Gemeen has been running a snack bar in Abdeen, a neigh-
> borhood of Greater Cairo, for 20 years . . . Gemeen has been
> a client of Al Tadamun, an Egyptian microfinance institution,
> for 10 years . . . Gemeen's first loan from Al Tadamun was for

250 EGP (less than 50 USD), and she currently has a loan of 3,000 EGP (less than 600 USD). Over the years, she has used the loans from Al Tadamun to buy stock for her business (bread, cooking oil, vegetables) and to buy and maintain equipment, such as the deep fryer. She has dependably repaid every loan with interest. With her revenues, Gemeen has helped support her family for the past two decades.[14]

During the 1990s, the growth in microfinance operations was so great and promising that a microcredit summit was held in Washington in 1997, launching a nine-year campaign to reach 100 million of the world's poorest. The UN declared 2005 the "Year of Microcredit." And, by the end of 2006, the Microcredit Summit Campaign claimed that its target of 100 million borrowers had been exceeded by 33 million. A new target of 175 million was set for 2015. It was almost guaranteed that claims about ending poverty very quickly, 100 million borrowers, and feel-good stories like these would eventually attract both appreciative attention and questions.

The emerging criticism can be broken down into three broad categories: comments about the role of microcredit in history, specific criticisms of the microcredit movement, and a discussion about borrowers. The historical arguments have to do with the claim that microcredit can short-circuit the economic lessons of history. Historically, the argument goes, microcredit, or more broadly, the democratization of financial services, was entirely savings-based. A credit-first approach ignores historical lessons about the need for savings and thrift. The German cooperatives, Desjardins, and others were based primarily on savings, and only began lending to their members as the institutions matured. When it did occur, lending was invariably for consumption purposes and possibly supplier credits for farmers, but it was rarely used to start a new business. Most small loans in the West, whether layaway plans, installment arrangements, or the modern credit card, are all about consumption, that is, obtaining goods and services in advance of payment.

Lessons from the West and from the past can, of course, be instructive, but they are not necessarily valid for all times and all places. Even if the Irish Loan Funds had been based primarily on savings, the fact would have held few lessons for BRAC or Grameen, struggling with the problems of very poor people without the wherewithal to save substantial amounts. BRAC's Outreach Program learned this lesson in spades. It was not that the poorest couldn't save. It was that they would have to save for years before they could accumulate enough for any meaningful investment.

There is another historical argument about the limitations of microcredit. Most lending for real entrepreneurs has historically come from the informal sector because the risks were so high. Developed countries did not begin with microfinance; microfinance came later with development. Entrepreneurial start-ups are risky experiments, and investment capital is typically provided by family, friends, and penny stocks that invariably remain valued in pennies or less. Formal credit for business has historically been the result of development, not the cause. "Growth came first." To believe, therefore, that microfinance will end poverty and bring about growth is to get history backwards, or so the argument goes.

But the history of economic development is instructive as much for its anomalies as for its lessons. While per capita incomes in the United States grew by a factor of 25 between 1820 and 1998, the average annual rate of growth was only 1.7 percent.[15] What lesson is there in those numbers for China, where the average rate of growth in recent years has been 8 percent or higher, or even Bangladesh, where the average growth rate after 1975 exceeded the 180-year American average? The issue here is not so much whether microfinance might lead development or follow it. The issue has more to do with whether microfinance for the poor is kick-starting millions of entrepreneurs or if it is actually about small and sustainable additions to a family's income, an issue that will be addressed in subsequent chapters.

There is an almost religious enthusiasm for microfinance that one critic has called "microcredit evangelism." The evangelical enthusiasm can be seen among those who exaggerate the numbers and the impact, treating microcredit as the solution to all ills. Depending on who provides them, the estimates of microborrowers worldwide vary by tens of millions. The Microfinance Information Exchange (MIX), which collects and posts information from microfinance institutions, shows a global total far short of the widely advertised 133 million, counting some 77 million in 2007, served by 2,200 institutions. The additional millions counted in Microcredit Summit statistics include two large traditional women's savings and credit groups in India, a number of government-run programs such as the Nigeria Agricultural Cooperative and Rural Development Bank, and others either not covered by MIX, not serving the poorest, or looking very much like the agricultural cooperatives of old.

Some critics hold that many microfinance operations actually lose money, and their success is bolstered by hidden subsidies and refinancing of loan defaulters. For years, there have been charges that Grameen Bank is not actually a viable business operation and there have been similar comments about BRAC and other microlenders. In April 2007, *Newsweek* quoted a former World Bank economist who said that only 300 out of an army of 25,000 microlenders had reached financial sustainability.[16]

The issue of whether microfinance operations can break even or make a profit is the subject of another book, but it is worth asking how important the issue is. If a poverty-based lending operation can be financially sustainable, that is certainly interesting because there would be no ongoing aid dependency. Many undoubtedly are financially sustainable. But some never intended to make a profit or even break even. They are not shy to admit that they and their clients' loans may enjoy, or may at some time enjoyed, a subsidy. The idea of a miracle cure that will emerge fully formed from the womb, end poverty, and be completely sustainable from the outset is little more than a fantasy.

Those who worry about subsidies might consider the subsidies enjoyed by farmers in the United States and Europe and ask themselves why subsidized loans for the poor in developing countries should seem any more strange or inappropriate. We will return to this subject later, because long-term financial viability is as important to borrowers as it is to lenders. In the case of BRAC, the numbers work. But the fundamental issue from a development point of view is not so much whether the lending agency makes money. It is the extent to which microcredit can end a borrower's destitution.

A further critique of the microfinance movement is that many microloans intended for productive purposes are actually used for consumption. Most microcredit institutions offer loans primarily for productive purposes. As Grameen states, "For creating self-employment for income-generating activities and housing for the poor, as opposed to consumption."[17] But Thomas Dichter has argued:

> Money is fungible. It can be used for anything. [This] . . .
> became real as we began to see poor borrowers use their loans
> for what the industry has come to call "consumption smoothing," ironing out the highs and lows in cash flow so that crises
> can be met or large purchases made.

But he says the microcredit movement is not comfortable with consumption loans, even if they are for education or medicine because this is "not really what microcredit started out to do." Rather than admitting that there might be some truth in the charge and dealing with it, many microfinance institutions simply deny it. The denial is understandable from a philosophical point of view because high repayment rates are based on the premise that the loan has generated new income. If repayments are coming from some other source, it suggests that they are not actually generating income and are not actually reducing poverty.

The truth in much of this critique lies somewhere in the middle. In 1980, BRAC undertook a detailed survey of what it called "credit needs" among the landless poor in a number of Bangladeshi villages. In very lean times, with a family's very survival in question, borrowing may be the only solution. The poor are not foolish, and they know that, if they convert a loan into food, they will soon be unable to repay. If they do not repay, they will not borrow again, and they may not eat for long. BRAC found that most loans were being taken for trading purposes. Borrowers used some or all of the money to buy farm produce or dry goods that they could offer for resale in another location, making enough money to feed their family and repay the loan with interest. Loans might be for periods of as little as a week, not surprising when the interest rate might exceed 100 percent if calculated on an annual basis.

A loan might be taken to cover a medical expense, but this would usually be very small and would almost certainly be viewed by the borrower as a productive loan. A sick family member cannot work, and, in poor families, all must work. BRAC found that few loans were taken by the landless poor for weddings, dowries, or even housing because there would be no chance of repayment unless work was plentiful. As for borrowing that might extend beyond sharecropping, chickens, livestock, and petty trading, BRAC found scant evidence of this among the poor. They found that village borrowers had little experience of entrepreneurial activities other than petty trading.

> They claim they cannot take the risk of setting up any productive schemes because of a lack of organizational skills, lack of public support services, and the unpredictability of future conditions.[18]

In fact, studies in the 1980s found that individuals regularly took loans that produced less income than the daily wage rate. The reason why people would borrow is easy enough to understand. The poor simply discounted the value of their own time, especially when paid work was hard to come by.[19] An individual might work for 100 days in a year for a landowner at Tk 10 per day. By working for himself for 200 days at Tk 7, he would earn significantly less in a day, but he would end up with double the cash income. As long as there was excess labor, that is, as long as there were not enough jobs to go around, microcredit could play an important role, even if it didn't actually yield the borrower very much money. The challenge for both microlenders and microborrowers was to find new opportunities that could earn people at least as much, if not more, than the unpredictable and infrequent daily farm wage that kept them in penury.

This is the basis for the most important critique of microfinance. The poor are not entrepreneurs. The idea that more than a few will turn tiny loans into a viable business is simply unrealistic. Yunus has said, "Entrepreneurial ability is practically universal. Almost everyone has the talent to recognize opportunities around them."[20] But Dichter disagrees, arguing that the distribution of entrepreneurial character is probably much the same everywhere in the world, that is, low:

> It is not surprising that many think the poor in developing countries are nascent business people; after all, most of them must take to the informal marketplace to generate small amounts of cash, and that is what makes it seem like they are engaged in business.

This is subsistence activity rather than business. It is enterprising strategies for survival perhaps, but not entrepreneurialism as it is normally understood.

This is borne out in BRAC's findings more than a quarter-century ago. But imagine what might happen if the effective rate of interest was not the standard 100 percent-plus that villagers know all too well. What BRAC found in its study was an opportunity. It did not see tens of thousands of potential entrepreneurs, but it did see what it called a "double demand." First, there was an essential and pressing demand among the landless for funds. Second, there was "a real demand for more favorable terms that might give them a genuine opportunity to gain some long-term advantage out of the loan process."

Grameen saw this as well, but that is essentially where it stopped. It would meet the demand for credit with better terms and conditions and leave it at that. Yunus explains:

> At Grameen, we follow the principle that the borrower knows best. We encourage our borrowers to make their own decisions. When a nervous borrower asks a member of the Grameen staff, "Please tell me what would be a good business idea for me," the staff member is trained to respond in the following way, "I am sorry, but I am not smart enough to give you a good business idea. Grameen has lots of money, but no business ideas. If Grameen had good business ideas also, do you think Grameen would have given the money to you? It would have used the money itself and made more money."[21]

That is why the bulk of Grameen Bank loans have focused on basic village activities, activities that had been known to villagers for a millennium, including poultry, rice husking, cattle fattening, and petty trading. These sorts of activities may be enough to get a family out of absolute poverty, that is, help it cross from an income of US$1 a day to something a little better. But it cannot be much better because there is only so much demand in a village for chickens, husked rice, and fatter cows. These are traditional subsistence activities, and lending money to the poorest simply moves the endeavor from one set of actors to another. The poorest may well have been helped, but, as long as "the borrower knows best," there is not likely to be much new productive activity in the village.

In a country where 93 percent of the population lived in the rural areas at the time of the BRAC credit study and where the population was projected to increase from 93 million to 150 million or more by the turn of the century, there would, of course, be a growing demand in villages for chickens, rice, and cattle. But BRAC knew the demand was limited and finite and it would not provide anything like the number or quality of new opportunities that would be needed to deal with hard-core poverty.

"The borrower may know best," Amin says, "but only if she is well-informed. Credit alone is not enough." Savings, credit, and everything that would eventually emerge under the heading of microfinance would be fuel for a new approach to development, but it would not be the engine. Malcolm Harper has written:

> The most frequent criticism is not really a criticism of microfinance itself at all. Nobody would criticize an obstetrician for not being able to do open heart surgery, but, if she or her friends claimed that she could do such a thing, we might be justified in expressing some doubt.[22]

The lessons of Sulla, Jamalpur, and Manikganj were identical where the economy was concerned. The engine had to be new productive enterprise—people moving beyond the kiosk economy and what had sustained villages in the past. It required people producing . . . and definitely producing new things.

Notes

1. David Bornstein, *The Price of a Dream* (New York: Simon and Schuster, 1996), 21.

2. David Freeman Hawke, *Nuts and Bolts of the Past: A History of American Technology, 1776–1860* (New York: Perennial Library, 1989), 8.

3. Bornstein, *The Price of a Dream*, 39.

4. Thomas Sheridan, *The Life of the Rev. Dr. Jonathan Swift*, 2nd ed. (London: Rivington, 1787), quoted in Aidan Hollis, "Women and Microcredit in History: Gender in the Irish Loan Funds," University of Calgary, 1999, http://www.econ.ucalgary.ca/fac-files/ah/womenandloanfunds.pdf, 3.

5. Information on the Irish Loan Funds taken from Hollis, "Women

and Microcredit."

6. Hollis, "Women and Microcredit," 13.

7. Appendix to Fourth Annual Report of the Central Loan Fund Board, quoted in Hollis, "Women and Microcredit," 16.

8. Akhtar Hameed Khan, *Orangi Pilot Project: Reminiscences and Reflections* (Karachi: Oxford University Press, 1996), 41.

9. Clifford Geertz, "The Rotating Credit Association: a 'Middle Rung' in Development," *Economic Development and Cultural Change*, 1, no. 3 (1962); Shirley Ardener, "Comparative Study of Rotating Credit Associations," *Journal of the Royal Anthropological Institute*, XCIV (1964): 201–229.

10. Malcolm Harper, *Credit for the Poor: Cases in Micro-Finance* (London: IT Publications, 1998), 7.

11. Thomas Dichter, "Hype and Hope: The Worrisome State of the Microcredit Movement," 2005, http://www.microfinancegateway.org/content/article/detail/31747.

12. http://nobelprize.org/nobel_prizes/peace/laureates/ 2006/yunus-lecture-en.html.

13. http://www.grameen-info.org/wallstreetjournal/index.html.

14. http://www.blueorchard.org/jahia/Jahia.

15. Jeffrey Sachs, *The End of Poverty* (New York: Penguin, 2005), 30.

16. Mac Margolis, "Lining up the Loan Angels," *Newsweek International,* April 9, 2007.

17. http://www.grameen-info.org/bank/WhatisMicrocredit.htm.

18. BRAC, *Peasant Perceptions: Famine, Credit Needs, Sanitation* (Dhaka: BRAC, 1984), 28.

19. Mahabub Hossain, *Credit for Alleviation of Rural Poverty: The Grameen Bank in Bangladesh* (Dhaka: International Food Policy Research Institute & Bangladesh Institute of Development Studies, Research Report 65, February 1988).

20. Muhammad Yunus, *Creating a World without Poverty: Social Business and the Future of Capitalism* (New York: Public Affairs, 2007), 54.

21. Muhammad Yunus, "Towards Creating a Poverty-Free World," Speech at Complutense University, Madrid, April 25, 1998, http://www.grameen-info.org/agrameen/speech.php3?speech=2. The words are repeated verbatim in Yunus's 2007 book, *Creating a World Without Poverty*, 13.

22. Thomas Dichter and Malcolm Harper, *What's Wrong with Microfinance?* (Rugby: Practical Action Publishing, 2007), 257.

CHAPTER 7

The Learning Organization

By the summer of 1978, BRAC was just over five years old. It now had a wide variety of projects under way in Sulla, Jamalpur, and Manikganj. It was starting to learn what worked and what did not. It was beginning to understand the power structure of the village and the political economy of poverty. With great disappointment, Abed and his colleagues had seen the bright promises of independence fade, as grand government- and donor-led development experiments fell, one after the other, under the wheels of bad theory, bureaucracy, and perverse management.

Bangladesh—the *"People's Republic of"*—was founded on well-articulated socialist principles of equality, justice, and fair distribution of national resources. When the country became independent, the new government nationalized huge swathes of the economy on principle, although there was a measure of expediency in it as well. The country's small industrial sector had been owned by West Pakistanis who fled at the end of the war. Factories stood idle, and nationalization had been, at least in part, an effort to get production moving again. Managerial talent, however, was in short supply, and many economic decisions were made for political reasons. The result was predictable: in the immediate postwar years, industrial production never rose higher than a tiny fraction of capacity. Inefficiencies drained the exchequer and contributed inexorably to inflation.

In October 1973, OPEC nations in the Middle East slapped an embargo on the export of oil to all countries that had supported Israel during the recently concluded Yom Kippur War. Within months the price of a barrel of crude oil quadrupled. The long-term effects of the oil crisis would be global in nature, but they were most damaging to poor countries without the foreign exchange necessary to withstand the shock. Bangladesh was doubly punished, because as oil prices skyrocketed, the price of its primary export commodity, jute, dropped by 25 percent. The irony of the situation could not have been lost on Bangladeshi economists: jute, which is used in carpet backing and burlap bags, was being crowded out of world markets by polypropylene, a synthetic product based on natural gas.

Then, in the autumn of 1974, Bangladesh suffered another natural disaster. This time it was not a cyclone, but floods—the worst in 20 years. The three-year-old regime of Sheikh Mujibur Rahman, mired in ineptitude, nepotism, and growing corruption, proved itself wholly inadequate to the challenges posed by food shortages. And then the country's biggest supplier of food aid, the United States, cut deliveries. As famine spread, hundreds of thousands of people starved to death. In places, the price of rice was four to five times higher than it had been before independence. Confidence was shaken in the man who had promised at independence to cut the price of rice in half, and people took to the streets in protest.

Responding in January 1975, Sheikh Mujib, the great democrat, imposed a state of emergency, banning all political activity. It was a short step from there to a permanent ban on all political parties except his own. A constitutional amendment proclaimed Bangladesh a one-party state, and the one party then declared Mujib "President for Life." It was a life, however, that was quickly running out of time. It would end on the sweltering monsoon night of August 14. Just after midnight, troops of the Bengal Lancers and the Bangladesh Armoured Corps left Dhaka's military cantonment, some heading for the airport, others for the radio station, and some for Sheikh Mujib's residence in Dhanmondi. When dawn broke, Mujib lay dead on the stairs of his house, murdered along with many of his family, and a new government took up the reins of power.

The majors who had led the coup appointed a civilian to replace Mujib, but Khondakar Mustaque Ahmed did not last long. A series of coups and counter-coups ensued until, in April 1977, the head of the army, General Ziaur Rahman finally took over the presidency, bringing stability to the situation. Unbeknownst to the broad collection of plotters and coup-makers, the politics of these tumultuous months would haunt Bangladesh for the next three decades. In due course, the vengeful daughter of one murdered president would return to seek her father's job, while the wife of another would carry the political torch of her murdered husband far into the twenty-first century. The two women would become implacable foes, as first one, then the other took the helm of state; and ultimately as—again—first one, then the other was arrested and jailed for mismanagement, nepotism, and corruption.

Against this backdrop of political instability and economic collapse, BRAC unveiled its plan for a new approach to rural development. Abed had seen the constraints on the poor: an absence of land and assets; dependence on a self-reinforcing village power structure; poor organization; and an absence of the knowledge required to make even small changes. BRAC now knew that it could target the poor. It could build awareness. It could provide the training needed for new kinds of enterprise. And by 1978 it had already put out more than Tk 1.5 million in microcredit (US$100,000 at the prevailing exchange rate). In the process, it had discovered that regardless of collateral, the poor were actually a good credit risk.

The Rural Credit and Training Programme (RCTP) that Abed proposed to Oxfam in August 1978 drew all of the strands together. BRAC would "combine agricultural extension, farmer training in resource management and vocational skills, and extension of credit" into a single package.[1] The lack of agricultural credit for small farmers was now widely understood to be a bottleneck to food production, and the government had established a specialized bank—the Krishi Bank—to deal with the problem. The purpose of the Krishi Bank was to undercut the power of the moneylender and village interest rates of 200–300 percent per annum. But like all financial institutions, the Krishi Bank required collateral. That alone cut out the landless. And BRAC discovered that even where institutional credit was available to small landholders at a nominal rate of 13 percent—the rate BRAC had charged in Sulla and Manikganj—the real cost to the farmer was much higher. "Running about and giving bribes to the bank staff often pushes the effective interest rate for a loan to an estimated 36 to 67 percent."

Abed had also seen that many projects starting with good intentions soon failed: "All the major delivery systems—cooperative banks, agricultural banks, rural development agencies—share the same problem: default, low impact and then a drift towards a large-farm clientele." And he saw additional problems from the farmer's point of view: "bureaucratic red tape, surety requirements, delay in processing, bribes and the costs arising from loss of work while traveling from the village to the bank."

He had read Indian studies showing that farmers would pay higher rates of interest than those typically charged by banks, if the loans were made by institutions deemed to be clean and efficient. Abed believed that BRAC could provide "clean and efficient" loans to those without collateral—if the borrowers were well known to BRAC, if BRAC worked closely with them on their investment plans, if training and extension were part of the arrangement, and if there was regular follow-up on weekly loan repayments.

The RCTP was nothing if not ambitious. The budget was set at US$3.8 million over five years ($12 million in today's dollars)—a very large sum then, as now. It would be a major financial undertaking for an organization whose entire income from all sources the year before had been $540,000.[2] The plan was to open 14 branches in the first three years in different rural areas. The next two years would be used to consolidate and evaluate "the success or failure of the experience." BRAC would apply its formula, but the formula would be tested and adapted as required, and each ingredient would be carefully analyzed for its contribution to the end result. Although BRAC presented a convincing case in its project proposal, it also understood very clearly that this would be an experiment.

Where self-financing was concerned, the idea was not to cover all costs but to break even on the credit operations within five years, perhaps making some contribution to the costs of training and extension. The difference, BRAC said, between its approach and others, was that lending institutions always started with the loan as the point of departure, on the assumption that development would follow. BRAC had started with development, "and only now feels confident to embark on a credit programme of substantial scale."

As promised, each set of loans and each set of borrowers were carefully studied as the project advanced. Solakaria, for example, was a Muslim village in Gheor Thana, part of Manikganj District. It was located on low-lying land that was inundated each year by monsoon floods. As in all other villages, the first step for BRAC was a baseline survey. All households were visited, and data was collected on landholding, occupations, number of people in each household, and so on. After the survey was conducted, BRAC's program officers spent days in the village, comparing it with others and assessing its potential. Once the targets had been identified, men and women were organized into groups. BRAC was now using the word *samity* for these groups, meaning "assembly" or "committee." Gone was the English word "cooperative," with all of its connotations of elite manipulation and hijacking. BRAC samities were for poor people who came from the same social and economic background, people who knew and understood each other's problems and who—with some organization and good fortune—might at last be able to work together.

In forming the groups, BRAC's first activity was the functional education program—based on Freire's concept of "conscientization"—aimed at building cohesion among villagers and an understanding of the possible. Savings programs were established, and discussions eventually turned to income-generating possibilities. In Solakaria a group of fifteen women took a loan of Tk 6,000 (US$416) in order to go into paddy husking, contributing Tk 576 of their own savings. They were divided into five teams of three members each. The paddy had to be bought, transported to the homesteads by boat, parboiled, and then husked. BRAC kept close tabs on the work and the costs involved. Between September and March, the women processed, on average, five and a half tons of rice a month, using the proceeds of the first sales to finance the next month's purchase. By the end of seven months, they had bought and processed an impressive total of Tk 93,000 (or $6,460) worth of rice. They had repaid the principal and the interest—now set at 18 percent—and they had spent Tk 807 to hire boatmen for transportation. Their net income was Tk 10,457.53.

A young woman named Ashiran spoke of what this meant to her. "I was the most unhappy woman of the village," she said, speaking of the time before BRAC. "My husband used to torture me physically ever since I married him five years ago. I was at one point sent to my father's house with the implied intention of divorce."[3] With the rice-husking project, all that changed. Her husband's attitude had been transformed, in part because he often had no work himself. "He now realizes my usefulness to the family," Ashiran said, adding with perhaps an edge in her voice, "He loves me now." But, she says, "BRAC is my *bap-maa.*" Literally, *bap-maa* means "father and mother," but it has a broader meaning as well—something more akin to "guardian," if not "guardian angel."

BRAC had calculated the number of person-days worked in Solakaria at 1,260. The per capita daily income, therefore, had been Tk 8.30. The daily wage rate for a male laborer was Tk 10 per day, so Tk 8.30 was a respectable addition to the family income, especially for an activity that could be carried out at home. It was clear, however, that the women had used all of their free time and had pushed their physical resources to the limit in order to do the work. Unless rice husking could be made more profitable, or less taxing, there were few advances to be made on Tk 8.30 a day. And there was another issue: mechanized rice huskers were springing up across the country, owned by wealthy entrepreneurs. There was a clear possibility—a probability, in fact—that mechanization would encroach more and more on this kind of traditional village work.

Cow rearing proved less labor-intensive in Solakaria. Twenty-three women borrowed Tk 18,255 to buy cows, fattening them up and selling them when market conditions were opportune. Here there was not as much labor involved; straw could be gathered from the fields by husbands as well as by the women. The opportunity costs were low, and the inputs were negligible. The net profit at the end of the season after the cows had been sold was Tk 3,500, just over Tk 152 per borrower—less in total than the Tk 697 earned by the rice-husking women, but still, not a bad lump sum, considering the smaller amount of time and effort required. But there were questions: What if one of the cows had died? Everyone in the group was liable for the work of each individual, but without some form of insurance, the risk was great, and one misfortune could wreck the entire samity.

In other villages, BRAC found that people had taken loans for one thing and used the money for another. In the village of Mailagi, the men's samity had borrowed Tk 3,900 for sugar cane and potato cultivation, but had instead turned all the money over to three men in the group who used it to buy bullocks. They paid off the loan and interest in three months, and when BRAC workers berated them, their response was not surprising: "We repaid the principal and the interest. Why should BRAC bother if we make cow business? They are not going to write us off if we suffer a loss."

In a village called Raghunatpur, three fishermen who had taken a loan for nets and twine borrowed additional money from samity members and went into a side business. They repaid the principal and the interest, and they gave the samity an additional "contribution" of Tk 111. BRAC was alarmed by these anomalies, as well as by the prospect that they would become more than anomalies if left unchecked. It did not see them as tolerable aberrations, but as a negation of the very idea of training, planning, and supervision. It wasn't the absence of supervision that had allowed them to happen, but its presence had not prevented them—an indication of managerial ineptitude.

Taking the money and running with it negated the whole idea of functional education, vocational training, and financial discipline—even if, as in these cases, the "projects" had made money. At Grameen Bank, Yunus worked on the principle of "the borrower knows best." At BRAC, the theory was different, and in a report to donors, BRAC said, "Wrong implementation of a plan under strict supervision makes little sense . . . a lot of work is required to set the credit mechanisms on the right track."[4]

In 1979, the Ford Foundation provided funding for David Korten to pay a visit to BRAC. Korten arrived in Bangladesh with an eclectic curriculum vitae. He had served during the Vietnam War as a US Air Force captain, but with a PhD in business administration, he must have stood out in the military. After a subsequent stint with the Harvard Business School, he joined Ford and was posted to Manila as a project specialist. Korten, who would go on to a distinguished career as an expert on voluntary organizations and who would produce several best-selling books— including *When Corporations Rule the World*—was thirty-two when he arrived in Dhaka. He was impressed by BRAC, and when he returned to Manila he wrote a paper about what he had seen, and the nature of learning. "A common error," he wrote, "is to assume that reliable adherence to a plan of action is a desirable characteristic in an agency engaged in rural development. In fact the need is for organizations able to engage in a continuing process of creative adaptation; organizations that have the capacity to deal constructively with error."[5]

Korten wrote about three types of organizations. First, the "self-deceiving organization" denies error and can always give visitors a polished briefing, "fully believing that their centrally planned program design has worked just as intended, producing results which meet or exceed their targets." Astute observers see through the deception soon enough. Second, the "defeated organization" speaks openly of its errors, but primarily as a means of pointing out the perversity of their environment and the impossibility of their task. In such organizations, "Error becomes impotence." Korten's third type was the "learning organization." The term "learning organization" may, over the years, have become trite and hackneyed, but in 1979 it was fresh, and Korten wrote about its chief attribute: embracing error. Learning organizations are "aware of the limitations of their knowledge of critical social dynamics which lie beyond their control, but not necessarily beyond their ability to influence."

"Error feedback," Korten said, "is seen as a source of vital data for making adjustments." In the learning organization, candor and practical sophistication are key: "Intellectual integrity is combined with a sense of vitality and purpose." BRAC, he said, "comes as near to a pure example of a learning organization as one is likely to find."

This was heady praise from a perceptive observer—one who could also be a tough critic. But heady praise and $40 wouldn't get you much more than a cow to fatten over the winter. As someone once said about poverty alleviation, "the rich get richer, and the poor get groups."[6] BRAC knew that creating samities, imparting planning and management skills, and parceling out loans was not enough, even if the on-time repayment rate was 99 percent. The biggest barrier to real economic change in the village was the absence of viable, new, productive enterprises that could be taken up with at least some confidence by very poor women and men.

Notes

1. Quotations related to the RCTP proposal are taken from BRAC, "Proposal for Rural Credit and Training Project: An Innovative Approach to Finance the Rural Poor in Productive Pursuits," Dhaka, August 1978.

2. BRAC Financial Statements, 1977: total income was Tk 7,779,076, and the exchange rate on December 31, 1977, was Tk 14.4 to the US dollar.

3. Statistics and quotations on RCTP outcomes are taken from BRAC, "RCTP Annual Report, 1979" and "RCTP Annual Report, July 1981–December 1981."

4. BRAC, "RCTP Annual Report, July 1981–December 1981."

5. Korten quotes are from David Korten, "Community Social Organizations in Rural Development," Ford Foundation Report, Manila, 1979.

6. Brian Rowe to author, personal communication.

CHAPTER 8

A Chicken and Egg Problem

White Babies Grow Up

BRAC's search for new income-generation activities would range far and wide over the years, but its work with poultry exemplifies the challenge in turning a good idea into a viable enterprise. BRAC was looking for ideas that poor people could invest in with confidence. First, the proposition would have to make money. As self-evident as that might seem, developing countries are littered with failed income-generation projects that have generated little more than loss and disappointment. While there has never been a lack of bright ideas and good intentions among aid agencies, there has too often been a surfeit of amateurism that, combined with money, can be deadly. Even where outsiders are technically competent, they may not understand the social context or the wider economic market. The perfect beehive and a new strain of bees might produce the best honey in the world, but, if it cannot be packaged properly or if the hive is too expensive, it may never get beyond the ubiquitous and heavily subsidized pilot stage.

Second, BRAC knew that any new enterprise would have to be technically feasible under the prevailing circumstances. There would be little point in promoting a silk-making project if there were no mulberry leaves for silkworms.

Third, there had to be a market or a way to reach the market. Producing milk for buyers in a town 50 kilometers away would doom a project from the outset if there was no way to move the milk to customers. And where women were concerned, there were two more considerations. First, any investment had to be something a woman could build into her already long workday without great additional burden. Second, the work would have to fit within the narrow confines of what was deemed suitable for women.

Of course, prevailing circumstances can be altered, techniques and technology can be added, and attitudes can change. Gertrude Stein was once asked, in an era when the idea was outrageous, whether she thought women should be allowed to smoke in public. "By whom?" she responded derisively. BRAC, however, was not exactly in a league with Gertrude Stein where attitudes about Bangladeshi women were concerned.

All things considered, poultry seemed to fit the basic criteria. Raising chickens was already women's work, and it could be done at home. But the issue was not just chickens. Anyone could raise poultry, and anyone did. The poultry question was how to create new opportunities and improved production. The potential was clear because local chickens had serious limitations. They were scrawny, and their egg production was poor. What's more, the technology to produce a better chicken was readily available. Better chickens could produce more meat and more eggs, which was good for the family diet and the family income, and it was good for the village. The cost of supplying a better breed of chicken would be offset against the higher income that it would generate. Simple.

The word "desh," as in Bangladesh, means "country." Bangladesh is the country of Bengalis. "Amar desh" means "my country." And just as a citizen of Bangladesh is a Bangladeshi, other things of the country are *deshi*. A country chicken, therefore, is a *deshi* chicken. While *deshi* chickens may have had some limitations, they also had their strengths. One was that they were disease-resistant. Another was that they cost very little to keep, scavenging rice husks, bugs, and garbage. So, to make new hybrid chickens economically viable, the cost calculation would have to go beyond supplying a better chicken. It would have to include the higher cost of raising it.

BRAC already knew that high-yield chickens fared badly in a village setting. Most died of disease, and those that survived eventually died of hunger because rice husks, bugs, and garbage were an inadequate diet. The first foray into poultry had been the introduction of White Leghorn cocks, and the arrival of a crossbreed of "white babies." BRAC then experimented with the castration of *deshi* cocks, a cock replacement program, and an arrangement where high-yield eggs were placed under sitting *deshi* hens. It also bought day-old chicks from a government hatchery and took them to villages, where they promptly died.

There was no question that crossbred chickens and new high-yield varieties produced more meat and more eggs. On average, it was at least 50 percent more. The question was how to improve the survival rate and keep costs manageable. By 1978, BRAC was in its third year of poultry experiments, and there were still very few answers to the hurdles in what had looked like an obvious money-spinner. The disease problem could be solved through vaccination if BRAC could procure vaccine and if it could figure out who might vaccinate chickens in a dozen or a hundred dozen villages. Another issue had to do with the chicken's diet. Could better feed be found or made locally?

That year, BRAC established its own poultry farm at the TARC in Savar and started to hire specialized poultry farmers and trainers. It trained village women to be paravets because, as it turned out, there was nothing very complicated about vaccinating a chicken. Alone, the average villager would never be able to get vaccine, so BRAC bought it wholesale and

BRAC villager with hen (Photo by BRAC: Syed Latif Hossain)

created a distribution network for its group members. In the absence of thermos bottles to keep the vaccine cool, ampoules were inserted into bananas, which at least protected the vaccine from body heat and the rays of the sun. Skill training was given to villagers in all aspects of poultry breeding and rearing, and BRAC started breeding its own chickens because it was learning the importance of a strong parent stock. Through a process of trial and error, by 1979, there was a solid little program, which provided almost everything, including trainers, a model farm, vaccine, vaccinators, hens, cocks, fertile eggs, and loan money for people at each step in the chain.

But the roads in Bangladesh were bad, and getting eggs to women who had been trained as rearers was not easy. Many eggs broke. Incubation also proved problematic, and losses were still uneconomically high. Initially, there were two solutions. The first was to train a much smaller number of women to become professional chick rearers. Equipped with better cages, pens, and incubation facilities, they could hatch eggs, raise the chicks for two months, and then sell them on through their village. Later, another system was developed. A trucking network was established to pick up day-old chicks from the government hatchery and take them to BRAC offices in rural areas. All of this, money for hatcheries, vaccine, and chicks, was provided in the form of small loans. What was gradually emerging was a system of connections that could make poultry much more profitable, serving as a new productive enterprise that would warrant and cover the costs of borrowing.

The poultry experiments were a lengthy process, but serious problems still remained unsolved. The issue of proper feed, especially for the youngest chickens, was a serious bottleneck to survival and optimum growth. There was simply no appropriate chicken feed available on the open market. By now, BRAC was developing a practical research capacity, and, when the focus turned to chicken feed, a formula was devised that could be made from locally available ingredients. By 1991, BRAC had trained and financed 95 feed merchants. There were more than 11,000 chick rearers countrywide, supplying 750,000 high-yield chicks to 132,000 key rearers in 3,500 villages. Some 9,000 vaccinators treated 12.6 million chicks and mature birds that year.[1]

Not surprisingly, the supply of eggs soon began to outstrip the demand in villages where the BRAC program was operating, but, with more than 70,000 villages in the country and a growing urban population, the demand existed if a marketing system could be established. BRAC's response was a new category of worker, an upgraded egg seller who would buy eggs from 15 or 20 villages and take them to market in nearby towns.

As the demand for quality chicks grew, the BRAC hatchery at Savar was expanded, and, by 1996, it was producing as many as 60,000 chicks a

month. None of this could have been done by an international development organization. Indeed, there are few, if any, examples of a foreign
development organization ever having developed anything this sophisticated. Nor is it likely that it could have been developed by a purely commercial enterprise. The challenge was not so much the technical
problems of breeding, vaccinating, and feeding a hybrid chicken. That
was tough enough, and BRAC needed its own experimental chicken farm,
a large residential training facility, and several years to perfect the system.
The real challenges in Bangladesh were the linkages, creating commercial and social connections between poor women who had borrowed
money for vaccine, eggs, and chicks, and backing it with the required
training and extension services. Taking it to scale and creating more linkages so the village could become part of a wider world required another
quantum leap that is simply beyond most companies and aid agencies.

Chicken Feed

Impressive as all this had become, by 1991, it was chicken feed in comparison to what came next. Rather, it was not chicken feed. Chicken feed
remained the ultimate stumbling block. The number of women taking
loans to finance poultry operations was growing exponentially. By 1992,
more than 200,000 women had become involved in the program, and
BRAC had loaned altogether Tk 326 million (more than US$8 million)
for poultry operations. But the demand for balanced chicken feed was far
outstripping the capacity to produce it from locally available inputs. And
the demand for high-yielding varieties of chicken had expanded beyond
BRAC as well, adding to the national demand for high-quality feed. A
stopgap effort was devised in 1993 with BRAC's creation of a centralized
poultry feed plant. The plant crushed dried fish, oil cakes, and oyster
shells and mixed it with vitamins to produce a balanced, standardized
combination that could be packaged and distributed for sale, first to
group members and then to the wider public.

From the beginning, Abed had kept an eye out for commercial possibilities that could help finance BRAC. The idea of institutional income-
generation activities had been mentioned in the very first BRAC report
after the 1972 emergency activities in Sulla. Now poultry feed was beginning to look like a good opportunity with a handy little profit in 1993 of
Tk 1.4 million (US$35,000) on gross sales of Tk 10.2 million.

But something was still missing. Free-range chickens, much promoted
in the West, by definition, run free. They eat grass and insects, and they
are given a variety of supplements. *Deshi* chickens are free-range, but the
range is not, in fact, very free. Poor people had no land, and the chickens
were not good producers. Moving to the higher-yielding varieties

White babies growing up: a BRAC member with her chicks
(Photo by BRAC)

demanded more than oyster shells and fish meal. If they cannot run free, chickens require grain. But, in a poor country where all manner of food is in short supply and where people starve, growing grain to feed chickens would appear to make little sense. Certainly people could not be placed in competition with chickens for rice or wheat. The option BRAC began to explore was maize, which could be grown on marginal land where it would not compete with food crops.

The problem (and there was always a problem every time someone came up with a promising new idea) was that maize was largely unknown in Bangladesh, and local varieties had very low yields. So BRAC imported maize seed and began to experiment with it. Through the microfinance program, they loaned money to farmers who bought and planted the seeds, and BRAC purchased whatever they grew. Now, with more appropriate inputs for feed, they could reexamine other problems. The handmade feed they were producing in Manikganj varied in quality, and the output was limited in relation to the growing demand. In fact, the demand for feed and the demand for day-old chicks now went far beyond BRAC's own groups.

In 2000, Abed and his board of governors made a decision. They would set up a modern, computer-regulated feed mill. Located in Sreepur, not far from Dhaka, the feed mill is today one of three owned by BRAC. The Sreepur mill is an impressive operation. It has four grain silos capable of holding 2,500 metric tons of grain each. It turns out 10 metric tons of feed every hour, 3,500 tons a month, with 80 percent of it for poultry, 15 percent for fish, and 5 percent for cattle. It has its own laboratory where samples are tested at regular intervals every day. Only 30 percent of the feed mill customers are actually BRAC group members. The rest of the feed goes onto the open market, generating income for BRAC. The net profit on BRAC's feed mill operations in 2007 was close to US$500,000.

With the new availability of poultry feed, BRAC could now consider a massive increase in its hatchery capacity. It had already opened a broiler hatchery in Chittagong, and, in 2001, it opened another in Bogra, this one with the ability to produce 300,000 day-old chicks a month. Today, BRAC has six hatcheries producing just under 13 million broiler and layer parent chickens each year for sale to its own members and beyond.

All of this is, literally, a chicken-and-egg story, a story about what had to happen first before something else could happen—cocks, day-old chicks, hatcheries, vaccination, distribution, maize, and feed mills. But the jump from the idea of maize to a 3,500-ton-per-month feed production capacity has glossed over an intermediate challenge. Deciding to grow maize is easier said than done. If a voluntary organization in Germany or France decided an entirely new crop needed to be grown domestically, for whatever reason, the prospects would be daunting. In fact, the idea would be laughable.

For BRAC in the mid-1990s, it did not seem laughable, but there were many challenges. It could introduce maize through its own groups and its own microfinance system, and its feed mills would purchase whatever the farmers produced. But the price had to be at least as good as whatever they would get for an alternative crop on the same land. Imported Thai maize was profitable, but soil and climate conditions in Bangladesh are not the same as those in Thailand, and the yields were suboptimal. BRAC knew yields could be improved, so they began to experiment again.

By 2008, they had produced 10 new breeds of maize, and others were in the pipeline. Their best, Uttoron, took three years to develop and had to be submitted to rigorous government-quality control tests before it could be placed on the market. Uttoron sheds water better than local varieties, and it produces larger kernels that do not break as easily. And from Uttoron, a farmer can get 4.5 tons per acre, against 1 ton for local varieties.

BRAC established its first seed processing facility at Tongi in 1998, but, by 2000, the demand had grown so much that a modern seed processing center was established at Sreepur, on the same compound as the feed mill. There, maize seeds and others are tested for moisture content, purity, and germination at the center's seed testing laboratory, and samples are also tested for pathogens at the Agricultural University in Mymensingh. After testing, the seeds are dried, cleaned, and fumigated. The treated seeds flow along conveyer belts, go into hoppers, and travel down chutes, where they are sealed into packets and bags by the plant's workers, almost all of them women. In 2006, BRAC seed farms produced 1,600 metric tons of maize seed.

Connections

The chicken-and-egg story does not even end here, however. A question about the sealed, waterproof packets and bags for seeds leads to yet another BRAC operation, the BRAC Printing Pack. Printpack was established to meet BRAC's growing packing and distribution needs for dairy products, salt, and seeds. The Printpack factory, also located in Gazipur, supplies about 80 percent of BRAC's needs and serves an additional 95 corporate customers, making and printing all manner of packaging. Their inputs give an indication of their output. Each month, the factory consumes 100 tons of packaging material and eight tons of ink for labeling.

There is another connection that can be linked back to the early ideas about putting high-yielding eggs under *deshi* chickens. In the search for better maize and higher yields in other crops, BRAC set up a small tissue culture laboratory in 1997. Its primary emphasis at first was on the development of better strains of bananas and potatoes. The shortage of high-quality seeds, seedlings, and tubers was a major constraint to increasing agricultural productivity in Bangladesh. Even today, less than 10 percent of the seed available to farmers is produced under controlled conditions that can ensure quality. The bulk of the seeds are produced from indigenous methods, while higher-yielding varieties are almost all imported.

The idea behind the tissue culture laboratory was to claim a portion of the import market with locally produced varieties that could increase farmers' productivity and income. Today, BRAC has the largest plant biotechnology laboratory in Bangladesh. It has a capacity for the mass multiplication of a wide range of plant species, including banana, starfruit, jackfruit, lemon, papaya, and others. Its tissue culture production facilities include three growth rooms that can handle 25,000 culture bottles at a time. The lab is especially proud of what it has accomplished with potatoes. The objective was a disease-free seed potato that could compete with imports in terms of cost and yield. They succeeded. The fourth-generation potato plantlets yielded over 400 tons of certified seeds, and, in the winter of 2006, the lab produced 6,000 tons of disease-free potato seeds in its adjacent fields. Where local seeds produce between 11 and 12 tons of potatoes per hectare, the BRAC variety produces between 35 and 45 tons.

In addition to commonly known fruits and vegetables, the biotech lab is experimenting with stevia, a medicinal plant known in other parts of the world as sweet leaf or sugarleaf. Stevia is grown for its leaves, which are up to 300 times sweeter than sugar. Stevia's taste has a slower onset and longer duration than that of sugar, but it contributes no caloric value to food. The plant has gained attention in some parts of the world as a low-carbohydrate, low-sugar food alternative. In Japan, it is widely used, notably as a sweetener in Coca-Cola. Stevia can be used to treat obesity and high blood pressure. It has a negligible effect on blood glucose, even enhancing glucose tolerance, so it has possibilities as a natural sweetener for diabetics and those on carbohydrate-controlled diets. With stevia, the biotech lab has a new opportunity for researchers and, it believes, a coming investment for small farmers.

For many years, the BBC produced a documentary television program called *Connections*, narrated by science historian James Burke. The series was an interdisciplinary examination of the history of science. It demonstrated how various inventions, scientific achievements, and world events have learned from one another in a myriad of interconnected ways in order to bring about particular aspects of modern technology. The analogy is a piece of yarn dangling from a sweater. If you pull on it, you will find that it is connected to the entire sweater—and perhaps the entire universe.

Had the BRAC poultry story been told backward in an effort to unravel the connections between its feed mill, its tissue culture laboratory, its seed processing center, a disease diagnosis lab, and the factory where it produces packaging material, it would have led to the same place this chapter began, that is, with the need to find viable new income-earning opportunities for poor people. Told in either direction, however, the poultry story demonstrates not just BRAC's genius for making important connections in a disconnected world, it demonstrates the imperative for these connections and the institutions needed to support them if poor people are to be linked to wider economies and better opportunities.

In its search, BRAC revolutionized the poultry business in Bangladesh. Over the years, more than 1.9 million women have joined BRAC's poultry program, but BRAC day-old chicks and feed have served a much wider community as well. In 2006, its feed mills produced just under 40,000 tons of poultry feed, and, in 2007, its hatcheries turned out 12.8 million day-old chicks. The business has helped poor women, and it has earned money for BRAC as well. And it has encouraged the growth of a much-wider poultry industry. There are now 130 commercial hatcheries in Bangladesh, where, 25 years ago, there was only one small government facility. Today, there are 80 feed mills in Bangladesh, where, 15 years ago, there were none. Explorer, pioneer, investor, and risk taker, all of these terms apply to BRAC where poultry is concerned, but other chapters will demonstrate that the entrepreneurial spirit was not limited to chickens or income-generation.

A Case of the Flu

In Bangladesh, however, there are clouds. The brighter the silver lining, the darker the cloud it seems to describe. It was unlikely that Bangladesh would avoid the avian flu that began to ravage Asia in the mid 2000s, and, for an organization with so much invested in poultry, BRAC had to take precautions. Hundreds of thousands of migrating waterfowl pass through the country between October and March each year, and public awareness of the problem was abysmally low. In 2005, there was a warning outbreak in India, and BRAC began to take precautions. It identified 275 hot spots, areas where migratory waterfowl gathered, and there it trained tens of thousands of poultry farmers. It bought disinfectant, masks, and protective clothing, and it worked with the government to set up an early warning system. In its surveys, it discovered that the rush to commercial poultry farming in the 1990s, sparked by BRAC's initial success, had been accompanied by little or no thought to zoning or distancing one farm from another. In suburban areas, hatcheries and farms were located disturbingly close to one another. It was a disaster waiting to happen.

In March 2007, the first case was diagnosed at the farm near Dhaka, which the national airline used to supply chicken meat for passenger meals. By the end of the month, it had spread. Every bird within a 1-mile radius was slaughtered, and no movement of poultry or poultry products was permitted within a 3-mile radius. Other restrictions were applied over a 10-mile radius. For a time, it seemed as though the outbreak had been contained, but, in January 2008, it returned with a vengeance, hitting 47 of the country's 67 districts.

BRAC imported 2,000 sets of personal protective gear from China for people who would use disinfectant and gave half to the government. It managed three of the country's 20 roadblock spraying facilities and stepped up its training and awareness program with special emphasis on wet market areas in Dhaka. This was no easy task because it meant finding and teaching traders in the safe handling of chickens, eggs, and waste disposal in more than 900 areas in a city of more than 6 million people. Because the symptoms of Newcastle disease and avian flu are similar, BRAC began a mass Newcastle vaccination and revaccination program for as many birds as could be reached so there would be no confusion if a bird fell ill. BRAC's 30,000 vaccinators and 3,000 poultry field workers were trained and retrained to watch for symptoms.

The impact of the flu was enormous. The government estimated, at the beginning of May 2008, when the incidence of new cases had abated, that one-third of the country's entire investment in poultry had been wiped out. The issue was not so much the 1.6 million birds that had been slaughtered. In the general scheme of things, this number was not huge. The problem was that public awareness measures had fright-ened the public, and, for months, people simply avoided both chickens and eggs. The price of broiler meat and eggs fell by as much as 50 percent in some areas, wiping out half of the country's commercial farms and 60 percent of the hatcheries.

BRAC survived the crisis, but at a cost. Its precautionary measures had worked. There had not been a single case of avian flu at any of its farms or hatcheries, but the downturn in prices had an impact on the financial bottom line and on related products such as poultry feed and maize farm-ing. By May, the demand for eggs and poultry had revived as people began to understand that the disease was not transferable to humans, at least not if eggs and meat were properly cooked. But the challenges ahead cannot yet be estimated. More training will be needed, along with more vaccination, better regulation, and more vigilance. Farmers can be more strategic with broilers, cutting back production during the most risk-prone months of the year. But broilers reach maturity in 35 days; layers have an 18-month cycle, and they don't stop laying on demand.

BRAC is studying the issue carefully. Most of the incidents were on large farms, and fewer broiler farms were affected than those with layers. Per-haps the problem was poorly disinfected trucks going from farm to farm to collect eggs. But *deshi* chickens running loose were a large factor, and infected birds that were supposed to have been slaughtered were some-times sold into the market. Whatever the case, it will take time before Bangladesh and the rest of Asia has come to grips with the problem.

In 1992, Catherine Lovell wrote a book about BRAC called *Breaking the Cycle of Poverty*. The poultry operation she described at that time was impressive, but it was nothing compared to what it had become 15 years later. What might it look like in 2022? Anything can happen, but, at BRAC headquarters in Dhaka, calculations have been made. Avian flu notwith-standing, the national demand for eggs is triple what is currently being produced. And the demand for chicken meat is 10 times higher than the supply. If economic growth continues to remain steady and if the influenza problem can be contained, chickens remain a good bet.

Notes

1. Catherine H. Lovell, *Breaking the Cycle of Poverty: The BRAC Strategy* (West Hartford, Conn.: Kumarian, 1992), 100.

CHAPTER 9

A Simple Solution

In 1977, BRAC had 200 staff. One of the newest was Mushtaque Chowdhury, a quiet-spoken young man with a freshly minted university degree and an interest in statistics. By the standards of the day, BRAC was growing, but NGOs were seen mainly as relief organizations and not a serious source of employment for up-and-coming, career-oriented young men. As a student, Mushtaque had been involved in a 1975–1976 world fertility survey carried out in Bangladesh by the Office of Population Research at Princeton University. He enjoyed the research he had done as part of his classwork, saying, "I liked statistics." So when Abed offered him work as a statistician in Manikganj, where so many of BRAC's early lessons were being learned, he accepted, working on a baseline survey of the area as a prelude to later evaluations of BRAC projects. He expected that his tenure at BRAC would be brief.

Like most at BRAC in those early days, Abed understood very little about poverty or the process of development, but there was an incredible thirst to know. That thirst was the origin of the organization's early monographs on poverty and its attempts to understand the political economy of village life. As part of this need to understand, right from the beginning, almost every project BRAC undertook had an evaluation component built into it, designed to help the organization learn from what it was doing. There is nothing particularly radical in this, except that research and evaluation were largely unknown among NGOs at the time. Even in the largest of the bilateral and multilateral aid agencies, research and evaluation were limited. In any case, evaluation was usually about verification, not learning. It was intended to demonstrate to funders that planned activities had been carried out efficiently and effectively. But effectiveness had a limited definition. A teacher training program, for example, would be assessed against the plan: how many teachers had been trained against how much training had been paid for. The training would be evaluated for its quality: how good was it? But whether teachers actually used what they had been taught when they went back to the classroom or whether they even went back to the classroom would be an afterthought in most cases. More fundamentally, the impact of their newly acquired skills on children might never be addressed, even though this would presumably have been the fundamental purpose of the effort in the first place.

It would be a generation or more before impact and results would become more firmly embedded into evaluative thinking among aid agencies, but, to BRAC in the 1970s, this was a no-brainer. Why would you work hard and spend money on something if you could not judge its impact on the ultimate target? Abed and his colleagues discovered that standard sources of research funding were not going to be much use to them. Funding proposals for research take time to work their way through academic approval systems, and, for an impatient NGO, the project might long be over before a funding decision could be made. BRAC realized it would have to build research and evaluation into each of its projects, even if it had to be called something else. In fact, this novelty set BRAC very much apart from the international NGOs that flooded into Bangladesh after the liberation war. They arrived with all the confidence and hubris of experts, developing their projects on the basis of quick-and-dirty field surveys with virtually all of the planning and senior decision-making firmly in the hands of people who had been in the country a few months, if that.

The need for information that could assist with the planning and evaluation of BRAC programs is what Mushtaque was supposed to address in Manikganj. Already bitten by the research bug, it was to become his passion. When he presented his first report, the accountant in Abed appealed to Mushtaque.

"He liked research. He wanted to know what was really happening and how you could use your findings to reduce the limitations of your programs," Mushtaque recalled.

Abed's response to that first study encouraged Mushtaque to abandon his early idea about looking elsewhere for work. Despite the misgivings of his friends and family, he decided to stay on.

"I thought I could develop myself here," he said.

The appreciation was mutual, and, as the programs became more sophisticated, BRAC sent him to Britain for a master's degree. This was a first for BRAC, but, by the late 1970s, Abed understood the organization had to work to keep its best staff. One of the most effective ways of doing this, in the absence of large salaries, was to ensure the greatest job satisfaction possible. A means of doing this was to send the best to study at the world's great universities. Mushtaque was the first, but, over the years, BRAC would send dozens of promising young people to study in Europe, North America, and Asia.

All of them had to post a bond before they went, promising to stay with BRAC for at least three years after their return, but the temptation to leave was sometimes great. The Pathfinder Fund, an American NGO specializing in family planning, offered not only to buy out Mushtaque's bond when he returned, but to pay him five times what he was getting at BRAC. In the end, Mushtaque declined. What kept him at BRAC was a project that was beginning to loom large on the horizon, one that would eventually set the pace for all of BRAC's endeavors, a project that would reach every corner of almost every village in Bangladesh, saving hundreds of thousands of young lives.

Scaling Up

In January 1992, 100 or more senior NGO people from around the world, along with as many academics and NGO watchers, gathered in northwest England at the University of Manchester to discuss the idea of "scaling up," that is, how to increase the developmental impact of NGOs. Many of the participants had come from developing countries, and they complained about a light covering of slushy snow and the inefficient heating in the university dormitories where they were billeted. The idea for the conference had originated in questions about whether NGOs really could make a difference. Although some NGOs had grown large by then, their overall influence was too often stunted, a patchwork of localized and transitory efforts, frequently advertised as models or pilot projects but with little subsequent uptake from a wider set of development practitioners.

Almost two dozen papers were presented at the conference,[1] and, although a dozen variations on the theme were discussed, there were essentially two basic kinds of scaling up. The first and most obvious strategies were additive, an NGO program simply gets bigger and reaches more people. The second were multiplicative strategies in which the success of an NGO initiative influences others. This influence might be felt in a variety of ways. It might happen through uptake by government or donors at a policy level. Or it might be through an expansion or spreading of the initiative in order to reach more people, not by the NGO itself, but by other organizations, government departments, donors, or individuals and families able to take advantage of new information and new opportunities.

If an initiative is to be scaled up, it must first be effective. The model, in other words, must work. And, of equal importance, it must be cost-effective. This is not exactly nuclear physics. But one of the most obvious limits to scaling up, even if an initiative appears to be effective, has to do with cost. There is nothing particularly magical about the nexus between effectiveness and efficiency. In the commercial world, many successful innovations fail because they are simply too expensive. Until recently, there has been little public uptake, for example, of electric-powered automobiles. The primary issues for many years were ones of reliability and functionality (effectiveness issues) and cost (efficiency). The few electric vehicles available to the public offered none of the positive features of mass-produced combustion engine vehicles. They were unreliable, expensive to operate, and costly to buy.

The advent of the hybrid automobile changed the equation, allowing manufacturers to move beyond concept cars. Toyota sold almost 200,000 Prius hybrids in the United States alone in 2007, and it expected to be producing a million hybrid vehicles worldwide by the 2010s. The Toyota experience represents an additive strategy. Its own production increased. Although other manufacturers had experimented with hybrid vehicles in parallel with Toyota, Toyota was the market leader, and the rest were playing a game of catch-up by the mid 2000s. At that stage, however, Ford, General Motors, Honda, Mazda, Nissan, Peugeot, and Renault all had hybrid vehicles on the market. That was a multiplicative outcome of Toyota's leadership and success.

BRAC's first major effort at scaling up, in the sense of making a small program very large, was in the somewhat unlikely area of diarrhea, through a program that eventually became known as the Oral Therapy Extension Program (OTEP).[2] In fact, it was probably diarrhea and the OTEP expansion between 1981 and 1991 that gave BRAC the experience, staff, and confidence it needed to put real meaning behind the concept of going to scale.

Diarrhea

Diarrhea is one of the biggest killers of children in the developing world. Diarrhea is not a disease in itself; it is a symptom of problems that can be caused by a virus, parasites, toxins, or bacteria, such as the one that spreads cholera. Diarrhea results in a loss of water and electrolytes from the small intestine, leading to dehydration, which, in extremity, can kill. It was not until the 1920s that a way was found through intravenous treatment to effectively replace both fluids and electrolytes. The problem with intravenous treatment is that it is expensive and requires both trained professionals and a clinical setting, neither of which are in plentiful supply in countries where diarrhea kills.

Although efforts had been made to find a way of administering water and electrolytes (such as simple table salt) orally, the problem was that, taken by mouth, neither was properly absorbed, simply making matters worse. Experiments in the Philippines in the early 1960s found that the addition of glucose helped, but it was not until later in the decade that a correct balance was found between the ingredients and the amount of fluid to be ingested. The real breakthrough was made in 1968 at the Pakistan-SEATO Cholera Research Laboratory in Dhaka. Until then, even intravenous treatment in Dhaka hospitals could not lower the mortality rate from diarrhea to less than 30 percent. Once the right mix of ingredients (water, glucose, and salt) was discovered, mortality rates fell to only 1 percent. Soon afterwards, the therapy was used with success in some of the refugee camps during the liberation war, and word of its success spread.

The news spread rapidly because it was so simple and yet so important. Soon, oral rehydration therapy (ORT) had become the treatment of choice for diarrhea patients. In 1978, *The Lancet* said it was "potentially the most important medical discovery of the twentieth century," and UNICEF credited it with saving the lives of 2.8 million children between 1980 and 2000. Soon, small packets of ORS salts, not unlike a small packet of table sugar, were available throughout the developing world and needed only to be mixed with the right amount of clean water. No medical expertise was required. Just add water and stir. Since 1981, UNICEF has been distributing 20 million packets of oral rehydration salts (ORS) annually and, with the World Health Organization, has been encouraging local production around the world. Brazil alone, for example, produces 20 million packets a year. Globally, it is estimated that 400 million packets are produced every year, about two-thirds of them in developing countries.

But there were problems. First, in a country like Bangladesh, the potential demand was high, an estimated 200 million packets per annum. But even at $US0.08 a packet, it would be too expensive for those who needed it most, and the overall cost of free distribution would have been beyond the reach of the Ministry of Health. And there were additional problems. The packets had to be delivered, which meant the creation of a complex supply chain from the factory to more than 75,000 villages. The ORS itself has a three-year shelf life. And the user must have enough knowledge to mix the solution, not just with clean water, but with the right amount. This sounds simple enough, but printed instructions had limited utility for mothers in a country where the female literacy rate in 1974 was only 16.4 percent. In the countryside, it was less than half that.

In February 1979, when BRAC began its first field experiments with ORS, the organization was precisely seven years old. It had accomplished a lot, and it had learned more, but, where health was concerned, it was still feeling its way. Taking a cue from China's "barefoot doctors," BRAC had started as early as 1973 to train locally recruited paramedics in Sulla to treat simple illnesses and provide basic family planning information. They were able to dispense from a list of essential drugs and could charge a small fee. BRAC also experimented with a prepaid health insurance program. There was more failure than success, however, in part because of BRAC's early emphasis on the entire community. Wealthier families soon dominated the health insurance scheme because the poor could not afford to participate. Some of the paramedics began to overstep their professional capabilities, setting up lucrative independent practices. The term "quack" is perhaps better known in Bangladesh than in most of the English-speaking world, and BRAC found it was contributing to the supply.

During the days of cyclone relief on Manpura, Abed had developed a professional as well as a personal relationship with Lincoln and Marty Chen. Marty had started to work with BRAC in 1975 on its programs for women, and Lincoln, an accomplished medical doctor, was the scientific director at the Cholera Lab. Lincoln knew instinctively that, even if enough packets of ORS could be produced, this was not the answer for Bangladesh. He also knew, or at least believed, that, if mothers could be taught to use the right amounts of clean water, they could also be taught how to mix a homemade solution. After all, it was nothing more than sugar, water, and salt. Getting the amounts right, however, would be a problem because mistakes could be fatal. And trying to equip each household with bottles and measuring spoons was no more realistic than shipping out 200 million packets of ORS a year.

The challenge also fascinated Abed, and, at one stage in the discussions, he actually started measuring out sugar, salt, and water in his own kitchen. What they eventually came up with was a simple, but ingenious, solution, a three-finger pinch of salt, two four-finger scoops of commonly available homemade sugar (*gur*), and a half-*seer* of water. A half-*seer*, the equivalent of about a half-liter, was a measure commonly understood, and a study showed that 90 percent of mothers could get the amount right within a range of plus or minus 25 percent. Mushtaque, now intimately involved in planning the project, recalled the objections that came from the medical establishment and the World Health Organization. Experts from Geneva were, in fact, dispatched in an effort to halt the experiment, on the grounds that ingredients incorrectly measured could be dangerous. Too much salt, for example, could kill a child. But BRAC was certain that mothers could get the formula right. Mushtaque said, "We decided to go ahead anyway, with or without their approval." But getting it right would be absolutely crucial.

In February 1979, they took the idea to BRAC's earliest development area in Sulla and tried it out over a period of three months in two villages. Harinagar had 95 households, and Anandapur had 150. BRAC created a simple message for mothers, and hired two women who would go from house to house, giving each mother a face-to-face training session. Over three months, the message was refined, and mothers who had received training were revisited later and asked to prepare the solution. Samples were sent back to the Cholera Lab for electrolyte analysis, and the result was encouraging. Illiterate rural mothers were capable of understanding and remembering the message, and they could produce the ORS properly. More than that, young, semi-literate village women could do the home-based training, and a simple monitoring system could be used effectively. The implications for the health of Bangladeshi children and adults were enormous, if it could be taken to scale.

Teaching a few dozen women in a small, tightly controlled experiment was one thing, but, if it were to become larger, there would be questions about hiring, training, organizing, and paying more trainers. There would be logistical issues in supporting and moving women trainers from one village to another. Monitoring would become a more complicated matter, as would evaluation. How effective is the training? How would they know if mothers were actually administering the ORS solution to their children?

BRAC decided to move from the first small experiment to a pilot project that would cover all of Sulla Thana. By then, BRAC was well-known in Sulla, and it had reached most of the villages with one sort of program or another. To test the pilot's effectiveness in areas where BRAC was unknown and where it had fewer logistical capacities, two neighboring *thanas* were added. BRAC then advertised for women who would become known as Oral Replacement Workers (ORWs). After selecting 20 from the 40 who applied, BRAC gave them a five-day training program.

Boats had to be hired to transport the newly recruited teachers. Camps had to be set up where they could be lodged without concern for their safety or their reputation, always an issue where female workers were involved. There was resistance in some areas because villagers feared the trainers were actually family planning workers in disguise, fallout from the overemphasis placed by government and donors on terminal family planning methods—tubal ligation and vasectomy.

When the pilot project began, there were few systems, but, in time, that changed. It became clear that a teacher, an ORW, could not reach more than 10 mothers a day. The 10 points to remember varied, rising at one stage to as many as 15, and, in monthly feedback meetings, trainers shared their experience in getting the message across. In some cases, they found that too much salt was going into the solution, so they modified and simplified the message. "One pinch of salt; one fistful of *gur.*"

Getting Results

Teaching is not the same thing as learning. A concern developed early in the pilot as to whether too much emphasis was being placed on getting the training done and not enough on whether trainees were absorbing and using what they had been taught. An ingenious incentive system was created to ensure that trainers were fully focused on results. Ten percent of the mothers were revisited a month after their training. They were asked to repeat the ten points and to prepare a sample *lobon-gur* solution, and they were graded. Grade A meant that all 10 points were remembered and the solution could be made correctly. Grade B indicated the solution could be prepared properly and at least seven of the 10 points could be remembered. C and D were essentially failing grades. The ORWs were paid only on the basis of results: Tk 6 for each A; Tk 3 for each B; Tk 2 for each C; and nothing for a D. An effective trainer could earn up to Tk 60 a day, depending on the number of women in each of the higher categories, so she had a real incentive to ensure that her students learned.

Monitoring for results was crucial, not just to the teachers, but to BRAC if this pilot was to be taken beyond three small *thanas*. Monitors were hired especially for the purpose. Remarkably, they found that 90 percent of the 58,000 mothers, who lived in 662 villages, scored either A or B in the follow-up monitoring. The pilot had worked.

Many of the papers presented at the 1992 Manchester scaling-up conference suggested that multiplicative strategies were the best route for NGOs. Their small efforts should be aimed at influencing others, notably government departments, and there was a disparaging tone in comments about NGOs themselves becoming bigger. The mind-set in this, however, was predominantly fixed on Northern NGOs operating in developing countries and the appropriateness of outsiders creating ever-larger programs and dependencies. Few at the conference were thinking seriously about Southern NGOs becoming larger. Abed, however, had begun to think about size during BRAC's first decade, and he has spoken about it frequently since:

> To me, with the kind of poverty we have in Bangladesh, with the kind of governmental ability to respond to the needs of our people, we basically have to act. We must act. It is not a question of whether we should or should not . . . Do we remain small and beautiful, or do we scale up and take the consequences? We have decided as a group that we would like to try to serve as large a number of the poorest people in Bangladesh as we can.[3]

Influencing government policy and inducing others to take projects to scale seemed like a fine idea in a British university setting, but, in reality, there were problems. Despite its best intentions, government efforts to take positive experiments to scale in Bangladesh had failed repeatedly. The apparent success of the Comilla Academy, described in chapter 4, led to the adoption of Comilla strategies as national policy in the early 1970s, a perfect example of the multiplicative approach. The government's IRDP aimed to replicate Comilla's success with two-tier cooperatives, irrigation, and rural works projects throughout the country. In the hands of bureaucrats, however, with poor motivation and weak monitoring, no research capacity, and little accountability, the IRDP consumed huge amounts of capital, but, in the end, achieved very little. In 1979, at the time of BRAC's ORS pilot project, the government established its own National Oral Rehydration Programme (NORP), which was to be the foundation of a countrywide program for the control of diarrheal disease. Although training and health education were to be important components of NORP, this failed dismally, and, within two years, NORP had been reduced to little more than the production of ORS packets.

In 1989, when OTEP was reaching its zenith, Abed said:

> When BRAC was started in 1972, we thought that it would probably be needed for two or three years, by which time the national government would consolidate and take control of the situation . . . But, as time passed, such a contention seemed to be premature. After 16 years, we feel we have not yet outlived our utility and need to do more and more.[4]

By then, BRAC had demonstrated with OTEP what "more and more" could look like. Nine years earlier, following the success of the pilot project, BRAC set out to take the ORS message across the entire country. Between 1980 and 1983, OTEP covered five districts. Between 1983 and 1986, it covered eight, and, by the end of 1990, it had covered another seven. The formula at first was based on what had been done in Sulla. A team of 14 to 16 young women, ORWs, would live and work together with one team coordinator and a cook. Each morning, starting at 7:30, they would begin to blitz a village, taking the message from one house to the next, spending about a half hour with each mother in the household. Each ORW had a quota of 10 mothers per day, and the team would spend about two weeks covering the villages in one area before moving on to the next.

Over time, the program was refined in several ways. Teaching aids were introduced in the form of posters and flip charts. The 10 points were revised several times and were finally reduced to seven. It was decided to include men as trainees because, in some places, their exclusion had led to skepticism about the message that was being promoted. The program was taken to primary and secondary schools, and the OTEP message was broadcast on radio and television. Because the cost of sending samples to the Cholera Lab for testing would have been prohibitive as the program grew, BRAC set up its own field laboratories in area offices under Cholera Lab supervision.

Monitoring was key. Even though BRAC was now doing its own laboratory testing, 10 percent of the samples still went to the Cholera Lab for backup testing. Monitors still visited a random sample of mothers weeks after the training to verify the retention rate. In order to ensure there was no cheating on this aspect of the program, an additional check was built into the system. Each mother who received training gave her own name and that of her youngest child to the trainer. When the monitor went back to the village for retesting, he had the name of the trainee, but not that of her youngest child. He had to fill in that name on his own report, and this could be cross-checked later against the original records.

During the first phase, there was concern that, even though women were retaining the message, many were simply not using the *lobon-gur* solution. In fact, in some cases, the uptake was as low as 10 percent. The quality of teaching and the ability of mothers to repeat the message a month later meant nothing if the ORT was not actually being used. That was one of the reasons for the inclusion of men as trainees in the programs. Another change was the length of time spent in a village. The blitz approach had the ORWs in and out of each village in a few days. By reducing the number of workers in a village by as much as two-thirds, the time required to cover all of the households tripled. It meant that BRAC workers stayed in villages longer, and they were able to build better rapport and trust. The usage rate improved dramatically. During the third phase, BRAC switched completely from individual training to working with groups of four or five mothers at a time. In groups, there was better cohesion and greater confidence. Mothers could reinforce one another, and the trainer could spend more time with them. It was significantly more cost-effective, and, most importantly, usage rates increased again by as much as 50 percent.

When the OTEP ended in November 1990, BRAC's simple solution had been taken to 12 million households in almost every village of Bangladesh.[5] BRAC workers had covered 20 districts, 423 *thanas,* 4,254 unions, and more than 75,000 villages. They had distributed three-quarters of a million posters and visited more than 35,000 primary and secondary schools. The monitoring component had visited 447,857 mothers for follow-up interviews, and more than 300,000 samples had been analyzed for electrolytes.

In their 1996 book about the OTEP experience, Mushtaque Chowdhury and Richard Cash, who had worked on Manpura in the days before BRAC, reviewed the elements that had made OTEP a success. Good planning and management had obviously been essential. The development of effective recruitment and training systems, a fundamental lesson that would be applied everywhere in BRAC, was key. When the program reached its peak, BRAC was hiring hundreds of ORWs a year, so the recruitment and training system became a constant, streamlined process. Instead of experts or even expertise, BRAC looked only for bright young people, mostly women around 20 years old with at least ten years of primary and secondary education. BRAC would provide the necessary training after that, and it created first one and then a series of training centers precisely for that purpose. This formula would be used successfully and repeatedly from program to program.

Years later, starting a program in Tanzania in 2006, BRAC applied the same principle, recruiting bright, young people straight out of high school and university and giving them the training it deemed necessary. It is a simple formula, one used in many other walks of life. The bulk of a bank's new recruits, for example, are not bankers. They are young people who become bankers, trained on the job by their employer. An air force does not hire pilots; it creates them. Among development organizations, however, there is a tendency to look for people who already have experience. For BRAC, of course, there could never have been enough, but it did not want (or need) other experience in its ORWs. Primarily, it needed energy, enthusiasm, and a willingness to learn. The development of commitment in the workers was important, along with training, performance-based bonuses on top of the basic salary, and careful monitoring for results.

Going from one village to the next was more than simple replication. It was about improving the product every time an opportunity presented itself. BRAC's development of in-house training facilities, teachers, and curricula served it well in other programs. The creation of its own testing labs became an approach used repeatedly in other projects. Training, monitoring, in-built checks, research, and evaluation, which were all hallmarks of OTEP, became standard fare in all of BRAC's endeavors as it moved from the experimental 1970s into a period of rapid growth in the 1980s.

Also key, BRAC avoided the tyranny of the four-by-four. During the 1970s, Abed had seen the build-up of huge vehicle fleets in UN agencies and international NGOs. In 1974, CARE alone had 75 cars, trucks, and motorcycles in Bangladesh, requiring a small army of drivers and mechanics and an enormous capital outlay.[6] "Development by *Pajero*," one wag called this kind of fleet dependency, referring to the ubiquitous Mitsubishi SUV used by aid agencies throughout the developing world. At the beginning, OTEP had no vehicles of its own, and ORWs traveled by country boats, rickshaw, bullock carts, and buses. As the program became bigger, faster transport became necessary for managers, and motorbikes were introduced, but, even at the height of the program in 1984, when there were more than 1,100 people working on the OTEP project, there were only three jeeps and 12 motorbikes.

BRAC was not shy in asking for support whenever it was needed. The Cholera Lab, officially known by its tongue-twisting name and acronym, International Centre for Diarrheal Disease Research, Bangladesh (ICDDR,B), had been a key player, providing technical and moral support throughout. This kind of strategic partnership would become a template for other experimental projects as BRAC moved ahead. Government support was essential, both centrally in terms of technical clearance and at local levels in terms of credibility and support for the ORW teams.

And funding, of course, was critical. As with many BRAC projects, it was an international NGO that provided the initial seed money, and, when the experiments were ready to scale up, larger donors stepped in. Oxfam GB funded the pilot ORS project, and Swiss Development Cooperation (SDC) and Swedish Free Church Aid (SFCA) paid for the first phase of expansion. Later, SFCA funding was replaced by support from the Swedish International Development Agency (SIDA), and UNICEF provided additional support in the third phase.

The OTEP project ended almost 20 years ago, and it is worth asking what happened next. Why did BRAC not renew the program year after year? In fact, several studies have been done to determine how well the simple solution has been remembered. A life skills study of 11- and 12-year-old Bangladeshi children in the mid-1990s found that *lobon-gur* was identified by 70 percent of them as the way to treat diarrhea. And a set of WHO core health indicators lists the percentage of children under five receiving ORS as a treatment for diarrhea in 49 different countries. The figure for Bangladesh in 2004 was 83.4 percent, by far the highest score among all of the countries surveyed.[7] The simple solution has become an accepted and widely known family remedy, one that has undoubtedly saved hundreds of thousands of young lives.

Mushtaque Chowdhury would later return to his studies. He was admitted to Harvard, but the degree he wanted would have taken four years, so, in 1986, he opted for the London School of Hygiene and Tropical Medicine where he could complete a PhD in two years. Again, he was the first of many who would be sent off into the world for a doctorate in studies that would be of use to BRAC and Bangladesh.

Mushtaque was the founding director of BRAC's research and evaluation division, and he would go on to author many papers and books. He would become dean of the BRAC University School of Public Health. In addition to his work on ORT, he helped pioneer important BRAC initiatives in tuberculosis, HIV/AIDS, immunization, as well as programs in sexual and reproductive health. He did a stint as clinical professor of population and family health at the Mailman School of Public Health at Columbia University in New York, and he serves on the boards of many international initiatives and journals. He eventually did get to Harvard, not to study, but for a yearlong sabbatical, where he co-authored *A Simple Solution* with Richard Cash. He has acted as a consultant to the World Bank, the Red Cross, and a wide variety of governments and development organizations. He was a co-recipient of the Innovator of the Year award given by the Marriott Business School of Brigham Young University in 2006. The list goes on and begins to read like a CV, but it is the CV of someone who might never have done that master's degree and who might never have gone beyond his master's had he not joined BRAC. He is someone who might never have contributed to BRAC's many health initiatives had his bond been bought out by the Pathfinder Fund in the late 1980s.

Not bad for BRAC . . . and not bad for a kid who liked statistics.

Notes

1. Michael Edwards and David Hulme (eds.), *Making a Difference: NGOs and Development in a Changing World* (London: Earthscan, 1992).

2. Much of the story of BRAC's OTEP program is drawn from Mushtaque Chowdhury and Richard Cash, *A Simple Solution: Teaching Millions to Treat Diarrhoea at Home* (Dhaka: University Press, 1996).

3. Chowdhury and Cash, *A Simple Solution*, 40.

4. Chowdhury and Cash, *A Simple Solution*, 39.

5. Only one district was not covered by OTEP. Civil unrest in the Chittagong Hill Tracts had made it impossible for BRAC to work there during these years.

6. Author's personal experience as CARE Deputy Director in Bangladesh at that time.

7. http://www.who.int/whosis/database/core/core_select_process .cfm?strISO3_select=ALL&strIndicator_select=DiarrhoeaChildORTFluids &intYear_select=latest&language=english.

CHAPTER 10

Of Pink Elephants and 9/11

The Pink Elephant

When Sharon Capeling-Alakija was director of the United Nations Fund for Women (UNIFEM), she carried a piece of cloth in her purse. It was a small rectangle of dull white fabric, badly hemmed, to which had been sewn a crude pink elephant. This handicraft had been produced by Liberian refugees in a training center in Ghana where women, young and old, bent over sewing machines in the hope, probably the desperate hope, of finding some way out of their harsh existence and their crushing poverty.

Capeling-Alakija carried the rather pathetic memento, not as a reminder of what women could do, but as a reminder of what women were still being encouraged, even driven to do, by well-meaning, but ultimately incompetent and demeaning, do-gooders. She carried this pink elephant, not in the early 1970s, before Women in Development (WID) had been coined; not in the early 1980s when a distinction, Women *and* Development, had evolved; and not even in the late 1980s when the concept of Gender and Development (GAD) began to analyze the problems of poor women in a broader and more political way. She picked up the elephant in the 1990s after three world conferences on women, a United Nations Year for Women, a full UN decade for women; after the creation of women's bureaus, women's ministries, and women's NGOs; after every development agency worthy of the name had practically signed an oath in blood that gender-sensitive programming was at or near the top of its agenda; and that it would never again encourage women to sew pink elephants onto scraps of old bedsheets.

For Abed, alternative forms of productive livelihood were essential, and, in the 1970s, BRAC was looking at any and all possibilities, especially for women, including new approaches to poultry and fish production; hand-rolled cigarettes known as *bidis;* snacks made of rice, lentils, and coconut, that could be sold in bazaars; spice grinding; pickles; chutneys; and embroidery. Many of the experiments took place in the Jamalpur and Manikganj projects, and Abed's wife, Bahar, led many of them. Bahar had

117

become one of Abed's two executive assistants. She and Marty Chen were given the same title, and they both joined on the same day in 1975. Bahar had special responsibilities for materials development and research, and she traveled extensively throughout the villages where BRAC worked in Sulla, Jamalpur, and Manikganj, often taking their young daughter, Tamara, with her. Gradually, she and Abed began to think seriously about the idea of craft revival as a means of income generation for women.

Bangladesh has a long history of folk art and crafts, well-known in village settings. Painting, weaving, embroidery, pottery, carving, and inlay, all have long traditions in Bengal. Bamboo is used for practical implements in fishing and around the home, and it is used for musical instruments and decorative purposes. Cane is used for mats, stools, shelving, and other furniture. Jute is used for bags and *shikas* (hangers to keep food away from animals in village houses) with designs readily adaptable for flower pots and other kinds of decorative use. Embroidered quilts (*nakshi kantha*) are used almost everywhere in Bangladesh, and the best are prized for their stitchcraft and picturesque designs. *Nakshi kantha,* traditionally made of layers of old cloth, are used as bedspreads, pillowcases, prayer mats, bags, book covers, and place mats. Silk also has a long tradition in rural Bangladesh. By the 1970s, some of this had been commercialized through shops in Dhaka and in exports to handicraft marketers in Europe and North America. But arts and crafts were infrequently exploited as a meaningful enterprise for the poor.

Block printing looked like an especially promising activity, and BRAC began experimenting with the idea early in 1978. But the designs were limited, as was production capacity. If the pink elephant syndrome were to be avoided, serious product development would be required. Karika, a handicraft marketing outlet in Dhaka, had obtained support from UNICEF to promote rural craft production, and a member of BRAC's fledgling block printing group was sponsored for a course in India. When she returned, she trained 10 more women, and soon a limited form of production was underway.

When the calculations were done, the results were positive. The cost of making a fancy bed covering, including cloth, dyes, laundering, sewing, and marketing, was Tk 53 while the sale price was Tk 65. The profit on a tablecloth was even higher. A single skilled woman could produce three bed coverings and two tablecloths a day for a net profit of Tk 82 (US$5.50), a staggering income at a time when the farm labor rate was between Tk 10 and Tk 12 a day. [1]

There were clearly other things that women could produce at home: *shikas, nakshi kantha,* embroidered goods, baskets, mats, and items made of cane, bamboo, or jute. There were two obstacles, however. Quality was one of Bahar's primary concerns, ensuring that whatever women produced would not be rejected because of poor design or inferior quality. The second was marketing. The major fair-price handicraft outlet at the time was the Karika shop in Dhaka. Karika, however, took goods on consignment, and the producer was not paid until the products were sold. If and when they were sold, the producer was paid by check. But, for the women in BRAC groups, with an account in Manikganj, checks took a month to clear. From the time their goods were delivered to Karika until the time they were paid, the women might wait as long as three months. Or, if the goods were not sold, they would be left high and dry with an unsellable product. The village women invested their labor and bore the cost of borrowing money to finance their work. They waited months to be paid, and they had to shoulder the risk that their product might, in the end, not sell at all in a marketing arrangement over which they had no control.

For these women, time was money, and unsold goods represented a high opportunity cost, one not far removed from disaster if the investment failed. BRAC might have solved the problem by acting as middleman between its village groups and Karika, but then it would have to carry the cost of inventory, providing a hand-holding service and a hidden subsidy, all too typical of well-meaning aid agency handicraft projects—and a slippery slope in the direction of pink elephants.

The Village Fair

The Mennonite Central Committee, the international development arm of the Mennonite church, had long experience of handicraft production for income generation. In 1946, they had established a program called Ten Thousand Villages, working with artisanal groups around the world and retailing their products through catalogue sales and shops in the United States and Canada. The Mennonites knew what sold. They knew about marketing handicrafts, and BRAC had the products. Abed approached them about a possible joint venture. The idea was a shop in Dhaka to be called *Aarong*, which means "village fair". The Mennonites would assist with the business side of the operation for the first year while BRAC worked to develop the skills of village women and their products. Abed said:

> I thought that, if we had a good marketing outlet, we could really develop the arts and crafts of Bangladesh, and, if we could market them properly, in the course of time, there might be an international market.

Bahar Abed and Marty Chen worked together in developing the effort. They began to study and catalogue the designs and motifs of traditional art forms, visiting museums, elderly craft masters, and private collectors.

Embroidery: building on a rich artistic heritage (Photo by BRAC)

They experimented with indigenous forms and materials, adapting them to possible new lines. They hired master craftsmen to help train village women, and they created a textile design center in Manikganj where they could experiment with materials and technologies in stitching, weaving, and dying. And they began to hold exhibitions in Dhaka to promote the products that were on sale at Aarong.

The most famous regions for *kantha* were not areas where BRAC worked, but, when they asked a group of women in Jamalpur what their grandmothers had made, they brought out some old *kanthas* to show them. Asked if they could still make *kanthas,* the women said, "A little. But not fancy ones."[2] Soon they were producing more than "a little," and, with the help of BRAC designers, their *kantha* became more and more intricate. Marty and Bahar began to study another traditional product. Bengal, famous through the centuries for the quality of its fine *jamdani* muslin, had lost much of the art with the Industrial Revolution and the end of cotton exports to Europe. This now became the subject of study and experiments at the textile workshop. An old master weaver was engaged. Traditional design motifs were collected and applied to *jamdani* saris, other garments, greeting cards, and leather goods.

There was one small issue in creating Aarong that would come back to haunt BRAC over the years. Should a nonprofit organization go into business? As a nonprofit organization, BRAC had advantages over commercial enterprises because any surplus would be turned back into the organization, so it was not taxed as profit. This freedom from taxes appeared to give BRAC an unfair advantage where private handicraft operators were concerned. The question will be addressed elsewhere in greater detail, but, as Aarong began, Abed's response was clear.

> Our prices have always been higher than the commercial sector for two reasons. We pay our workers a living wage, and we pay them on time. We also insisted that we would not compete with low-quality stuff; ours would be of the highest quality. Even if we paid no taxes, nobody could blame us for undercutting the commercial market with lower prices. Our prices were higher.

He added, "I didn't think we would make huge profits. We were quite content to cover our costs."

That was a sensible idea, at least in the short run, because, in 1978, its first year, on sales of Tk 23,000, Aarong lost Tk 70,000 (about US$5,000). The second year showed a surplus, but only because there had been a large infusion of cash from the German NGO, Bread for the World. With the external donation removed from the calculation, there had actually been a loss of Tk 38,000. The loss, however, was an improvement over the first year. And on an impressive turnover of Tk 1.4 million (US$93,000), BRAC was very quickly demonstrating that it had essentially reached the breakeven point, and it had found a significant new enterprise for village women. The proof of the pudding came in 1981 when Aarong's surplus, stripped of donor contributions and BRAC's own inputs, was Tk 1.5 million.

By 1980, in its seventh year, BRAC was clearly well established, and it was gaining recognition in Bangladesh and abroad. That year, Abed was awarded the Ramón Magsaysay Prize. The award, established in 1957 by the Rockefeller Brothers Fund, commemorated the late president of the Philippines, promoting his example of integrity in government, service to the people, and "pragmatic idealism within a democratic society." At the time, Tamara Abed was six. She recalled:

> As a kid, you think that what your parents do is normal. We used to go to Sulla a lot, but I think the first time I realized that there was something special and different about my dad when he got the Magsaysay Award. I realized that my dad did something that was different from other people, and it was special.

The following summer, Bahar was expecting their second child. There were complications, and she was advised to spend the last trimester resting. Unexpectedly, on July 11, during the birth of their son, tragedy struck. A complication developed, a thrombosis that might have been routine if the right kind of medication and care had been available. It was not. The baby lived, but Bahar did not.

"He deals with his sadness in a very quiet way," Tamara said:

> [H]is sadness was very quiet. He's got one world that he func-
> tions in, and another world inside his head that nobody is
> really let into . . . You know he is grieving, but outwardly there
> is no sign of it. When my mum passed away, he went straight
> back to work after two days . . . he is addicted to BRAC; BRAC
> is where he can find peace.

Marty Chen said:

> They really were soul mates. Bahar understood his mission.
> She had old-fashioned grace and elegance. She was a healer.
> She was important to BRAC because people could go to her if
> they had a problem they couldn't discuss with Abed. She was
> deep, and she was philosophical, and she was so important to
> BRAC . . . and to him.

They had planned to take a short sabbatical after the baby was born. Abed
was to be a visiting scholar at Harvard. Now he was lost, Marty recalled. Soon
he did go to Harvard, living at the Chen household, but it was hard. Back in
Dhaka, a sister looked after the children, and the family offered to take both
Tamara and the baby boy, Shameran, permanently, so Abed would not have
to raise them alone. "He was like a ghost," Marty recalled. It was uncertain if
he would return to Bangladesh. But, at the end of the sabbatical, he chose.
He would go back to BRAC, and he would raise the children.

Tamara said:

> My dad is a very private, introverted person. The way he dealt
> with us, was through a quiet kind of guidance—not quiet in
> the sense of his interaction with us. Every evening after he
> came back from work, we sang songs, we recited poetry, the
> names of capital cities. He would tell me about great explorers
> and wars and things like that . . . he never told us what we
> should do or not do, like many South Asian parents. He never
> told us what we should study . . . he always seemed to commu-
> nicate with us as if we were adults.

September 11

Tamara Abed sits in her office on the ninth floor of Aarong House. It is
October 2007, and she is trying to divide her time as best she can between
her job as director of both Aarong and the foundation named after her

mother, and planning for her wedding, which will take place in December. In the 25 years since her mother's death, much had changed at Aarong. It stands as a remarkable testament to Bahar's work and her vision. The Ayesha Abed Foundation was created in 1983 as a tribute to her memory, funded initially by her family and Abed's, to further the work she had started in rural arts and crafts. Today, the overall enterprise is huge. Aarong buys whatever village women, working through the foundation, can produce, and it buys from other NGOs and handicraft producers as well. In 2004, its sales totaled almost US$14 million, and it returned a surplus of US$1.96 million to BRAC, distributed among its agriculture, education, and health programs, with the bulk going to a special program for what BRAC called the ultra poor.

After several years alone, Abed remarried. His second wife, Shilu, was a widow who combined a strong artistic flair with good business sense. First advisor and then manager of Aarong, she presided over its growth from a single outlet to an enterprise with a string of shops in Dhaka, Chittagong, Sylhet, and Khulna. But in 1997, tragedy struck again when Shilu died unexpectedly. A memorial trust was established. Each year on her birthday, an award is given to an exemplary Bangladeshi craftsperson in her name. When Shilu died, her daughter, Maheen, already a fashion designer in her own right, took up the reins. It didn't work, however, and, in 2001, there was a massive restructuring in the organization.

Tamara had never seriously considered working at BRAC. Abed, perhaps understanding from his own career that one's ultimate calling in life can develop in odd ways, had not pushed his children in any particular career direction. He had cast about in an unstructured fashion himself until, at age 36, he had found a calling that would make him happy. In similar fashion, Tamara had taken off in her own direction, studying at the London School of Economics and then returning to Dhaka in 1995 where she joined Peregrine Capital Ltd., a Hong Kong investment bank. When Peregrine collapsed in 1998, Tamara took a year off to gather her thoughts.

She spent some time with BRAC, opening a couple of coffee shops in Dhaka's Aarong outlets. But, before long, she had obtained a student loan and was off to Columbia University to do a graduate degree in business. Graduating in the spring of 2001, she decided she would stay in New York. She found a flat in Chelsea and quickly landed a job with Goldman Sachs, one of the world's largest investment banks. During that summer, Goldman put her through a training program, and, in September, she began her new career.

The morning of September 11 was bright and clear in New York. It was a Tuesday, her second day on the job, but the subway she was riding to the Wall Street Station stopped between stations. It stopped for almost thirty minutes.

Tamara thought, "Oh my God! I'm going to be late my second day on the job."

The train eventually reached Wall Street, and, as she emerged from the station, she realized something was wrong. There had been an accident. A plane had crashed into one of the twin World Trade Center towers. Goldman Sachs was at 85 Broad Street, not far from the World Trade Center, and Tamara could make little sense of what was happening. In the office, somebody had a television, and she found herself watching the fire in the first tower and then hearing, not from the television, but from just outside her own window, the explosion as the second plane hit. The phone lines went dead. When the towers collapsed, the Goldman Sachs building was engulfed in black smoke. Nothing was visible from the windows except darkness and burnt papers wafting aimlessly through billowing clouds of smoke.

> It was absolutely terrifying; we didn't know what was going on, who was doing it, what the next target would be. They couldn't evacuate us because we couldn't have breathed if we went outside, so finally they decided to take us to the basement, which was a safer area in a building like that.

They sat in the basement for what seemed like hours, and Tamara and a friend finally took matters into their own hands. They left the building, and, like thousands of other New Yorkers that morning, they started walking. Someone near the Brooklyn Bridge was handing out face masks, and they walked for hours until they were finally able to get a cab in the East Village.

It was never the same after that. The smell of the smoke and decomposing flesh lingered for months. The glamour of Goldman Sachs and the excitement of New York had vanished. At Goldman, Tamara was in mergers, but there were no mergers. The topic of every conversation was September 11.

> [A]t lunch, during coffee breaks, that was all people talked about every day. There was a lot of Muslim-bashing too. Nobody ever bothered me, but I heard conversations all the time.

The world had changed. Tamara had lived in India, London, and New York, but, now for the first time, she felt as though she was very far away from her family. Many people living and working in the financial district were revaluating their lives, and working nights and weekends, she "began to wonder whether it's all worth it. There was no sense of purpose . . . there were so many other things I could be doing."

She called home.

"I spoke to my dad, and he encouraged me to stay," just as his own father had encouraged him to stay in Glasgow almost 50 years before.

He said, "Why don't you give it a year? It may pass."

"People couldn't believe I would give it all up and go back to Bangladesh," Tamara said.

But, after five months at Goldman Sachs, it was time to go home. She arrived in Dhaka without a plan. She had sublet her New York apartment and left a lot of her belongings there, not having a clear idea about staying or going. She thought she might join another investment firm or a UN organization, perhaps in Dhaka.

"That's when Aarong happened," she said.

She agreed to spend a couple weeks as a volunteer, looking at management issues in Aarong. She found that, although the people in charge were creative and artistic, there was a serious problem of professional management, especially after the restructuring that had taken place the year before.

But there was more.

"There was an immediate connection," she said. "I could see all the things that needed to be done in Aarong . . . it just happened."

She started as general manager in the design and product development department. Then she set up a marketing department. The export manager left, so she took that on as well. Finally, in 2004, she became director. That year, Aarong contributed almost US$2 million to BRAC's development activities. By 2007, its US$30 million in sales had tripled, and it contributed a whopping $4.6 million to the organization's development effort. How does Tamara like her new job after the glitz and glamor of London and New York?

"I'm having a ball!" she says.

Notes

1. Figures from BRAC, "BRAC's Economic Support Programme in Manikganj, Phase I, April 1976 to March 1979," Dhaka, 1979.

2. Martha Alter Chen, *A Quiet Revolution: Women in Transition in Rural Bangladesh* (Cambridge, Mass.: Schenkman Publishing, 1983), 127.

CHAPTER 11

The Mulberry Bush

Up and down the city road
In and out the Eagle,
That's the way the money goes,
Pop! goes the weasel.

There are several versions of this old children's nursery rhyme, which dates from the 1700s. In one version, there is no weasel. It is a simple rhyme for children doing chores. The first verse, "Here we go round the mulberry bush," leads to others: "Here is the way we wash our clothes," "Here is the way we bake our bread," and ending with everyone going off to church, "so early Sunday morning."

The original version was darker, describing poor Londoners with little more than "half a pound of tuppeny rice, half a pound of treacle" spending more than enough time in the Eagle, a well-known pub of the day. "That's the way the money goes," the rhyme says, ending with Cockney slang of "Pop goes the weasel," meaning to pawn a coat in order to survive another day.

There is another version that is not far removed from the story of BRAC's work to revive the Bangladesh silk industry:

A penny for a spool of thread
A penny for a needle
That's the way the money goes
Pop goes the weasel

Here, the "weasel" is the shuttle or bobbin used by silk weavers, being pawned in the same way as coats in the earlier version.[1]

Poverty and the mulberry bush make good framing devices for the story of BRAC's involvement in silk production. As with everything BRAC has done, the beginnings were modest, but they were based on Abed's drive to find alternative rural livelihoods for the poor in Bangladesh.

The origins of the silk industry go back 4,500 years to the twenty-seventh century BC and the time of China's third emperor, Huangdi, the Yellow Emperor. Legend has it that his 14-year-old third wife, Xilingji, accidentally dropped a silkworm cocoon into a cup of hot water while making tea. She discovered that the silk fiber could be loosened and unwound and that, by twisting several fibers together, a thread could be produced and woven into cloth. Whatever the origins, the secret of silk production was closely guarded for many centuries. Production was at first limited by law, and the use of silk was restricted to the Chinese nobility.

Gradually, silk became an export commodity, an important one that gave its name to the caravan routes that carried it across China to Western Asia and the Middle East. There are references to silk in the Old Testament, and silk has been found in Egypt's Valley of the Kings in the tomb of a mummy dating to 1070 BC. Chinese silk was known to Alexander the Great, and it was highly prized in ancient Rome. During all this time, for almost three millennia, China managed to protect the secret of how silk was produced, and it was not until 300 AD that the technology at last escaped to Japan. Two hundred and fifty years later, silkworm eggs were obtained from smugglers by the Byzantine emperor Justinian, and silk production spread gradually around the shores of the Mediterranean.

By the sixteenth century, silk production had reached France and Spain, growing dramatically thereafter with the advent of the Industrial Revolution. But the seemingly well-established European silk industry was not immune to problems. In the 1850s, a series of silkworm diseases turned into an epidemic, and viruses affected the mulberry trees on which silkworms feed. The European industry declined, and it contracted even further when the industry in Japan began to mechanize. Today, after several turns around the mulberry bush, China has once again become the world's preeminent silk manufacturer, producing over 70 percent of total world production. India, a relative latecomer to the industry, produces about 17 percent, with Thailand, Vietnam, and Brazil each producing about 2 percent.

Silk production in Bengal dates from as far back as the thirteenth century, and it has been said that the expression "Golden Bengal" from "Sonar Bangla," a Tagore song that became the national anthem of Bangladesh, was derived from the color of the silk thread for which the region was once famous.[2] The lure of silk brought many of the first European traders to the region, and, by the late 1700s, silk production and the overall trade was dominated by the East India Company. During the nineteenth century, however, with trade in the hands of a growing number of private companies, the quality of production deteriorated, and, along with it, the tonnage produced. As exports dropped, the colonial government began taking an interest.

In the 1920s, there was an effort to form silkworm rearers into cooperatives in order to rid them of "oppression by the *mahajans* (moneylenders)."[3] This effort and others failed, as did a brief revival in the fortunes of Bengal silk at the beginning of World War II when there was a sudden new demand for silk parachutes. Silk parachutes, however, soon gave way to nylon, and, with partition in 1947, East Pakistan found itself with two obsolete mulberry nurseries, a few thousand people involved in silk production, and all of the silk processing capacity located across the border in India.

As in colonial times, the Pakistan government took a halfhearted interest in the possibilities of silk, establishing a factory at Rajshahi in the 1960s, but the effort was as inept and as feeble as the province's overall production. In the 1860s, production had topped 1,000 tons a year. A century later, in 1966, a grand total of 29 tons of raw silk was produced in East Bengal. After 1971, the new Bangladesh government placed a higher emphasis on sericulture (the rearing of silkworms for the production of raw silk), perhaps because silk had been adopted as a Swiss aid project. But efforts to make the Rajshahi factory run at a profit proved futile, and it only served to depress prices paid by the factory to cocoon producers, ensuring the business would be as unattractive to them as it was unprofitable.

Despite the problems and perhaps because of the once-attractive production figures, sericulture seemed in many ways a ready-made opportunity for BRAC. From ancient times in China, it had been a cottage industry, dominated almost entirely by women. The demand for silk in Bangladesh was considerable, and production techniques were known. In addition, through Aarong, BRAC had learned something about the marketing of village-produced handicrafts.

The basic silk production process is not complicated. The silk moth lays eggs, and, when these hatch, the caterpillars are fed on mulberry leaves. When the caterpillars or silkworms are 35 days old, they begin to spin their cocoon. Within two or three days, the worm will have spun as much as a mile of silken filament. In due course, the worm becomes a moth, emerges from the cocoon, and flies away, starting the cycle again. In order to obtain the silk spun by the worm, the cocoon must be heated to kill the moth before it emerges and damages the silk. The silk filaments are unwound from the cocoon and rewound onto reels, after which they are spun into thread. A silk thread normally contains 48 individual silk filaments, and different amounts of thread may be combined to create different weights of yarn.

BRAC began its silk experiments in 1978 after learning some of the basics from other NGOs that had already begun sericulture projects. At the beginning, it decided to put its emphasis on ericulture (the cultivation

Smiling faces going places: the children
of BRAC members (Photo by BRAC)

of a silkworm variety that feeds on castor rather than mulberry leaves).
The resulting *endi* silk was seven times stronger than cotton and considerably cheaper than mulberry silk. Three women were sent to be trained
by one of the other NGOs, and they, in turn, trained five more. Two test
villages were chosen, one for producing silk and another for spinning it.
Problems were quickly identified, including the need for steady supplies
of *endi* eggs and castor leaves; the problem of diseases that could strike
the cocoons; and low prices for spun thread. BRAC started working with
the Bangladesh Sericulture Board, sending more trainees to study disease
control and the growing of both castor and mulberry plants, and it
thought about how to make the effort more cost-effective.

The production approach was reorganized, because while a woman
could make a reasonable sum from spinning, there was little to be made
from raising silkworms. It was decided that women should do both rather
than have one earn significantly more than another. BRAC service centers
would provide spinning wheels, and they would also supply worms from
BRAC's own grainage centers to cut down on the problems associated
with disease. Where leaves were concerned, they would provide seedlings

in order to reduce the loss from planted *endi* seeds. The parent stock of worms and plants was supplied by government, along with whatever technical assistance was required. The government would also buy any amount of silk thread that was produced.

The biggest problem, one that would continue for years, was access to enough leaves. Even with its own nurseries, BRAC could not keep pace with the demand. Part of the problem had to do with land. All land available to farmers is planted throughout every growing season, and the castor plants had to compete with established food and cash crops, no easy thing when the prime beneficiaries of the project were women from landless households. Some found that they were using their spinning wheels at only 40 percent of capacity for want of the leaves needed to feed their worms.

Nevertheless, by 1979, BRAC was ready to build on its achievements with ericulture and begin experimenting with the more difficult, but more lucrative, mulberry silk. It decided as well to experiment with silk weaving, producing its first batch of silk and cotton cloth in June of that year. By the end of 1982, the project had grown considerably, with more than 800 women involved in rearing and spinning castor silk and another 50 working with mulberry silk.[4]

Feroza Begum, who lives in the little village of Kaliganj, 300 kilometers northwest of Dhaka, explained what silkworms mean to her. She recalled a famine that struck the previous year. Her neighbors had been reduced to eating leaves to survive. "Ever since I started this business with the silkworms," she said, "this household has never known what hunger is."[5] With loans from BRAC, she and four other women had set up home-based worm-rearing five years earlier. None of them owned land, two of them were widows, and all survived by scraping together money from sharecropping, earning less than US$10 a month. Feroza said:

> We couldn't afford schoolbooks and pencils for our children, so they didn't go to school, and I worried that my eldest daughter, Mukta, would never get married because I had no money to pay for her dowry.

The "worm business," as she called it, got Feroza and her friends through the famine, and she credits it with saving the life of her four-month-old son, Alam. "Because I could eat enough, there was also enough breast milk for Alam." Now Feroza has two cows, and, after five years in silk, she has been able to buy a small plot of land where she grows maize. And Mukta was married at a wedding ceremony that Feroza paid for. "I spent Tk 30,000 (about US$440)," she said proudly.

By the early 1990s, the BRAC approach had changed. The expansion of many BRAC programs during the 1980s, made possible by a growing infrastructure of training and research centers, was mirrored in the silk project. By 1991, some 2,000 women were rearing silkworms and cocoons, and many more were involved in spinning. BRAC members were now producing one-fourth of Bangladesh's silk, but mulberry leaves remained the major constraint. Each rearer needed access to about 100 mature trees in order to make a decent income, and the trees had to be near the silkworms because the leaves lost their nutritional value within a few hours of being picked. BRAC was, by then, buying half of all the seedlings produced by the Sericulture Board, but it was still not enough. Trees were being planted wherever BRAC members had access to land, and BRAC worked with CARE and the World Food Program on additional tree-planting projects, paying women to care for trees over the three years needed for them to become productive. BRAC established nurseries of its own and used its credit program to help establish women in the creation of backyard nurseries.

But land remained the major handicap until BRAC hit on an ingenious solution. The Forestry Department owned and managed the strip of land on the verges of the country's highways, even though most roadside trees had long ago disappeared. This land, often set at a 45-degree angle between the surface of the road and the field below, was not useful for much, but mulberry trees could certainly be grown on it, and they would help stabilize the banks. Once the idea had been broached, it was not long before leases were arranged, covering hundreds of miles of roadside land. In 1992, BRAC efforts resulted in an annual planting of 2 million mulberry trees across the country.

By then, BRAC had established a vertically integrated system, not unlike its poultry operation. Thousands of independent operators, each financed through small loans from the credit program, were supplied in one way or another by BRAC or another woman in the chain, each selling onward to the next person in the process. BRAC's sister organization, the Ayesha Abed Foundation, bought all of the silk not purchased by government for its own textile mill, establishing weaving, dyeing, and block printing operations at several centers across the country. And, by 1990, there were six Aarong shops in Dhaka, Chittagong, and Sylhet, where any amount of silk that might be produced could be sold.

A 1992 cost-benefit analysis of cocoon rearing showed how successful it could be. Assuming adequate access to mulberry leaves, a cocoon rearer could expect to earn about US$228 in a year, not a bad part-time income. The cost to BRAC of mulberry trees, amortized over 30 years, plus the cost of organization and training, added up to about US$57 per new rearer per year.[6] Not only did this represent a 400 percent return on investment, it demonstrated how little was required to create a job. Raising silkworms, of course, is not a job. It is a livelihood, a part-time activity that allows the individual to remain at home and deal with all of the other demands on her time.

During the 1990s, the program expanded both vertically and horizontally. The Bangladesh Sericulture Board foundered and was replaced by the Bangladesh Silk Foundation, supported in large measure by a World Bank project that sought to emphasize research rather than commercial activities. To deal with a growing demand for better quality silkworms, BRAC expanded into its own seed production, importing improved silkworm varieties from India and China. It established its own grainage facilities to raise disease-free eggs, and it worked on producing its own variety of egg, one that could resist weather and disease better than imported varieties.

In 1991, BRAC planned for 250,000 women to be involved in all aspects of sericulture. At that time, there were 2,000 women rearing silkworms. Thirteen years later, in 2004, there were four times that number, supported by 18 silk seed production centers, six sericulture resource centers, and three reeling centers. By then, BRAC members were responsible for a significant proportion of all the silk produced in Bangladesh. But the overall number of women involved in the program was nothing like the 250,000 that had been projected in 1991, and even the number of rearers had declined by almost half from a high of more than 15,000 in 1998.[7]

The Worm Turns

Several things conspired to make silk production something less than the great success that had been projected. World prices for raw silk had been rising through the 1980s. In 1989, the price reached US$51 per kilo, up by more than 13 percent in one year alone. But that was its peak, and the decline was rapid. Oversupply conspired with two other international factors. First, a Western fad for hand-washed silk had created a boom that, like so many Western fads, ended in a bust. Second, the bust coincided with fast-growing competition from ever-more sophisticated synthetic fibers that looked and felt very much like silk. By 1998, the world price for raw silk had plummeted to US$26 per kilo. Japanese production fell by 75 percent in less than a decade, and Korean production dropped from 1,343 tons in 1988 to 110 tons in 1997.

Growing mechanization in China, combined with cheap labor, added to the woes of other producers. In 1998, Lou Yuming, general manager of a necktie factory in Shengzhou, visited Como on a scouting mission. Como, the traditional center of Italy's silk business, would soon feel the impact of the visit. When Lou got home, there were only eight computer-controlled looms in Shengzhou. By 2003, there would be 672, more than double the number in Como. And where an Italian factory worker earned

US$1,800 a month, a Chinese worker earned less than that in six months. "We have lost almost everything," said Guido Tettamanti, head of the silk section of Italy's industrial union, speaking in 2003. He estimated that 80 percent of the region's business had been lost since the mid-1990s.[8]

In Bangladesh as well, the impact was enormous. Chinese silk yarn undercut BRAC costs by a factor of 30 percent. But there were other problems. Home-based rearing had the social advantage of being home-based, but high humidity and heat in cramped living quarters affected the quality of cocoons. The volume and quality of BRAC silk was directly affected by the mediocre quality of mulberry leaves harvested from the roadside plantings. The ingenious idea had its limitations, with roadside trees affected by vehicular, pedestrian and livestock traffic. Not only that, as the Bangladesh road network improved, roads were widened, and many mulberry trees vanished. Recognizing the value of its roadside land, the government now began leasing it to higher bidders. Religious fundamentalists, opposed to the idea of women spending time on the roadside tending their mulberries, added to their woes by chopping down trees. A devastating 1998 flood wiped out huge numbers of the remaining trees and killed a large proportion of the silkworm population.

An independent review carried out in 2001 was pessimistic, saying that, despite BRAC's detailed feasibility assessments during the 1980s and 1990s, "even the worst-case scenarios turned out to be rather optimistic, given the changes in the macro economic environment." On the productivity side, it said:

> While BRAC has contributed to developing a national infrastructure through the silkworm egg grainages, reeling centers, and mulberry plantations, it is unlikely that BRAC can turn around the viability of silk production in Bangladesh on its own.[9]

Pop goes the weasel? One observer in 2001 said that, despite efforts to increase productivity and cost-recovery, the BRAC program was running at a loss of 30 percent. The supply of inputs was fixed, and demand was falling, which, in turn, limited the opportunities for individuals involved in the program to grow without some kind of subsidy. This seemed to have turned sericulture into more of a make-work employment operation than a successful rural enterprise.

But losing battles can be an important part of winning wars. If lessons are learned, defeat can serve to redefine strategy for a wider victory. BRAC's revival plans began to turn on a new approach to mulberry trees and the organization of larger plantations on marginal land in North Bengal where rice yields were low. New, better mulberry bushes were imported from India, and, by 2007, more than 2,000 acres in small half-acre plots scattered across North Bengal had been planted with the new variety. BRAC imported 300 tons of cuttings from Indian plants that year, and these were expected to yield 10 million saplings, which, in turn, would become part of an expansion to 5,000 acres in 2008.

A widow named Halima said the new arrangement was an improvement. She and her family settled in Feroza's village 30 years ago after the eroding Jamuna River had washed away their riverside land in Sirajganj. They had arrived in Kaliganj as landless vagrants, but, as a silkworm rearer, Halima was able to set up her three sons in business over time. She had also been able to buy a plot of land where she could grow mulberry trees. She said:

> When I earned a little bit of money, I bought this land so I wouldn't have to venture to the highways and roadsides to collect the leaves, but also because the quality of the leaves is much better on well-irrigated land, compared to the roadside plantations.[10]

BRAC had also learned that better spacing of the bushes improved production, and it began experimenting with intercropping, interspersing a row of mulberries with two rows of potatoes. Or onions, groundnuts, or other vegetables that grow during the winter season, yielding an income when the mulberries are dormant. On top of that, the price of Chinese silk began to rise faster than the new cost of production in Bangladesh, and, by the end of 2007, BRAC had a 20 percent advantage over Chinese yarn.

Abed again sees a bright future for silk in Bangladesh and expects to have a million people involved in the business by 2012 or 2013:

> We have all of the infrastructure. We produce disease-free eggs; we have six grainages that were built with donor money in the early days. These will flourish as we get more people involved . . . So, in a village, you will find maybe 20 families involved in silkworm rearing and silk reeling and others specializing in weaving.

Just as the industries in Japan, Korea, and Thailand gave way to lower production costs in China, he sees an inevitable shifting away from China where labor costs are rising and the yuan is appreciating. He looks out of his office window and talks about the next 10 or 15 years:

> China and India produce silk, but it is not as good as the Italian and the French. A fine Italian brocade silk tie costs

$100 because the technology is more sophisticated. We will have to invest a lot more money in technology and design . . . maybe we will get into some kind of connection with designers like Versace or Armani.

He is trying the idea out for size, but anyone who saw that distant look in his eyes when he spoke of health and education in the 1970s, a bank in the 1980s, or a university in the 1990s would know that Versace and Armani are the easy parts—and this is no pipe dream.

Notes

1. Lost Lyrics of Old Nursery Rhymes, http://www.rhymes.org.uk/a116a-pop-goes-the-weasel.htm.

2. Willem Van Schendel, *Reviving a Rural Industry: Silk Producers and Officials in India and Bangladesh: 1880s to 1980s* (Dhaka: University Press, 1995), 40.

3. *Annual Report on Sericulture Operations, Bengal, For the Year 1918–19,* quoted in Van Schendel, *Reviving a Rural Industry,* 56.

4. Chen tells the story of the early years of the project in Martha Alter Chen, *A Quiet Revolution: Women in Transition in Rural Bangladesh* (Cambridge, Mass.: Schenkman Publishing, 1983) 130–134.

5. Feroza Begum quotes are from "Worms of Fortune," *Slate,* February 2006.

6. Catherine H. Lovell, *Breaking the Cycle of Poverty: The BRAC Strategy* (West Hartford, Conn.: Kumarian, 1992), 107.

7. Rahman, Chowdhury Akter, "Environmental Investigation," BRAC, Dhaka, 1998.

8. "China's Silk Noose Tightens," *Washington Post,* Dec. 18, 2003.

9. Simel Esim, "See How They Grow: Business Development Services for Women's Business Growth," 2001, http://www.cefe.net/forum/Seehowtheygrow.pdf.

10. "Worms of Fortune", *Slate,* February 2006.

CHAPTER 12

Water and Milk

Deep Tubewells

If you ask Amin about projects that have not worked, he will get a faraway look in his eye. "Deep tubewells," he will say without a great deal of pause.

Bangladesh is probably the wettest country on earth during the monsoon, but, in winter months, the rain stops, rivers recede into their channels, evenings are cool, and, for weeks, the sun shines in a warm, blue sky. Historically, there was little winter farming in Bengal beyond oil seeds and vegetables, but, with irrigation pumps, things began to change. With irrigation, winter was now a season for more vegetables, maize, pulses, wheat, and *boro* rice. Tubewells with motorized pumps provide the water. Shallow tubewells were introduced during the 1960s, but they are unreliable because of fluctuating water tables. Deep tubewells, however, reaching 60 to 90 meters into the earth, are more reliable and can pump between 50 and 80 liters of water a second when fitted with a 20- or 30-horsepower engine.

In irrigation pumps, BRAC saw an opportunity. The poor might not own land, but those who did needed water if they were going to plant during the winter months. Water under the land was not owned by anyone. If the poor could be organized around pumps, they could sell water for irrigation. Experiments began in the mid-1980s, but problems soon arose. The pumps needed trained mechanics and operators. Pump managers had to know about canal construction and drainage, how to organize farmers around the operation of the pump, pricing, and recouping their outlay. If the pump was to be profitable, farmers had to be able to pay for the water. That meant they had to use new higher-yielding seed varieties. That, in turn, meant they had to have access not just to seeds, but to the fertilizer and pesticides they required.

BRAC was not alone in these experiments. Other NGOs also saw merit in the concept if the bugs could be worked out. For a time, BRAC partnered with CARE on pump training and management, and the program began to grow. Landless men and women were organized into groups that bought shares in a pump. They then elected a management committee that would receive training in pump maintenance and operation. The groups took two types of loan from BRAC: one for the pump itself and one for the operating costs. Most of the groups were paid by farmers with a percentage of their crop, usually between 25 and 30 percent of the total.

In December 1990, BRAC had 112 deep tubewell groups, and the program was expanding quickly. Over the next six months, the number almost tripled to 309 groups. By then, there were 25,000 shareholders in the system with 309 pump operators and 600 drainage workers. The pumps increased agricultural production, benefiting farmers and the people they employed. But there was more. BRAC believed that, by turning rural dependency on its head, the deep tubewell program might fundamentally alter social relations between farmers and the landless, and the program looked set to grow even faster. The program did grow, doubling once more to a peak of just over 700 pumps, covering an estimated 27,000 acres during the winter of 1992–1993.

Deep tubewells were a phenomenon. They were springing up across Bangladesh like daisies, and BRAC's 1992–1993 coverage alone was more than all 1970 deep tubewell irrigation in the entire country.[1] But, by then, BRAC's project was in trouble. As part of its agreements with donors, the organization has always hosted a variety of review teams and evaluators. Abed welcomed specialists who could provide fresh insight and new ideas. Although it was rare that an outsider would spot a problem before BRAC did, that was not the case with tubewells. Two reports at the end of 1991 found that the overall loan repayment on all lending programs was only 82 percent of target, considerably lower than what was needed for financial sustainability.[2] Although BRAC categorized loans as current, late, and overdue, it had no way of measuring the quality of the current loan portfolio, that is, no way of knowing whether specific types of loans were performing well or not. The overall recovery rate did not, therefore, paint a complete picture of what was going on.

Branch offices, of course, did know what was going on. Repayment rates on the pumps were poor. But the staff were uncertain what to do about it. The emphasis from headquarters seemed to be on more rather than better. And, once village groups began to see that delinquency might be tolerated, the problem spread. There were, of course, more fundamental reasons for delinquency than the absence of pressure for loan repayment. Many of the pumps were simply not profitable. The price of rice was lower than forecast, and yields per acre were also lower than predicted. BRAC argued that the financial picture could be painted more positively if the return on pumps was calculated on gross rather than net profits because interest charges would decline over time as the capital loan was paid off. But, for the borrower, the bottom line was the net profit at the end of the most recent harvest.

By the end of the 1993 harvest season, almost half of the pumps were in a loss-making situation, and many loans were in significant arrears. The pumps represented less than 9 percent of BRAC's total loan portfolio, but this level of difficulty had a serious negative effect on the overall bottom line. BRAC worked hard to salvage the operation, because if it could be made to work financially, it stood to make so much difference socially. Reporting systems were improved so loan performance could be analyzed faster and more critically. Loan officers focused more on motivating borrowers and their repayment rates. They worked to help groups increase the command area of their pumps. They reduced operating costs by pumping more precise volumes of water against crop requirements rather than against demands made by farmers. Wherever possible, they converted from diesel to electricity, which was cheaper, and they promoted second crops and higher yields through the use of better seeds, fertilizer, and pesticide. BRAC also repurchased 35 percent of the shares from defaulting members, reselling them to individuals with better motivation and training.

It didn't work. Here was a project with the best potential in the world, not just for income generation, but for altering the rural social contract and improving the country's food security. Where it worked, it did all of that. But BRAC was not interested in promoting income-losing ventures. This project had far too many moving parts over which BRAC and the pump operators had insufficient control. In 1996, Abed decided to shut down the operation.

BRAC wrote the loans off against a reserve it had established for this purpose, so, in overall financial terms, the failure was not grave. And it sold most of the pumps into the thriving private market. Many development organizations would chalk a failure like this up to experience and move on, leaving the participants with little to fall back on. But BRAC was different. It refunded 100 percent of the Tk 2.2 million loan payments that group members had made on their purchase and operations loans. The irrigation project was over.

A Dairy

In 1986, BRAC amalgamated its various rural development efforts, including the pump projects, under a single banner. It was called the Rural Development Program, and it comprised most of the organization's activities from institution building to agriculture, education, health, income generation, and microfinance. Where credit was concerned, at something between 15 and 20 percent of the total, livestock loans represented a significant proportion, and experiments with cattle had started as early as 1984. Borrowers purchased cattle for three reasons. Some wanted calves that could be fattened and sold when the market price rose. Others wanted draught animals. Some wanted cows for their milk. Problems in the live-stock sector were similar to those BRAC had encountered with poultry, including poor breeds, extremely limited veterinary services, and shortages of fodder. The risks in borrowing money for a cow, however, were more seri-ous. A dead cow represented a much greater loss than a dead chicken.

In 1987, BRAC started an animal husbandry training program. It worked with the government's Livestock Department on a vaccination program, and it began training its own paravets who could vaccinate, deworm, and diagnose simple ailments in cattle. The paravets earned their keep, as in other BRAC programs, not by joining the BRAC staff, but by purchasing vaccine and supplies from BRAC and selling services to their neighbors. In 1987, 37,000 animals were vaccinated, but that was only the beginning.

The following year the paravet training program was improved, becom-ing a 45-day course that was followed up with refresher sessions. At the end of 1989, there were 396 paravets, and three-day sessions had been cre-ated for cattle rearers. A fodder extension program was started, along with a loan program for fodder seed, and BRAC began to promote artifi-cial insemination as a means of improving local breeds. By 1989, they had opened 34 insemination centers, and 20 qualified veterinary graduates now staffed the animal husbandry program. By then, in all of its mature programs, BRAC was in serious escalation mode. By the end of 1995, it had trained more than 2,100 paravets. Its 68 AI centers had inseminated more than 100,000 cows. It had trained over 36,000 model cow rearers and dispensed more than 5 million doses of vaccine. The results were impressive. The borrowers made money. The new breeds produced 50 percent more meat. And, where traditional milk cows produced an aver-age of 1.5 liters a day, the new breed produced four.[3]

Where poultry was concerned, BRAC had learned that critical services were missing at almost every step in the chain between the egg and a potential market and that, if village women were to benefit from poultry, especially from an approach that looked beyond the family and the small market in the borrower's own village, it was going to have to create the services and the connectors itself. The same was true where cattle were concerned. Fodder remained an issue, so BRAC began to develop and dis-tribute grass seed and molasses salt licks. Artificial insemination had severe limitations because semen required refrigeration, and, in any case, it had a 24-hour shelf life. In a country plagued by power outages in the few places that actually had electricity, a standard cold chain and speedy delivery were impossibilities.

Some of these problems were solved when BRAC established its own bull station. To assist, it brought cattle experts and geneticists from India's renowned Bharatiya Agro Industries Foundation, and it sent its own staff to India for training. It imported tested Holstein, Friesian, and Shahiwal semen in order to create its own hybrid bulls, and it set up a more reliable cold chain by using inexpensive liquid nitrogen to preserve frozen semen as it made its way to the client. The result was a cow able to produce as much as six or seven liters of milk a day, a vast improvement on the *deshi* variety that produced less than a quarter of that amount.

Where milk was concerned, however, there was only so much that could be sold beyond the homestead. A cow might produce more milk, but the village demand was limited, whether the cattle were local breeds or not. It was not space technology to say that other markets had to be found, and markets certainly existed. There was an enormous unmet demand for milk in the towns and cities of Bangladesh, but over 85 percent of the country's milk was being imported. For new rural milk producers, the sky might have looked like the limit.

But there were two difficulties. First, if there had been a problem getting perishable bull semen to farmers, there was a much larger problem in getting volumes of milk across country roads to urban areas. Microorganisms grow quickly in milk. Unchilled, milk can start to go off in as little as two or three hours. Here was a problem that liquid nitrogen was not going to solve.

More importantly, however, there was a pricing issue. A liter of fresh milk produced in a Bangladeshi village was more expensive than the equivalent in imported powdered milk. Imported powdered milk was inexpensive because it was produced in Europe and North America under generous farm subsidies. Bangladesh's one dairy, Milk Vita, established in 1974 with aid from FAO and the government of Denmark, lost money hand over fist, and it was occasionally reduced to converting free powdered milk imports into liquid milk in order to modify its negative bottom line.

It is a sad commentary on countries in Europe and North America that provide foreign aid with one hand—dispensed with lashings of advice about how poor countries must liberalize their economies and eschew subsidies—while simultaneously undercutting the world price of grain, dairy products, and other goods through generous subsidies to their own producers. What is good for the goose is apparently not good for the gander.

"We looked at the idea of a dairy in the 1980s," Abed said, "because I thought it might be possible to develop an industry. But we just couldn't make it. The economics were not there."

Amin went two or three times to Gujarat to study the famous Amul dairy cooperative that had revolutionized milk production in India, but the obstacle was not organization. It was price. The price break did not come until the 1990s when changes were made in the Common Agricultural Policy of the European Union. Although European subsidies were not removed, there were enough changes to start pushing up the price of imported milk powder in Bangladesh, and Abed saw the opportunity.

He spoke of going to a village at the time and meeting a woman who had borrowed Tk 5,000 to buy a cow.

> She was getting four liters of milk a day, and I said, "You must be doing well." She said, "No, I'm not doing well because if I sell at Tk 7 per liter, I don't make any money." It left me thinking about why she was getting only Tk 7. In Dhaka milk was now selling for Tk 25. If I could buy her milk at Tk 15—double her income—I could still bring it to Dhaka, pasteurize it and then sell it in town.[4]

The first concept paper for a milk processing plant was drafted in 1995. Abed sent a study team led by Amin back to the Amul Dairy, and, before the machinery came from Europe, a BRAC team of six went to study milk processing in Denmark. Six Danish experts arrived with the equipment to set it up, provide more training, and get the dairy into production.

Today, BRAC organizes its cow rearers into milk producer organizations of 40 members. Each organization has one milk collector, who waits for members to bring their milk to a collection point once every morning and once every afternoon. At first, the collector took the milk to one of 17 chilling plants that were set up around the country. Each chilling plant served about 25 groups, and, before the milk was purchased, it was tested for its fat content and priced accordingly. Every day, tanker trucks would arrive from Dhaka to collect the milk and take it to the processing plant.

By the beginning of 2008, the system had expanded. There were 67 chilling centers, each equipped with a small cooling tank capable of reducing the temperature to 4° centigrade. No milk remains at a chilling center for more than 24 hours. Sixteen trucks with stainless steel tanks ranging in size from 6,000 to 9,000 liters leave the Gazipur processing plant near Dhaka every day, 365 days a year, fanning out across the country to collect the milk. At the plant, they process 70,000 liters of pasteurized milk a day, along with UHT milk and milk powder, which is still preferred by poor villagers without access to refrigeration. The plant also produces butter and yoghurt, *ghee*, chocolate milk, and fruit juices. The dairy's enthusiastic general manager, Mohammad Ali, said in 2008 that he could process 120,000 liters a day if he had the supply and the ability to collect more milk. That will, no doubt, come. He spoke of an intermediate processing plant and 30 more chilling plants over the coming three years. And he spoke with pride of the dairy's 2007 sales record: US$14 million and a contribution to BRAC's education, health, and development projects of more than US$1.2 million.

In 2007, the dairy processed enough milk to fill almost nine Olympic-sized swimming pools, and all of it was produced by women and men with only one or two cows. There are no herds, cattle barons, or even cattle farms as they are understood in industrialized countries. And all of it—from the vaccinators to the inseminators and from cow rearers to milk collectors—operates on a self-employment basis through BRAC's very small loans and microfinance program.

Notes

1. A.R. Khan, *The Economy of Bangladesh* (London: Macmillan, 1973), 49. The total devoted to deep tubewell irrigation in 1969–1970 was 22,000 acres.

2. Doug Salloum and Lorna Grace, "BRAC Donor Consortium Review: Savings and Credit Activity January 1990 to September 1991," November 1991; David Wright, "Report on Selected Investments by BRAC's Village Organization Members," December 1991.

3. Catherine H. Lovell, *Breaking the Cycle of Poverty: The BRAC Strategy* (West Hartford, Conn.: Kumarian, 1992), 103; BRAC, "RDP Phase II Report," December 1995.

4. Ashoka, *Innovator for the Poor: The Story of Fazle H. Abed and the Founding of BRAC,* Recorded Interview, DVD, Arlington, Virginia, 2005.

CHAPTER 13

Millennium Development Goal 6 (Target 8)

Tuberculosis and the Community Health Worker

BRAC began its health efforts in Sulla in 1972, but it was not until 1975 that the idea of the female village health worker (*shasthyo shebika*) was developed. Even then, the idea was experimental. BRAC was providing curative services through paramedics, but a fully trained paramedic could not be posted to each village, and, besides, it was not necessary. Many of the most common ailments could be diagnosed and treated at a lower level of expertise. An estimated 60 percent of all treatments handled by paramedics were for diarrhea, worms, dysentery, scabies, malaria, and pneumonia, most of which could be managed without difficulty by a health auxiliary.

BRAC saw that traditional healers and midwives had a prominent position in the village, but attempts to train them in new approaches had not worked. Under the *shasthyo shebika* plan, young women without any background in health were selected from each BRAC village for training. They had to be a member of the BRAC village organization and acceptable to its members. They had to be over 25, and married. Their youngest child had to be more than two years old. All of this contributed to acceptability, stability, and mobility. Over that first month-and-a-half, they spent two days a week in training and the rest accompanying paramedics on their rounds. The *shebikas* were trained to recognize and treat a dozen common ailments and to refer those they could not handle to BRAC paramedics or government health services. A s*hasthyo shebika,* of course, could do much more than treat common ailments. As a member of the village organization, she could teach women about nutrition, hygiene, safe water, immunization, and family planning. She could go directly to the homes of members and nonmembers alike because she knew the village and the village knew her, and because she had an important service to offer.

Originally, village organizations created a health fund to provide a stock of medicines that could be made available at cost, but this changed in time. Medicines for common aliments were sold to *shasthyo shebikas* through the microfinance program, and they, in turn, provided a fixed-price charge for their services and the medicine to villagers. The *shasthyo shebikas*, therefore, were soon self-financing, requiring neither salary nor subsidy from BRAC. There was no thought at the outset that the *shasthyo shebikas* might eventually turn the health establishment of Bangladesh on its head, or that they might become the leading edge in the fight against tuberculosis.

Tuberculosis (TB) has been present for thousands of years. It has been found in Egyptian mummies, and there is evidence of its presence in the Americas for more than 2,000 years. Known as consumption in the nineteenth century, it was the cause of one in four adult deaths in England in the mid 1800s. As late at 1918, it was the cause of one in six deaths in France. When milk was discovered to be one source of infection, pasteurization was introduced. A vaccine known as BCG* was developed in 1906, although it was not widely used until after World War II. Public health programs in the 1940s and the advent of antibiotics made huge inroads on the disease, and, for a time, it was thought that TB might be wiped out completely.

In the 1970s and 1980s, however, there was a dramatic resurgence, in part because of new drug-resistant strains, but also because many countries had let down their guard, reducing their public health facilities and treating TB as yesterday's problem. It was far from that. In 1993, the World Health Organization declared TB a global emergency, the first disease to be classified that way in the history of the organization. TB, which is curable if properly detected and treated, was killing an estimated 2 million people a year. It had become the world's number one infectious disease killer, and it was growing fast. Between 1993 and 1996 alone, there was a 13 percent increase. One-third of the world's population was infected, and TB accounted for more than a quarter of all preventable adult deaths in developing countries. HIV/AIDS was exacerbating the problem. HIV/AIDS victims are more susceptible to TB, so the spread of one disease was leading to an increase in the other.

BRAC's first encounter with TB was inauspicious. Because of the high incidence of TB in Sulla, BRAC began a curative service at three of its clinics in 1975. Statistics survive from two of those clinics, in Anandpur and Markuli, where 127 patients were enrolled. Six of the patients died, two moved away, and 59 dropped out before their treatment was complete. Although TB is completely curable and the treatment and medicines were

---

*Albert Calmette and Camille Guerin developed the BCG vaccine in 1906. BCG was named for them, "Bacillus of Calmette and Guerin."

free, fewer than 40 percent had completed the course. A terse comment in a 1978 evaluation says that "fresh enrollment to the service was stopped at the end of 1977."[1] In fact, BRAC's health workers could not ignore people suffering from TB, so a low-key approach to the disease continued in Sulla, but with limited success. In the early 1980s, for example, a mini laboratory was set up for testing sputum samples. Of 90 people tested, 13 were found to be positive. Nine patients began treatment, but four dropped out before completion.

Being village-based, BRAC had an obvious advantage over government TB services, which were all city-bound and hospital-based. But the dropout problem was severe, even where medicine was free. People dropped out for various reasons. Some complained of side effects, but the biggest problem was the length of the treatment. A patient had to receive 30 injections of streptomycin every other day for two months and take tablets every day for a year. Treatment caused the symptoms to disappear quickly, and, far too often, when patients began to feel better, they would simply stop taking the medicine. In fact, one of the main contributors to the evolution of drug-resistant TB is the fact that so many patients over the years and around the world did not complete the course of medication. When the disease returned, it was more virulent.

BRAC did not examine the problem of TB seriously until 1985 when it finally sent some of its health technicians from Manikganj to a monthlong training course at the National TB Control Board in Dhaka. When they returned to Manikganj, they set up another lab for sputum testing and began to treat patients. By the middle of 1985, they had enrolled 43 people in a course of treatment. Their caution with numbers was merited because, at first, dropouts continued. By 1987, however, the success rate had improved because they had developed two very simple innovations. Money was the first. Under the new arrangement, the patient had to make a deposit of Tk 100, the equivalent of several days' labor. At the end of the yearlong treatment, Tk 75 would be returned, and the balance would be given to the shasthyo shebika.

The shasthyo shebika was part of the second innovation. In order to earn the money, she and BRAC both knew that the patient had to test negative at the end of the treatment, and that meant that all of the medicine had to be taken as prescribed. The only way to be sure of that was for the shasthyo shebika to administer it directly or watch as the patient swallowed the pills. This came to be known as directly observed therapy (DOT). By mid-1987, BRAC was treating 152 patients, and only seven dropped out.[2] And, during the period from 1992 to 1994, having switched from a twelve-month to an eight-month regimen, they cared for more than 3,000 patients with an 81 percent cure rate. Fewer than 4 percent dropped out.[3]

Connecting the DOTS

Although there had been experiments with DOT during the 1950s and 1960s in India and Hong Kong, there was little uptake. By 1997, however, things had changed. That year the director-general of the World Health Organization, Dr. Hiroshi Nakajima, declared, "DOTS* is the biggest health breakthrough of this decade in terms of the lives we will be able to save." It was, he said:

> [T]he single most important development in the fight against humanity's oldest and most deadly disease since Robert Koch discovered the TB bacillus in 1882.[4]

WHO gave credit to five NGOs for developing and testing the DOTS strategy, one each in France, Netherlands, Germany, Norway, and Japan. BRAC, which had been using the technique for a decade by then, improving its cure rate to 90 percent and working with the government on wider DOTS application, was not mentioned.

Today, DOTS is the accepted treatment for TB in more than 150 countries. Diagnosis remains problematic, and it still is in some parts of Bangladesh. Many victims are ashamed of having the disease, and, for women, it can mean the end of a marriage or marriage prospects. There are problems with the basic DOTS concept as well. In order to observe patients taking medicine, a small army of health personnel is required, something that few developing countries have. BRAC, of course, could make DOTS work because it had created exactly that, a small army of health personnel based in tens of thousands of villages across Bangladesh. By the end of 2008, there were more than 70,000 *shasthyo shebikas* at work.

The BRAC experiments had worked for other reasons as well. First is BRAC's commitment to learning through careful monitoring and evaluation. Its work on TB began very slowly and was not taken to scale until the approach had been fully tested.

BRAC's quiet tenacity is undoubtedly a second reason. In experiment after experiment in health, education, and income generation, BRAC refused to accept failure, pushing ahead with new ideas and improvements until there was a clear answer.

And BRAC's innovative spirit is the third reason. BRAC's health programs exude innovation—from the invention of *shasthyo shebikas* and *sheboks* to the arrangements for their financial sustainability; from the

---

*DOT refers to the twelve-month directly observed treatment; DOTS refers to the eight-month directly observed treatment-short course.

financial incentives it created in the TB and oral rehydration programs, and to the directly observed therapy they pioneered.

A fourth factor is the location of the *shasthyo shebikas*. They were not outsiders or visitors; they lived in the communities they serviced. They knew the village; they could speak to village women in ways that outsiders never could. They had a personal, professional, and monetary stake in the patient's cure.

A fifth factor, one that has made a significant difference in many other BRAC programs, is that the *shebikas* went straight to the patient's house. The patient did not have to leave the village for treatment, and women did not have to leave the family compound. This is crucial enough in sustained treatment, but it is even more important in the detection of TB. Many victims do not volunteer their illness until very late in its progress. Home visits made early detection more possible.

The bond money made a big difference as well, and it is perhaps the ultimate key to the program's success. On top of all that, unlike other drugs provided by the *shasthyo shebika*, TB pharmaceuticals are free, provided to BRAC without charge by the government.

Finally, BRAC's ability to manage a far-flung program and its talent for breaking a complex delivery chain into simple and verifiable component parts paid huge dividends.

A Global Fund to Fight AIDS, Tuberculosis, and Malaria was launched in 2002 as a new funding mechanism to deal with these three most debilitating diseases. A financial package of US$4.4 billion was established to support efforts in 128 countries. The money was to be allocated on a performance basis to recipient governments and organizations that could demonstrate effective and measurable results. Where HIV/AIDS is concerned, Bangladesh is one of the more fortunate countries in Asia, with a prevalence rate of only 0.1 percent. Malaria is a major public health problem, but it is nothing like an epidemic. Of the three diseases, TB is, by far, the greatest killer. The Global Fund committed a total of US$88.44 million for TB eradication in Bangladesh between 2004 and 2011, and there were two principal recipients. The government of Bangladesh was allocated 47 percent, and 53 percent was allocated to BRAC.

The arrangement is a partnership with a coordination mechanism that includes government, civil society, and the private sector. Government provides coordination, management, and national guidelines for treatment. It provides training, lab, and hospital facilities. It also provides the drugs. The funding managed by BRAC is for a consortium of 11 NGOs, of which BRAC is the largest. Between July 2005 and June 2006, BRAC diagnosed 84,035 people with TB and began their treatment. The cure rate was 92.6 percent.[5] BRAC had come a long way in 30 years from its first 127 patients and 60 percent dropout rate.

In September 2000, the largest-ever gathering of world leaders took place at the United Nations General Assembly in New York City. The leaders had come together to adopt the United Nations Millennium Declaration. The Declaration was hugely important because it set specific and tangible targets for reducing world poverty over the next 15 years. The targets included universal primary education, reductions in child mortality, improvements in maternal health, and movement toward greater environmental sustainability. Goal 6 aimed to halt and begin to reverse some of the world's most serious diseases. Target 8 referred to malaria and tuberculosis.

As economist Jeffrey Sachs put it:

> The Millennium Development Goals are the down payment on ending poverty. They are specific, quantified, and already promised in a Global Compact of rich and poor.[6]

They are less ambitious than earlier targets, such as the false promise of "health for all by the year 2000," solemnly pledged at a 1978 UN gathering. But, in 2000, with the right political will in developing countries and adequate financing from the rest, the Millennium Development Goals were judged to be achievable.

But there is a problem. Many world leaders have learned that pledges and promises, especially those with target dates falling after their likely departure from office, can be ignored, if not forgotten. This is unlikely to be the case with the Millennium Development Goals because they are so specific and include hard targets for poor countries as well as rich. Halfway through the 15-year target period, however, deep concerns about progress had developed. UN Secretary-General Ban Ki-moon said that the results had, by mid-2007, been mixed. He called for "urgent and concerted action" and said "the MDGs are still achievable if we act now."[7] This is UN-speak for serious pessimism.

Where TB is concerned, however, there is room for optimism. DOTS and widespread BCG vaccination have made huge inroads on the TB problem in South Asia. The number of cases per 100,000 people dropped from 531 to 290 between 1990 and 2005.[8] In Bangladesh, the incidence rate has dropped to 227, farther than the regional average. And, in the ten years between 1995 and 2005, the application of DOTS as a treatment has risen from 41 to 99 percent of all cases. The cure rate is a remarkable 90 percent. The World Health Organization still ranks Bangladesh sixth among the world's 22 high-burden TB countries. There are an estimated 300,000 new cases and 70,000 TB-related deaths a year. But the WHO says that the global epidemic is on the threshold of a decline. WHO's 2005 targets for DOTS programs (70 percent case detection and 85 percent cure) were only narrowly missed. The world is on target to stop TB. One reason is the DOTS breakthrough, pioneered by organizations like BRAC.

Millennium Development Goal 6 aims to "combat HIV/AIDS, malaria, and other diseases." Target 8 under this goal is to have halted and begun to reverse the incidence of malaria and TB by 2015. In its annual report for 2007, the World Health Organization said:

> If the global TB incidence rate is indeed falling, Millennium Development Goal 6 (Target 8) has already been satisfied, more than ten years before the 2015 deadline.[9]

Notes

1. BRAC, "Evaluation of BRAC's Programme on Health Care in Sulla," Dhaka, December 1978.

2. BRAC, "Manikganj Integrated Project; Extension Report, July 1986–December 1987," Dhaka, 1989.

3. Mushtaque R. Chowdhury, "Success with the DOTS Strategy," *Lancet*, 353 (March 20,1999).

4. World Health Organization, "Breakthrough in TB Control Announced by World Health Organization," Press Release WHO/23, March 19, 1997.

5. BRAC, "TB Control Program Annual Report July 2005–June 2006," BRAC, November 2006.

6. Jeffrey Sachs, *The End of Poverty: Economic Possibilities for Our Time* (New York: Penguin, 2005), 365.

7. United Nations, *The Millennium Development Goals Report 2007* (New York: United Nations, July 2007), 3.

8. United Nations, *The Millennium Development Goals Report 2007*, 21.

9. WHO, "WHO Report 2007: Global Tuberculosis Control; Surveillance, Planning, Financing" (Geneva, WHO, 2007).

CHAPTER 14

Educating Bangladesh

For BRAC, education came in various experimental shapes and sizes at first, eventually expanding into a stunning array of schools, libraries, training facilities, and, eventually, a full-fledged university. Almost from the beginning, BRAC was all about education. Its very first development plan for Sulla, written in 1972, aimed to make the entire adult population of the area literate, and a campaign was planned to get all primary school dropouts between the ages of five and eleven back into school. The organization was soon to learn, however, that education is about a lot more than schools and teachers.

"Functional education" was the term that emerged in the 1970s to describe an underlying fundamental in BRAC's organizing principles. This was where everything began. The first step in entering a new village was to identify households in BRAC's target group, the poorest. A BRAC program officer would then organize discussions to identify priorities. Eventually, after several weeks, separate organizations would be formed for men and for women. While a savings program might begin early, the basic platform on which everything else would be built was functional education.

Abed read copiously about development. During the early 1970s, he discovered three writers who were having a profound impact on the world's development discourse. One, a descendant of African slaves, hailed from Martinique. Franz Fanon, a psychiatrist, had structured his most famous book, *The Wretched of the Earth,* around the Algerian fight for independence from France, but its transcendent theme was the struggle for a decolonization of the mind. The second writer was a Brazilian, Paulo Reglus Neves Freire. Freire, trained in philosophy and admitted to the Brazilian bar as a lawyer, turned from a legal career to education, teaching Portuguese for many years in Brazilian high schools. During the 1960s, he embraced what would become known as liberation theology in his approach to education. He developed his ideas first with sugarcane workers in Brazil and then with Chile's Christian Democratic Agrarian Reform Movement during the turbulent pre-Allende years of the 1960s. Influenced by Fanon and combining his work as a social organizer with his background in philosophy and education, in 1970, he produced his most influential work, *The Pedagogy of the Oppressed.*

This book explored the relationship between the oppressor and the oppressed and explained why the powerless in society are often frightened by the idea of greater freedom. He argued that freedom had to be taken rather than given. It is an indispensable condition in the quest for human completion. Freedom came from what he called "praxis," a balance in action between theory and practice. Where education was concerned, Freire wrote derisively about what he called the banking approach to education, an approach that treats students as empty bank accounts awaiting deposits by the teacher. He argued that it dehumanized both teachers and students. He argued for an approach that would allow people to become aware of their incompleteness and strive to be more fully human. Freire called his effort to use education as a means of shaping the person and society "conscientization", coining a term and an approach that would become widely used in community development during the 1970s.

The third writer Abed discovered was Ivan Illich, the author of *Deschooling Society*, a radical critique of formal education as practiced in modern economies. Illich was a Vienna-born educator who lived much of his life in Mexico, resigning from the priesthood in the late 1960s after coming into conflict with the Vatican over his views about education and society.

Today, Fanon, Freire, and Illich are regarded as pioneers in thinking about the psychological liberation of the poor and the concomitant role of education, but, in their day, they were feared by the educational establishment and reviled as left-wing radicals. And perhaps with good reason. Fanon took his title from the first line of the Socialist Internationale. *"Debout, les damnés de la terre."** Freire had been arrested as a dangerous radical by Brazil's right-wing military junta in 1964, and Illich came into direct confrontation with the Vatican over his attempts to deschool the clergy in Latin America.

Kushi Kabir, the first person to join Abed in a paying staff job at BRAC, and therefore employee number two, recalled this time in BRAC. She said:

> In 1973, Abed started reading Freire. His reading was quite revolutionary, and he made me read *The Wretched of the Earth* and Ivan Illich. And then we all got hooked on Freire, and we thought about how to use Freire's methods in our literacy work.

There were two parts to the functional education course that had emerged by the end of the 1970s. The first part, delivered in 30 sessions,

---

*The line has been variously translated into English, none with the drama of the original French. "Arise, ye workers, from your slumber." "Stand up, all victims of oppression." "Arise, you victims of starvation."

was about awareness, helping villagers to analyze their environment, their relationships and dependencies, and the constraints and possibilities in their lives. The objective was to build a sense of solidarity and group cohesion, create a savings mentality, and prepare people for income-generation projects and other activities that would come with time.

The second part was about literacy and numeracy, also taught in 30 courses that were three hours each. In the early years, both courses were compulsory, but, by the start of the 1980s, the literacy and numeracy courses had become optional. Literacy for its own sake was not always useful, and some people had limited opportunities to sustain their newfound reading skills.

Trainers for BRAC's functional education were drawn from young people with a basic high school education. Background training was given at BRAC's TARC in Manikgang. Over time, as programs expanded, more TARCs would be established throughout the country. To supplement the training, BRAC had to develop its own learning material in the form of posters, flip charts, and booklets. To produce these, it established its own small printing facility with two used offset presses manufactured in 1956. By the end of the 1970s, BRAC already had the makings of a comprehensive educational system, including a community development curriculum, a literacy and numeracy curriculum, an internal training and research capacity, and a publishing operation where it developed and printed its own educational material.

To someone from the West, there would have been nothing particularly radical about what BRAC was doing, but, in Bangladesh, it was all new. Helping people to understand the context in which they lived, understanding rights and responsibilities, and just learning how to count past 10, all of this was deeply revolutionary. For many of those who joined BRAC groups, especially those who continued with the literacy training, new worlds soon began to emerge. Twenty-five years ago, for example, a young woman named Rohima lived in a village called West Shanbandha, miles from any place that a car or a jeep could reach. She spoke of what she had learned after joining a BRAC group in those early days.

> After I joined the group, I acquired knowledge gradually: how I can bring up my son in a decent way, how I can bring changes, and how I can live better . . . Even my mother said yesterday, "You did not used to visit others' homes, did not speak to others. How have you learned to speak so many things?" I said, "Ma, how I have learned, I cannot say. Whenever I am alone, I sit with the books." Mother asked, "What do you see in the books?" I said, "Ma, what valuable things there are in the books you will not understand because you cannot read and write."[1]

BRAC's first 1950s Heidelberg presses: still going strong
(Photo by Ian Smillie)

Another woman, Mallika, of Dapunia Village in Jamalpur District, spoke of obtaining some books from a BRAC trainer.

> I thought, "If I can read Bengali, it will help me." I started reading. Then I could read well and remember. I used to finish my housework quickly, cooked and fed my children, and then went to study. When I came back home, the children started crying. I told them not to cry. If I could read and write, that would be good for them. This is how I did my housework and studied. After one year I could read and write very well.[2]

Mallika was right. Her ability to read and write, and, perhaps more importantly, her ability to imagine things beyond the confines of the narrow world in which she had grown up, would be good for her children. But, not surprisingly, many parents asked BRAC to do something more directly for their children as well. As early as 1974, BRAC had started to engage with the primary education sector, producing a monthly magazine for children. *Gonokendra* contained stories on health and social issues, and

BRAC sent it to every one of the country's 45,000 primary schools. By 1981, BRAC's materials development unit was also beginning to think about an improved primary school curriculum. But it would take more years of examining how the formal education system did and did not work before BRAC would intervene.

There were several fundamental problems with the country's formal system. First, it was inadequate in terms of its geographical reach. Huge numbers of villages were nowhere near a primary school, and many parents were simply not prepared to let their youngsters spend hours trekking to and from a distant school. Second, the quality of education was abysmal. Dropout rates for those who did enroll were high, and there seemed to be little economic or social reward for those who struggled on through the system.

This seems counterintuitive, flying in the face of known facts. Historically, in both older and newly industrialized countries, the relevance of education to development and poverty reduction is well-known and well-documented. The same was true in Bangladesh. For example, the average salary of a secondary school-educated Bangladeshi woman in the 1980s, that is, the few who were actually employed in a job, was as much as seven times higher than that of a woman with no education.[3] Skilled construction workers earned double the wages of unskilled construction workers. Four years of schooling, on average, increased the output of farmers by about 8 percent.[4] Generally, increasing the average amount of education in the labor force by one year raises GDP by 9 percent, a statistic that holds for the first three years of education.[5]

The poverty-reducing impact of basic education goes further, however, than employment and income opportunities. Cross-country research conducted by the World Bank had shown that a mother's schooling of one to three years could be associated with a 20 percent decline in the risk of childhood death because the household was better able to manage basic health care, sanitation, nutrition, and the diagnosis of disease.[6] Child immunization rates increased, and there was a strong link between female literacy and fertility. According to another World Bank study, contraceptive use among uneducated Bangladeshi women was 27 percent, while, for those with primary education, it was 35 percent. There is an old adage borne out in these statistics. "Educate a man and you educate a person; educate a woman and you educate a family."

Education is an important element of social cohesion and of national and civic consciousness. It is also an important part of the democratic process. Yet another World Bank study showed, for example, that only 3.6 percent of illiterate Bangladeshi women had the confidence to go alone to a political meeting in the 1980s, but, among those with a primary education, the number doubled.[7]

As the South Asian *Human Development Report* put it:

> The role of education in reducing absolute poverty is decisive.
> Many research studies . . . [have] concluded that rising levels
> of education in a society were often accompanied by a sharp
> decline in absolute poverty. When poverty levels were corre-
> lated with such variables as mean years of schooling, adult
> literacy, and gross enrollment rates, it was clearly established
> that absolute poverty declines as education increases.[8]

So why then were only 40 percent of school-aged children enrolled in
primary school in 1984? Why were three out of every four of those who
did enroll dropping out before class five? Why were 98 percent of the girls
who enrolled in class one no longer there by class five? Why had the
country's overall literacy rate dropped from 24.3 percent in 1974 to
23.8 percent in 1981?[9] One of the answers, obviously, was about the distance a child had to walk to school. Some of the answers had to do with
poverty. Illiterate parents could not support their children at home, and
this was a contributing factor. Others had to do with the quality of education, and a lot had to do with corruption and mismanagement.

Poverty was perhaps the most important factor where the student was
concerned. In poor families, the child is part of the livelihood system.
Eight-year-old boys can go to the fields; girls as young as six can become
involved in rice processing. The entire family goes to work during the harvest season, and schooling only serves to reduce the family's immediate
income. For parents without education, there may be no appreciation
that a better-educated child might eventually earn more. In fact, a better-
educated child may well leave home, creating greater problems for the
family as the parents age.

And there was another economic factor, extortion. Although education in Bangladesh was free, it was not at all uncommon for teachers to
demand money from students for sports, a flag day, or some other fic-
tional event. This is perhaps not surprising, as a prospective teacher might
have to bribe the powerful teachers' union, the local educational authority, and perhaps several others in order to get an appointment. In 1988,
the *New Nation* reported that a typical set of bribes required to obtain a
teaching job might run to Tk 30,000 (then worth about US$840).[10]

Poverty, distance, and corruption were not the only reason for keeping
a child out of school. In many cases, the education on offer was so bad
that it was simply pointless to send a child. Even when they did enroll, students were absent much of the time, mocking the whole point of
enrolling in the first place. In the early 1980s, only one out of five were
actually in class more than 80 percent of the time.[11] The absenteeism was

understandable, however. Why bother going if there are no books, playgrounds, and teachers? A 1985 study found that 70 percent of the schools had no latrines, and 25 percent had no blackboards. Out of 76 schools in one survey, only one had any textbooks.

It gets worse. The teacher problem was not so much that there were no teachers; it was that the teachers played as much hooky as the students. Many ran side businesses or had their own gardens and farms to attend to. And, on top of the lack of teaching resources, many were simply incompetent. Teacher training was dismal, commitment was low, and supervision was largely absent. A 1985 report on one school was emblematic of the problem. Most class three students could not read, and many could not even pronounce common words properly. Class two students could not do subtraction. Class five students could not do division.

"In English, students of class five cannot even construct a simple translation such as 'I go home.'"[12]

It is not surprising that many parents believed they could give their child a better education at home than they could ever hope to receive from a bad teacher running an extortion racket with a tea stall on the side.

It is important to say that, throughout this period, there were good teachers, dedicated principals, and competent education authorities. Bangladesh could not have produced the many capable professionals that exist today in all walks of life if the primary education system had been universally abysmal. But quality and dedication were, during the 1970s and early 1980s, the exception rather than the rule.

The government's answer to all this, with much donor prompting, was to build more schools, improve teacher training, hire more teachers, print and distribute more books, and declare that universal primary education would be achieved by 2000. Despite a tripling of the primary education budget in the early 1980s, and even with 80 percent of the project costs covered by donors, it was not going to happen. Each new five-year plan, in fact, could be likened to a new idea from a group of passengers standing around a bus that was mired up to its headlights in mud. Plan as they might, few were actually pushing, and the vehicle remained stalled in despondency, confusion, and vested interests.

Twenty-two One-room Schools

In 1985, BRAC began an experiment with 22 one-room schools. The idea was to demonstrate that education could be made relevant and cost-effective, high standards were achievable, dropout rates could be reduced, and the imbalance between girls and boys could be rectified. They called it the Non-Formal Primary Education Program (NFPE).

One of the first principles was to involve parents. Because they were dealing with children from the poorest families, the experiment had to be relevant and convincing for both mother and father. The physical distance between the students and the school had to be shortened, and the pedagogical distance between the teacher and the students had to be dramatically reduced.

With assistance from Dhaka University, a team of educators gradually evolved a plan. The approach would be based on a one-room schoolhouse for children from the village in which it was located. The aim was to take children who had already dropped out of the formal education system and give them basic literacy and numeracy over a three year period. To BRAC's surprise, 94 percent of the first batch got themselves admitted to high school, so high school entrance was adopted as a more ambitious standard. This meant that, while BRAC could develop its own curriculum, teaching material, and textbooks, it would have to conform sufficiently with the formal system in order for children to return to it.

Instead of looking for teachers for its schools, BRAC followed the formula it had developed successfully elsewhere. It would look for people with enough basic education and the right mix of motivation and enthusiasm, and it would turn them into teachers. Typically, BRAC looked for a young woman in the prospective village who had at least nine years of schooling. She was given 12 initial days of teacher training and a one-day refresher course each month. She could expect regular visits from a field supervisor and a further six-day training session at the end of her first year.

The schools were simple affairs, either rented buildings or newly constructed from bamboo and corrugated tin roofing. BRAC maintained that the vast sums being spent on new schools during the 1980s ignored some of the fundamental problems in the education system. The most serious issue was not the quality of the school building; it was the quality of what happened inside it.

Parents were involved in two critical ways. First, they helped to establish the school day and the school calendar. The calendar could vary from school to school in order to accommodate needs during the harvest or other periods when children might be needed at home. The school day (two-and-a-half hours for the first two years and three for the third) might differ from one village to the next as well, starting early in the morning or later in the day. The school year, however, would be 253 days long rather than the 200-plus common to government schools. Schools would run six days a week, and no holiday would be longer than two weeks. These schools had a lot to accomplish, so time and continuity were important. Second, parents helped with the selection of the teacher and supervision. Being local, the teacher would be known to parents, who could ensure she was actually in the school during the prescribed hours. A monthly parents' meeting helped to ensure trust and commitment, and it provided opportunities for corrective action when it was required. There were other issues. Most of the students were first-generation learners whose parents were illiterate. Because children would be unable to get much support at home, homework was out, and everything had to be accomplished during the school day.

For BRAC, gender was an essential ingredient. The organization aimed for as many female teachers as possible, and it set a target of 70 percent for the enrollment of girls. Because girls were so disadvantaged in the formal school system and in society more general, BRAC intended to correct the social imbalance. It soon discovered that there were two categories of recoverable dropouts. There were those in the 6- to 10-year-old category who were still of primary school age. But there were older children who could also, in a sense, be rescued. So a second model was developed for children between the ages of 11 and 14. This Primary Education for Older Children (PEOC) program covered the same ground as the one for younger children, but did so in two rather than three years. The BRAC schools offered a curriculum with three basic areas of study: language (largely Bangla and some English), mathematics, and social studies. Social studies emphasized nutrition, hygiene, sanitation, safety and first aid, ecosystems, community, country, the world, and basic science.

When the 22-school experiment ended in 1987, BRAC had learned a lot of what it needed to know, and it was ready to scale up. It opened what seemed like a very ambitious 642 schools. The most important numbers, however, came three years later when the first graduates were emerging, and they were spectacular. One hundred and ten schools for younger students had enrolled 3,300 children, 65 percent of them girls. Only 10 of the kids had not completed the course. Of all of the students, 3,256 (99 percent of those who started) were subsequently admitted to government schools, 75 percent of them to class four, and 25 percent to class five. The numbers for the older children were even better with 15,960 enrolling in 532 schools. Only 71 had not completed the course. More than 73 percent were girls, and, of the graduates, 33 percent had gone into class four at government schools, and 66 percent had gone into class five.[13]

In five short years, BRAC had recovered almost 20,000 children who had been failed by the formal system. It had proven that girls could stay the course, and it had proven to parents and the formal education system that a curriculum could be relevant to the needs of children. It had proven that the involvement of parents mattered, and teachers could be found and trained locally. Whatever happened to those 20,000 children next, no matter how long they stayed in the formal system, they would keep the basic awareness and skills they had been taught. Twenty thousand of today's parents are literate, and they have an education they would never have received without BRAC.

As with so many BRAC initiatives, however, 20,000 students were only the beginning. By 1995, at the end of what was eventually referred to as Phase I, BRAC had opened 19,000 schools, graduating more than 500,000 children. Seventy-one percent of the children were girls, and 98 percent of the teachers were women. At each step of the way, changes and improvements were made. The number of students per school was reduced from 33 to 30 in order to provide more teacher-student contact. More and better learning materials were developed for mathematics and social studies. Concentrated language programs were developed for Bangla, and interactive radio programs were developed for English. Some teachers who had been through two teaching cycles were upgraded to the position of teacher-supervisor; others became master trainers, improving both the quality of teacher training and classroom support.

BRAC had learned a lot about the management implications of scaling up with its oral rehydration project. With the schools, it had to recruit and train teachers. It had to set up field offices, develop staff and teacher training materials, produce textbooks, and deliver these and other educational material to distant sites across the country. The program was and is intensely managed. One team office is responsible for a cluster of 80 schools. Each team office has program organizers and program assistants, each, on average, supervising and accountable for 14 or 15 schools.

In order to educate, staff themselves had to be educated, and BRAC arranged to send key people for training to regional centers such as CENIT in India and the Asian Institute for Management in the Philippines. Four BRAC staff were sent to Queen's University in Canada to complete master's degrees in education, and Queens assisted BRAC in setting up an audiovisual center, which led to the production of radio programs and educational films for its own use and television broadcast.

Phase III, which ran from 1996 to 1999, increased the program again, taking the number of schools from 19,000 to more than 34,000. Textbooks were revised, and reading centers were established for villages where the school program had been completed. A typical reading center would have about 120 books (novels, reference books on health hygiene, the environment, and legal rights), some magazine subscriptions, and games such as ludo and chess. More than 5,000 of these small libraries had been opened by the mid-1990s, and larger libraries were established at union level. By 1997, 200 of these had been established with more than 100,000 members, all operated by locally hired, BRAC-trained female librarians.

By 2004, the education program had grown to about 34,000 schools, now called BRAC Primary Schools and BRAC Adolescent Primary Schools. By 2008, the number had increased to 38,250. There had been a plan to cut back somewhat because more children were staying in government primary schools, the quality of formal education was better, and the gender imbalance had improved as well. But there were still at least 5 million children missing a primary education, and, with donor support, BRAC decided to keep the numbers up. A donor-led evaluation in 2007 supported the move, speaking of BRAC's amazing capacity to:

> [M]aintain high standards across its many schools, to supervise classroom interactions, to offer continuous and regular in-service training to teachers and support staff, to deliver supplies on time to even the most remote schools, to recruit train and retain women teachers, and to achieve relatively high levels of literacy and numeracy among the students.[14]

The implications were enormous. Already BRAC had graduated more than 3 million students, and it was producing new graduates at a rate of almost 600,000 a year, accounting for about 11 percent of all primary school students in the country. In addition, BRAC worked with other Bangladeshi NGOs, helping them both professionally and financially to set up their own primary education facilities on the BRAC model.

Beyond Primary

Despite BRAC's Herculean achievements in education, there remains a frustration that more has not been accomplished. BRAC's critics charge that it is doing little more than running a parallel education system and it lets government, which has the ultimate responsibility to educate its citizens, off the hook. Abed is impatient with this kind of criticism, saying that BRAC is a Bangladeshi organization, and, if the government can't educate Bangladesh children, others with the capacity to do so should. And, as long as BRAC can, it will. But he has another frustration:

> BRAC schools are looked upon by government as a separate entity, and "we have nothing to learn from them." So our real challenge in the future is to transfer some of the things that we do in our schools to the national system . . . that part of it we haven't achieved yet.[15]

Some have likened the primary schools to a Bailey Bridge, a temporary structure that will eventually be replaced by something more solid and permanent. Government will perhaps assume full responsibility in time, or a foundation might be created to manage the schools, with government providing funding and the regulatory framework. Bailey Bridges are common in Bangladesh, however, and many have a way of assuming an odd kind of permanence. In fact, not far from the BRAC office in Dhaka, in a fast-growing area called Niketon, there is a roadside sign that says "Baily [sic] Bridge Ahead—Only for Light Vehicles." The bridge, which crosses a channel connecting two lakes, has been there for years, and every kind of vehicle (small and large, heavy and light)—probably thousands a day—passes over it. Such is the life of a Bailey Bridge in Bangladesh.

BRAC sees the education challenge now not so much in terms of maintaining its status quo, but in deepening its engagement with the national educational system. It has developed an extensive network of pre-primary schools, almost 25,000 in all, giving young children a head start before they enter the formal system. This will help to reduce the problem of early dropouts. It has expanded the reading centers and library programs to take into account a growing demand for information from older adolescents about reproductive health, dowry, drug addiction, women's rights, and legal information, including inheritance law. It has developed a continuing education program for its union libraries, known locally as *gonokendras*. Fifteen hundred of these *gonokendras* had been established by 2008, more than 500 of them equipped with computers and a basic collection of educational CDs. All were started on a matching grant basis, with BRAC putting money into the effort only after local subscriptions had been raised. And there were 500 low-cost, rickshaw-based mobile libraries operating from *gonokendras*, making some of the material available to homebound village women.

There are two ministries of education in Bangladesh: one for primary and one for post-primary levels. Where high schools are concerned, BRAC has had more success in working with government. Perhaps here the effort is on assisting government schools, and BRAC's efforts do not show up their incompetence. But, in the high schools, the problem Freire observed 40 years ago persists. Students sit like empty bank accounts, waiting to have deposits made by teachers. The flow is all one-way. Students lack confidence, remaining disengaged and uninvolved.

BRAC has ideas and new interventions to counter the problem. It has introduced a computer-based pilot project, rewriting the math text for online use and introducing computers into the system. It runs teacher training programs, and it is training head teachers in both teaching and school management.

Shafiqul Islam, who heads BRAC's education program, is particularly excited about a new high school mentoring effort. A school's brightest children, half of them girls, are identified for a special kind of program at BRAC training centers, along with one teacher per group. The idea is to give 25 to 30 young people in a school guidance on how to encourage greater student participation in the educational process. When these

Abed visits one of BRAC's 34,000 schools (Photo by BRAC)

young mentors return to their schools, they organize a variety of projects. They run what are called "free writing groups" where students are encouraged to express themselves, where they are not judged on the quality of their work and made to feel inferior. They organize wall magazines to encourage writing, and they set up debates to encourage confidence and critical thinking. In 2006, a nationwide debating contest, involving 2,000 students in 100 schools, held its finals in Dhaka with ministry officials, Abed, and other prominent people in attendance. Taken for granted in many countries, the debating contest was a first in Bangladesh.

"It is just amazing to see what these kids can produce when they are given an opportunity," said Shafique, with obvious pride in the program's success.

The overall pilot in these 100 schools was judged a success. School attendance was up by 10 to 25 percent. Pass rates were higher. Schools were cleaner, and many had even started gardens. As with all successful BRAC programs, this one was rapidly scaling up in 2007 and expected to reach 3,000 of the country's 18,000 high schools by the end of 2008.

Abed had other ideas about how to make the public system more effective. When Manzoor Ahmed retired from UNICEF, Abed saw an opportunity for something more ambitious. Ahmed, who holds a doctorate in educational management from the University of Northern Colorado and did postdoctoral studies at Princeton, had been UNICEF's senior advisor on education and served in many capacities in the organization, including a stint as its country director in China. Ahmed had a long background in education for development, and he had encouraged UNICEF to use BRAC as a technical consultant on its own education programs in Africa during the 1990s. So, when he returned to Bangladesh, it was not surprising that he and Abed would start talking and that they would collaborate on something. The something turned out to be BRAC's Institute of Educational Development.

The idea of an educational institute was ambitious enough, but, once established as part of the BRAC University in 2004, the institute set its own ambitious course, aiming to became a center of excellence for professional development in education. It has focused on several key areas during its start-up years, developing strategic partnerships with NGOs and universities in Asia, North America, and Europe. One program deals with early childhood development for pre-primary children, a natural, given BRAC's growing emphasis in this area. In many Western countries, pre-primary education aimed at three-, four-, and five-year-olds has proven to be extremely important to children's social and cognitive development. Done well, along with parental involvement, it can build the self-esteem, self-confidence, curiosity, and self-discipline that are invaluable to future success in school. In 2001, an experimental group of 814 pre-primary feeder schools was started in collaboration with the Ministry of Education. The reaction from parents and the ministry was so positive that, by the end of 2008, nearly 25,000 of these schools, with almost 700,000 children, were in operation.

In primary education, the institute's efforts deal mainly with improvements to the curricula in Bangla and mathematics, and, in secondary education, the focus is math, science, and English. This means improved teaching, improved curricula and texts, and more and better supplementary material. The institute also works on professional development for teachers and educational managers and more detailed educational research, policy studies, and advocacy. Advocacy is critical because breaking through the glass ceilings on every floor of the educational structure in Bangladesh is a daunting task. Oddly, however, BRAC's work has been made more difficult by the donor community, which has locked itself into what is known in the development world as a SWAp, a sector-wide approach to education.

According to UNESCO:

> Sector-wide approaches, or SWAps, as they have come to be
> known, comprise one of several relatively new aid modalities
> that emerged as a means of overcoming the lack of sufficient
> recipient ownership and the fragmentation of many individual
> projects, which, even when taken as a whole, have not neces-
> sarily resulted in adequate support for a country's own, identi-
> fied priority development.[16]

This is development-speak for a simple idea. Historically, donors have
supported a patchwork of projects, rarely giving much attention to a government's overall plans or what other donors are doing. The result is very
often an ineffective stew with some projects well-funded (even double-
funded) while important areas may be completely neglected. Life, of
course, and ministries of education do not march to the beat of a donor
drum, donor timetables, or donor funding cycles. After 30 or 40 years of
chaotic hit-and-miss projects, therefore, the idea of the SWAp emerged in
the mid-1990s. A typical sector-wide approach would see all of the donors
sitting around the same table with the government, making a plan for a
whole ministry—for example, education. Targets that everyone could
agree upon would be established, donors would pool their money, and
the government could step down from the project treadmill.

In addition to greater efficiencies and synergies, the SWAp concept was
based on an additional idea, recipient ownership. The plan had to be
owned by the government rather than by a collection of donors micro-
managing their own individual projects. "Putting the government in the
driver's seat" became the donor watchword of the late-1990s, and this is
what happened when donor representatives got together with the
Bangladesh Ministry of Education to create the giant Primary Education
Development Program (PEDP).

A donor consortium led by the World Bank had helped to fund the
General Education Program between 1990 and 1996 at a cost of
US$159.3 million. Then came the PEDP, which lasted for five years
between 1998 and 2003, costing US$741 million. Next, an Asian Devel-
opment Bank-led consortium of 10 donors pooled more than US$650
million into a new project, the PEDP II, which was to last through 2009.
These projects were supposed to contribute to a growth in primary enrollment, particularly for girls, but a study carried out by 10 NGOs in 2007
found that the net enrollment rate of 6- to 10-year-olds had actually
declined between 2002 and 2005 and the dropout rate had increased
from 33 to 47 percent.[17] The quality of education had barely improved,
and, in the view of many, it has actually deteriorated.

Despite the huge advance in having donors coordinate their assistance, there are two fundamental problems with the SWAp approach in Bangladesh. First, putting an ineffectual government department in the driver's seat does not improve either management or governance, and it certainly does not guarantee better use of foreign assistance.

Second, insisting that all NGOs should line up behind the SWAp and march to the tune of a badly managed ministry—backed by a collection of foreign donors—works against everything that has given Bangladesh an edge in the delivery of primary education. Many donors actually believe that NGOs should now stop innovating, limiting themselves to service delivery. The ultimate goal for them is a ministry that will farm out service contracts to NGOs prepared to follow its policies and direction.

It is no doubt a good thing that NGO innovation is helping to set standards that donors can at least request from government. But to insist that NGOs should give up their innovation and work exclusively inside the government-donor box is not just shortsighted. It is foolish.

Some donors have continued to support BRAC's primary education program, not least because the pretentious PEDP II has simply failed to meet targets. But, at a policy level, BRAC's Institute of Education remains underfunded and frustrated by what it sees as willful donor collaboration in the dumbing of educational policy and management. The ministry's problem is not the articulation of an appropriate education policy for Bangladesh. It is the difficulty of translating it into action at almost every level of the system. Decisions are made by donors on the basis of consultancies conducted by outsiders and senior ministry officials, many of whom have no professional background whatsoever in education. And decisions are frequently made, not on the basis of technical or professional considerations, but on the basis of who might get a contract from a huge SWAp awash with money.

Manzoor Ahmed said:

> In principle, the sector-wide approach is a very good idea, a logical idea, but in practice it seems to compound the problems of fragmentation and centralized decision-making. PEDP II has two major objectives: one is to improve quality in terms of the performance of students and children, and according to the document, to build greater authority, accountability and responsibility at the school level. Now we are at the mid point and I don't think they have really made progress on either of these things. They claim success, and they have spent quite a lot of the budgeted money, but it has been mainly in constructing classrooms and appointing teachers. These are necessary, but they do not necessarily contribute the main objectives.

In fact, a draft 2007 midterm donor review of the PEDP II was apparently so critical of the achievements that the report was suppressed through much of 2008. "Not exactly suppressed," as one Dhaka official put it, "but not exactly available." When it finally appeared, it contained long lists of achievements, although it was much heavier on quantity than quality. A subsequent review of Norwegian assistance to Bangladesh listed many of the project's inputs, to which Norway had specifically contributed. But it also said that "the government lacks the capacity to manage and implement the program effectively" and there was a problem with the PEDP II impact.

> For a program of USD 1.8 billion, the Team is surprised that it lacks the proper baseline data and procedures for the evaluation of impacts . . . no impact methodology seems to have been developed.[18]

The Digital Divide

By the mid-1990s, BRAC was considering not just the development potential in new information and communications technologies (ICTs), but the possibility that Bangladesh, especially poor Bangladeshis, might be left behind in what was already being termed a "digital divide." The rate of advancement of ICTs in the industrialized world during the 1990s was revolutionary. E-mail, videoconferencing, the Web, computer networks, and CD-ROM were transforming ways in which governments, the private sector, and individuals worked. ICTs were building new markets, products, and productivity. They allowed faster generation, manipulation, and transmission of information. ICTs clearly offered special new opportunities and some very real challenges for development. As the 1998/1999 World Bank *World Development Report* put it:

> The explosion of new knowledge, accelerating technological progress, and ever-increasing competition make life-long learning more important than ever . . . [The] new technology greatly facilitates the acquisition and absorption of knowledge, offering developing countries unprecedented opportunities to enhance educational systems, improve policy formation and execution, and widen the range of opportunities for business and the poor.[19]

This statement illustrates one of the basic problems in understanding what information technologies are and can do, confusing information with knowledge. T.S. Eliot pointed out the difference in 1934 when he asked, "Where is the wisdom we have lost in knowledge? Where is the knowledge we have lost in information?" Confusion and hype notwithstanding, communication technologies had become so important by the late-1990s that the International Telecommunications Union (ITU) was talking about the "right to communicate." Its secretary-general, Pekka Tarjanne, said that, in order for people to enjoy the benefits of the Universal Declaration of Human Rights, they must have access to basic communications and information services.

In 1998, he argued:

> Without action on the part of the world community, there is a very real danger that the global information society will be global in name only; that the world will be divided into the "information rich" and the "information poor"; and that the gap between developed and developing countries will widen into an unbridgeable chasm.[20]

His worry had a real basis in fact. At the time, USAID had devoted US$15 million over five years to global information infrastructure technologies, aimed at extending full Internet connectivity to 20 or more African countries. It might have been instructive to compare this small price tag with the US$450 million invested by the state of North Carolina and the local telephone company in building the North Carolina information highway between 1994 and 1999 and with the US$1 billion they expected to spend on it before 2007. US$3 million a year for 20 African countries. US$77 million a year in North Carolina.[21] This is not to suggest that USAID is responsible for spending more on new technologies for Africa, but it points up the very large gap between what is available for these technologies in developing countries and what is available in the West.

Most developing countries lack affordable access to basic information resources. This includes the technologies as well as the capacity to build, operate, manage, and service them in instances where they are available. One of the key measures of telecommunications access is teledensity, the number of main telephone lines per 100 people. Teledensity ranges from a high of 99 in Monaco to only 0.4 in Bangladesh. In fact, more than a quarter of ITU member states have a teledensity of less than one. Historically, it has taken most countries 50 years to move from that threshold to a teledensity of 50. This was borne out in the Bangladesh government's 1999 plan to get the teledensity up from 0.4 per hundred to four by 2010.

Of course, the technology existed, even in the olden days of the late-1990s, to skip the need for landlines and go straight to radio and satellite connectivity. These technologies, however, looked as if they would be constrained for some years to come by cost, local capacity to use and maintain them, and a shortage of satellites in the Southern hemisphere. Cellular telephones were something of an exception in all of this, and investments like Grameen Bank's in this new technology bore early fruit. Within a decade, Grameen Phone, launched in 1997, had become the country's largest mobile phone company with over 10 million subscribers. While no doubt extremely useful to users, however, voice connections are essentially a high-tech variation on Alexander Graham Bell's "Come here, Watson; I want you." With adult literacy rates under 40 percent (and much less for women) in Bangladesh, the knowledge-based application of ICTs looked like they would remain a luxury for many years to come.

The Internet came late to Bangladesh, with the first UUCP e-mail connections beginning in 1993. A major opportunity for change came three years later in 1996 when the government decided to allow private entrepreneurs to become Internet service providers (ISPs) using low-bandwidth VSAT technology. Fast off the mark, Grameen Bank set up Grameen Cybernet, and several NGOs became service providers. BRAC was one of them, establishing BracNET in 1997, backed by an information technology institute it established the following year.

But the problems in making the new technology available to poor people in remote areas (and even in not very remote areas) were enormous. And even if the problems could be overcome, there was a final issue in the assumption that the medium is the message. Computer security network specialist Clifford Stoll, writing in the dark ages of 1995, said:

> Perhaps our networked world isn't a universal doorway to freedom. Might it be a distraction from reality? . . . Nobody can offer utopia-on-a-stick, the glowing virtual community that enhances our world through discovery and close ties while transcending the coarseness of human nature.[22]

"Utopia-on-a-stick" is not a new phenomenon where ICTs are concerned. The London *Times* hailed the 1858 completion of the transatlantic telegraph cable saying, "Since the discovery of Columbus, nothing has been done in any degree comparable to the vast enlargement which has thus been given to the sphere of human activity."[23] The telegraph would bring an end to war and promote "the exchange of thought between all the nations of the earth." There were hundred-gun salutes in New York and Boston, parades, fireworks, and special church services.

"Our whole country has been electrified by the successful laying of the Atlantic telegraph," wrote *Scientific American*.

Similar declarations were made in their day about the peace-building and educational values of radio, film, and television. The message (content) has always been the number one issue in Bangladeshi education. Government and donors may build schools, but the most important part of education is not and never was the building. It is what goes on inside. The same is true of educational radio, film, and television. That said, Internet technology has huge potential, and, in the hands of organizations like BRAC, it could revolutionize education. But getting the Internet to remote villages is no easy task in a country where electrical connectivity, not to mention telephone connectivity, has remained elusive for over a century.

Much has been made recently of rugged, ever-cheaper, battery-powered computers that draw energy from the sun. An American project, One Laptop per Child, developed over several years by MIT professor Nicholas Negroponte, has produced an inexpensive computer and program that aims to get hundreds of thousands of US$200 laptops into the hands of poor children. The laptops can be loaded with books and other educational material, so they appear to have crossed several educational Rubicons in one go. There are two problems, however. The first is that, in most poor countries, there is no localized material available for the computers. In Bangladesh, BRAC is leading on this with development of CD-based programs for secondary school students and their teachers, one in math and the other in English.

The second is more serious. According to *Newsweek*, the Negroponte laptop's "Wi-Fi connectivity finds more hot spots than your average Windows laptop can hope to locate."[24] The problem is that Wi-Fi is a short-range system, reaching a few hundred meters at most. The average Bangladeshi village might wait as long for this technology to arrive as it has for electricity.

In less than a half-decade of limited Internet connectivity, however, BRAC could see how useful the technology might be, if people could access it. BRAC had internal management requirements for it as well. Most of its 1,500 offices across the country had been computerized by 2005 in an effort to speed up microfinance operations and keep closer tabs on remote financial operations. But, at the end of the day or the end of the week, someone still had to mount a motorbike and take a CD to a town or a city with e-mail connectivity. It was space-age computer technology combined with Pony Express connectivity.

Given the rapid uptake of computer technology and of the Internet where it was available, BRAC was nothing if not frustrated by this final hurdle. By 2007, it had established 30 E-huts, commercial cyber cafés with training facilities and all the technological mod cons. More than 500 of its *gonokendras* had computers, and they were on standby for connectivity. And with ever-cheaper computers coming onto the market, the educational applications were obvious. Connectivity remained the issue. But that was on the way. Working with international investors, BRACNet began in 2007 to install a new wireless broadband technology, WiMAX, in Dhaka, Chittagong, and Sylhet. WiMAX, a wireless technology capable of transmitting wireless data over long distances, is sometimes called last-mile wireless broadband, and, in due course, it may be as common as mobile telephony. An initial investment of US$6 million was expected to be enough to demonstrate the value of the technology and attract the larger investment required to take it nationwide. In Bangladesh, BRAC is the WiMAX technology leader and will no doubt use it to revolutionize education throughout the country.

Paraphrasing what T.S. Eliot had said 75 years earlier, management guru Peter Drucker wrote:

> What we call the Information Revolution is actually a Knowledge Revolution. What has made it possible to routinize processes is not the machinery; the computer is only the trigger. Software is the reorganization of traditional work, based on centuries of experience, through the application of knowledge, and especially of systematic, logical analysis. The key is not electronics; it is cognitive science.[25]

Abed put it more succinctly, "We need not only to get children into schools, but to provide a quality education, and this is not happening in Bangladesh yet."[26]

Notes

1. Martha Alter Chen, *A Quiet Revolution: Women in Transition in Rural Bangladesh* (Cambridge, Mass.: Schenkman Publishing, 1983), 202.

2. Chen, *A Quiet Revolution*, 214.

3. World Bank, "Staff Appraisal Report on Female Secondary School Assistance, Report No. 15496-IN, 16 February 1993.

4. D. Jamison and L. Lau, *Farmer Education and Farm Efficiency* (Baltimore: Johns Hopkins University Press, 1982).

5. World Bank, *World Development Report 1991* (Oxford: Oxford University Press 1991), 43.

6. World Bank, *The East Asian Miracle: Economic Growth and Public Policy* (New York, Oxford University Press, 1997).

7. World Bank, "Staff Appraisal Report on Female Secondary School Assistance," Report No. 15496-IN, 16 February 1993.

8. Mahbub ul Haq and Khadija Haq, *Human Development in South Asia 1998* (Karachi: Oxford University Press, 1998), 29.

9. Styrbjorn Gustavsson, *Primary Education in Bangladesh: For Whom?* (Dhaka: University Press, 1990), 30, 37.

10. *New Nation,* Feb. 12, 1988, 63.

11. Ibid.

12. S.A. Qadir, cited in Gustavsson, *Primary Education in Bangladesh,* 83.

13. Catherine H. Lovell, *Breaking the Cycle of Poverty: The BRAC Strategy* (West Hartford, Conn.: Kumarian, 1992), 55.

14. "BRAC Education Programme 2004–2009: Midterm Review," 15 March 2007, 1.

15. Ashoka, *Innovator for the Poor: The Story of Fazle H. Abed and the Founding of BRAC,* Recorded interview, DVD, Arlington, Virginia, 2005.

16. http://portal.unesco.org/education/admin/ev.php?URL_ID= 10217&URL_DO=DO_TOPIC&URL_SECTION=201.

17. The study, funded by the Commonwealth Education Fund, was reported at http://www.irinnews.org/Report.aspx?ReportId=75139.

18. Arne Wiig, Farah Ghuznavi, and Alf Morten Jerve, "Midterm Review of the Country Programme (MoU: 2003:2008) between Norway and Bangladesh," (Dhaka: Royal Norwegian Embassy, 2008), 13–14.

19. World Bank, *World Development Report 1998/99* (Oxford: Oxford University Press, 1999), 8–9.

20. ITU, *World Telecommunications Development Report 1998,* Executive Summary, www.itu.int/ti/publications/WTDR_98.

21. Benton Foundation, *Losing Ground Bit by Bit: Low-income Communities in the Information Age,* Washington, 1998, http://www.benton. org/library.

22. Clifford Stoll, *Silicon Snake Oil: Second Thoughts on the Information Highway* (New York: Doubleday, 1995), 2–3.

23. Tom Standage, *The Victorian Internet* (New York: Walker and Company, 1998), 83.

24. Steven Levy, "Give One, Get One: The $100 (well, $200) laptop is ready to change the world if people will buy it for the kids who need it," *Newsweek,* Oct. 1, 2007.

25. Peter Drucker, "Beyond the Information Revolution," *Atlantic Monthly,* October 1999, 57.

26. Ashoka, *Innovator for the Poor: The Story of Fazle H. Abed and the Founding of BRAC,* Recorded interview, DVD, Arlington, Virginia, 2005.

CHAPTER 15

Challenging the Frontiers

The Ultra Poor

BRAC learned at the beginning that, if it was going to help the poor, it had to be able to identify and work directly with them. Comfortable ideas from the 1960s about community development simply did not work in villages where wealth and power were rigidly stratified and where the poor were social and economic outcasts, living and dying like serfs from a bygone age. The BRAC approach had worked. Poor people had been assisted out of abject poverty through a combination of organization, education, better health, and microfinance, backed by the creation of new, productive enterprise opportunities.

By the end of the 1990s, however, BRAC had started to consider an issue that some of its staff and outsiders had pointed out for years. There was a substratum of deeply ingrained poverty that BRAC, Grameen Bank, and other NGOs were simply not reaching. There were people so poor, so weighed down by ignorance, ill health, and fear, that they were unable to join a BRAC group or any other. Their social skills were minuscule, and their self-esteem could be described only by its absence. Training and microfinance were beyond the physical and psychological resources of these individuals. Many were women who had been abandoned, widowed, or divorced. Left to fend for themselves, their children, and sometimes their elderly parents, they had nothing, not even the social skills required to succeed at begging.

Take Mongli, the youngest of five children born to a day laborer named Jyotish in a village called Putimari.[1] Growing up, Mongli never had more than one meal a day. She and her siblings never saw the inside of a school, and, at twelve, she was married off to a man who soon began to abuse her. When he tired of her, he arranged a divorce through village arbitration, which meant little more than ridding himself of unwanted chattel. Mongli returned to her parents' house and took whatever day labor she could find, but, when her mother died, the economic pressure

175

on her to leave mounted. At 16, she married again, this time to a man named Dhormu who worked as an assistant to the village blacksmith. Dhormu, more than twice her age, married Mongli because his two sons from an earlier marriage had left home, and he needed someone to look after his hearing-impaired daughter. At first, life seemed to improve. Frequently, there were three meals a day. But they slept on the mud floor of their hut, and, during the monsoon, they were often flooded out. Her husband became ill and worked less, so they ate less. On some days, they ate nothing. Each of three pregnancies resulted in abortions brought on by severe malnutrition. Mongli was what demographers refer to as a member of the ultra poor.

Fulmala came from a family like Mongli's. Her father was also a day laborer, and Fulmala grew up with her parents, three brothers, and three sisters in a tiny shack on the edge of their village. They had nothing, and her father counted himself lucky to marry Fulmala off when she was only seven. Her husband, Lokman, was, at age 16, no more ready for marriage and certainly no better off. Fulmala was lucky in a sense because she did not become pregnant until she was 16 and she and Lokman were able to earn enough to survive by working for a village worthy. By the time she was 40, however, Lokman was dead, and Fulmala was an old woman with five sons, two daughters, and a life of abject penury.

Jahanara, who lived in Hajirgol village in Kishorganj District, was sent away by her parents to work as a domestic when she was seven.[2] For a while, she worked in a garment factory until her parents married her to a man of 50. They knew so little about this man that they had no address for him and did not know he had already been married seven times. Before abandoning Jahanara, he beat her with an iron rod. She was three months pregnant.

BRAC had worked with many women like Mongli, Fulmala, and Jahanara over the years, but there were limits both to their success and the numbers they had been able to reach. One effort started in 1985 was a program called Income Generation for Vulnerable Group Development (IGVGD). Under this program, BRAC provided training for vulnerable women in income-generation activities. They were also given training in health care and basic human rights. While they were being trained, they were paid with food supplied by the World Food Program, gradually becoming eligible for loans to finance an income-generation activity. By 2006, BRAC had provided training to 2.2 million women through this program, and it had been able to bring almost 70 percent of them into the microfinance program. But what about the rest?

Studies during the 1990s had shown that the numbers of people living in poverty could be disaggregated for the purposes of targeting and programming. Almost half of the people in Bangladesh were poor, meaning

they consumed less than the 2,122 calories now judged to be the minimum intake for a healthy life. Almost 16 percent were judged to be very
poor, not consuming even 1,800 calories. And almost 10 percent were
ultra poor, consuming less than 1,600 calories a day.

Other studies during the 1990s had begun to demonstrate that, while
BRAC had been able to reach some of the ultra poor through its regular
programs and the IGVGD program, many were simply being left out.
There were two basic reasons. First, the very poorest were sometimes
being screened out. A BRAC group would normally have 40 or 50 members,
but, if there were about 100 very poor households in the village, BRAC
staff and other group members might screen for those more likely to succeed than others. All would be poor, that is, falling below the marker of
2,122 calories, but the very poorest might slip through the net.

There was another explanation, self-exclusion. BRAC undertook
detailed studies in four villages where it and Grameen Bank had programs in order to try to understand the problem better. They found that,
out of 498 ultra poor people eligible to join a BRAC or Grameen group,
43 percent had stayed away. About half had done so because they were
fearful of programs based on borrowing. They were so poor and may
already have been carrying such an unbearable debt load that the idea of
joining a program based on microfinance was too frightening to consider. A quarter of the women had stayed away for religious or social considerations while others complained they didn't have the time required
to participate in group meetings. A few said the rules were simply too
complicated.

Only 13 percent said they had been screened out because other villagers or program staff had decided they were bad credit risks. The broad
conclusion was not that BRAC couldn't reach the poorest, but that its
now-standard health plus education plus microfinance package was not
the way out of poverty for many of those on the bottom rung of the economic ladder.

After considerable internal debate, BRAC now proposed something
new, something that seemed contrary to the self-help ethic they had themselves espoused and perfected, something that went completely against
the grain of an increasingly single-minded development orthodoxy
inspired to believe that microfinance could solve all problems and all
microlending should be financially sustainable from the outset.

They called the proposal "Challenging the Frontiers of Poverty Reduction." All projects inevitably wear acronyms, and this one, CFPR, was no different. But the substance was. The idea was to use the standard BRAC
approach, but to tailor it specifically to people like Mongli, Fulmala, and
Jahanara, drilling down into the core of their misery and working closely
with them over time. The first part was an update on BRAC's functional

Abed with villagers in the countryside (Photo by BRAC)

education. Here they would have to start at ground zero with people who had absolutely no standing in the community, people with no social capital. They would create special organizations of and for these people, organizations that could help build self-esteem as well as knowledge and courage, in addition to awareness. They would work on legal issues such as child marriages, the ruinous dowry system, and abusive divorce arrangements. It was a 24-month immersion program that went beyond formal training to the very roots of what Paulo Freire had talked about years before.

The second part was about health. Illness, malnutrition, dangerous pregnancies, and child mortality were among the greatest barriers to any kind of advance among the very poorest. Their access to health services was restricted in almost every way, by distance, affordability, and understanding. Even the most basic information about sanitation seemed beyond their reach. Improvement to economic and psychological health would have to be accompanied by improvements in physical health. CFPR would reorient BRAC's health services to the very poorest, ensuring that health information would be both accessible and understandable. It would develop water, sanitation, and curative services they could reach and afford. BRAC would extend its own health activities, but it would also arrange for better access to government health clinics and hospitals. It would develop advocacy programs that would push government policies in a pro-poor direction from the national level on down. Improved governance in the country's health system would become a growing focus of attention.

Breaking with Orthodoxy

The third and most important aspect of the program dealt with income. BRAC would work more closely with these participants than it did with others, developing specially tailored investment opportunities and the skills they would require, whether in poultry, vegetable farming, or fish production. The major difference between the CFPR and other programs, however, was that BRAC would pay participants to join the program. Participants would be given a cash stipend for one year so they would be freed from begging, prostitution, or whatever menial work they were doing in order to participate meaningfully in group education and training. Some of the payment would be set aside in savings accounts that would be redeemable at the end of the program. And BRAC would also give each participant some form of income-producing asset, for example, a cow, goats, poultry, or a nursery.

This was the controversial part, cash payments and assets that would be handed over for free. It went against the entire ethos of the ballooning microfinance juggernaut, which boasted that even the very poorest could borrow a bit of money and haul themselves up out of poverty. BRAC was not only saying that this was wrong, but that handouts and subsidies would be required if microfinance was to ever reach some of the people it was supposed to have been serving all along.

This would be a hard sell. It was, as BRAC said in its proposal to donors, "a radical departure from conventional poverty reduction interventions in Bangladesh."[3] Self-financing, market-based microfinance was not reaching the poorest, and safety net schemes like food-for-work during lean periods did not lead to any kind of sustained development.

> Not all BRAC programs can aspire to financial self-sufficiency, at least not in the immediate future. Service delivery activities— credit, training for enterprise development, health services— can support themselves either individually or through cross-subsidies . . . But the special investment program for the ultra poor, with its asset transfer and stipend program, is inherently dependent on external financing, from BRAC or elsewhere.

BRAC was looking for more than US$60 million for the program over five years, and, given the economic heresy that was inherent in its concept, donors were unlikely to part easily with that kind of money. Abed began discussing the idea with donors in 1999, and BRAC drew up a concept paper in January the next year. A concept paper would take no skin off any donor's nose, so it was not surprising that a full proposal might be encouraged. This was completed in June 2000, and, in September, an appraisal team visited Bangladesh to place the idea under the donor microscope. The team issued a report in several volumes, hundreds of pages in length. It was a useful report in two respects. First, it helped BRAC to refine its proposal. The report's major concern was that BRAC had become so large and grown so fast that it had become overly task-oriented. This essentially meant that its approach had become formulaic, focusing too much on inputs and targets rather than on the participatory, qualitative approach that would be required in dealing with the very poorest.

Second, the report served to convince donors that the effort would be worthwhile. A BRAC team, including Rabeya Yasmin, Sonia Sultan, and Jalaluddin Ahmed, along with Amin and Mushtaque, worked on a new version of the proposal. Marty Chen returned to Bangladesh to assist.

The proposal was completed in 2001 with a somewhat reduced budget. The total over five years would be US$53 million, of which US$47.7 million would be provided by donors and the rest by BRAC. The biggest contributor, with 40 percent of the total, was Britain's Department for International Development (DFID), followed by the European Commission with 28 percent. The balance was made up of inputs from the Canadian International Development Agency (CIDA), the Dutch NGO NOVIB,* and the World Food Program.

There would be two challenges for the CFPR program after it began in 2002. The first was to make it work, and the second, if it did work, was to prove its success. Like so many BRAC efforts in the past, it was billed as an experiment. The first two years would be a pilot and the subject of intensive study. BRAC's research and evaluation division would follow the progress of three slightly different models in order to determine which might be the most effective. And the donors would watch it like hawks. Between April 2004 and September 2006, BRAC would produce more than a dozen research reports on its progress, covering virtually every aspect of the program, from numbers and the effectiveness of targeting to community perceptions and the impact of the project on the health and incomes of participants.

One innovation that had not been part of the original design involved engagement with villagers who were better off, a first for BRAC. As the

*NOVIB (Nederlandse Organisatie Voor Internationale Bijstand) has been a longtime supporter of BRAC. In 2006 it joined the Oxfam consortium of organizations and became known as Oxfam-NOVIB.

poorest in a village started to become better organized, the pool of cheap, subservient labor that wealthier households had depended upon started to dry up. There was grumbling, and it seemed that an incipient conflict was brewing. Amin, who, as a student Marxist in the 1960s, had gone to villages to meet the poor, came up with an idea. Instead of confrontation, why not actually engage the rich? The message for the elite was simple. For hundreds of years, they had been obliged to support the poor. Now BRAC was helping the poor to stand on their own two feet, but it could not do so alone. It would need the help of the better-off: "BRAC needs your help in assisting the poorest and in making sure that other elements in the village don't get in the way."

A system developed. Now, after widespread and very careful consultation, a poverty reduction committee is created, consisting of some very poor and some very wealthy villagers, ensuring all come from good backgrounds and none is politically partisan. In addition to providing social cover, the committees also provide tangible assistance. They help get children from poor families into school. They provide tutorial support. They contribute resources, including shoes and schoolbags for children, building material, and even money for latrines and house repair. Oddly, perhaps some of the "community" that had been missing for so long in Bangladeshi villages began to develop in this fledgling contact between the very poorest and wealthiest.

By 2008, more than 3,000 of these committees had been established, and BRAC calculated that their cumulative contribution to the program (in cash and in kind) could be valued at Tk 30 million. This amounted to less than US$150 per village, but it was a start, not just of additional resources, but of a possible new way of thinking about community development.

The main part of the project dealt with 5,000 women each in the first two years, and, in January 2004, the donors fielded a team of six international evaluators to investigate the results. The team carried out interviews with women in six different districts, examining changes in their human capital, their social capital, and the return on investment (ROI) made by BRAC and the donors. They also examined the health, income, and attitudes of the beneficiaries.

Benefactors and Beneficence

The careful reader may have noticed that the word "beneficiary" has not appeared in this book until now. "Beneficiary" is a word commonly used throughout the world of development organizations, but it is almost never used within BRAC. It is absent from even the earliest project proposals and reports. There is a reason. A beneficiary receives a benefice from a benefactor. Benefactors are, by definition, beneficent. In English, these words all have a distinctly charitable, semi-religious connotation, and, for BRAC, they smacked of paternalism and condescension. For Abed, education and health are basic human rights, not a gift to be handed out at the whim of the beneficent. The ability to live a decent life and be able to provide food and shelter for one's children is also a basic human right. Abed believed the conditions for these things should be provided by the state, as elsewhere in the world. But, in the absence of government, elements of the framework, along with connections and opportunities, could be provided by others. As a Bangladeshi organization, BRAC would help build an environment in which all Bangladeshis could exercise their innate abilities and potential as a right, not a gift.

This avoidance of the word "beneficiary" may seem like a quibble. Certainly everyone who came in touch with BRAC was meant to benefit from the experience. But it reflects a state of mind, an important one that permeated BRAC's programs and its dealings with those who joined its programs through the years. Mongli, Fulmala, and Jahanara were people before all else.

The 2004 evaluation found that, where human capital was concerned, the program was achieving its aims. Confidence-building, awareness-building, basic literacy, and numeracy training had all contributed. Legal aid clinics had helped with problems relating to marriage, divorce, and property rights. BRAC developed a traveling theatre group that staged plays aimed at an entire village, plays that could educate while they entertained. The women interviewed by the evaluators were articulate and self-assured, and they took pride in their newfound ability to earn money from something other than begging and menial tasks. [4]

Where social capital was concerned, there were also important changes. The women were no longer regarded as social outcasts, and the better-off no longer disparaged the groups that had been formed. There was, in fact, some envy, even difficulty, for members who had hitherto lived rent-free because of their previous penury. Health conditions had shown a vast improvement. An intensive program to sink tubewells for clean drinking water had paid off. Latrines had been built for most participating households. BRAC had created a new level of health worker to deal specifically with pre- and postnatal health care. It had introduced participants to government clinics where they existed, and it built and staffed its own clinics where distances were too great.

The evaluation was tentatively positive. There were no big surprises and no major criticisms. It looked as if 70 percent of the participants had built the base for a sustainable livelihood. "Conclusions on the results," the report said, "and their sustainability are necessarily tentative at this stage," but the project was "off to a good start." It was "producing results and is on track to achieve its purpose, to bring about sustainable improvements in the lives of rural ultra-poor women."

A second team of international evaluators arrived in 2005, this time to look more deeply into the program's cost-effectiveness and make recommendations to donors about taking the pilot to a second phase. This one found that all of the output indicators were being achieved or surpassed. In other words, the numbers of women, groups, training programs, latrines, and loans that had been planned had been met. In more qualitative terms, the team reported that the economic progress of participants was significant:

> [T]he social development components are on track to meet targets and appear to have had positive effects in improving the sociopolitical position of ultra-poor beneficiaries and ensuring that their voice is heard.[5]

"Cost-effectiveness," the report stated, "is central to the replicability of the CFPR model." The team noted that costs were higher than standard microfinance models, "however, the traditional microfinance programs bypass the ultra-poor." At a cost of US$291 per participant, the value for money was good. The team had two major recommendations. One was for BRAC. The organization needed a more coherent advocacy strategy, an issue that will be addressed in chapter 18. The other was for donors. Extend Phase I, and approve Phase II "on an urgent basis." This is what one might call a positive recommendation.

The donors did extend and approve. In fact, the original plan was to bring 5,000 women into the program in each of the first two years, 10,000 in the third, and, if it all seemed to be working, 25,000 each in years four and five. The planned total was therefore 70,000. So successful were the results after the first three years that DFID added enough money to bring the total to 100,000, and, in 2007, Canada, Australia, Britain, and the Dutch NGO, NOVIB, came up with US$204 million to expand the program over the next five years.

By the end of five years, the CFPR had been studied extensively. The studies, both internal and external, concluded that BRAC's targeting had been accurate, health conditions had improved along with confidence, and there was improved acceptance of the poor and their projects in the village. All graduates had been able to join BRAC's mainstream development groups. Not all had stayed, and only 60 percent had taken loans to augment what they had already received from BRAC. But the enterprises that had been introduced worked. Somewhere between 75 and 80 percent of the women were on their way to some kind of sustainable economic improvement.

What next? Imran Matin, who left the World Bank to join BRAC and became director of BRAC's research and evaluation department in 2003, believes this should not be viewed as a five- or ten-year program if extreme poverty is to be eradicated in Bangladesh. It will probably be needed for the next 50 years, and donors certainly will not pay for that. He believes, however, that there is enough money in government safety net programs (feeding, relief, and various allowances) to devote substantially more funding to an approach like this that could graduate people out of permanent dependence.

Is this realistic? After all, BRAC developed cost-effective models for primary health care and education, and government never picked up on them. And, even if it had, would a government approach have been even half as effective as BRAC's own go-it-alone versions? Imran Matin believes that, if an approach is so sophisticated that only BRAC can do it, there is a fundamental problem. Any model has to be replicable, and not just by BRAC. If it is too sophisticated, it will not work.

And he believes that mainstreaming this kind of ultra-poor program will not be as difficult as it was in education and health:

> The politics of reforming the education system or the primary health care system are far more complicated than the politics involved in a safety net program from which people can graduate.

First, where the poor are concerned, there are fewer vested interests than there are in the education and health systems. "Here, we are dealing with the politics of sympathy and the politics of empathy, something that is very much rooted in Bengali culture," he says. For evidence, he points to the allocation by village and union committees of cards entitling the very poorest to test relief, emergency food, and other special allowances. These are no longer as routinely purloined by the rich, as had been the case when BRAC first went to Sulla.

Mainstreaming the approach, however, will undoubtedly take time. In his office at BRAC, Imran tacked a card to the wall. On it, there is a quotation from Albert Einstein: "The significant problems we face cannot be solved at the same level of thinking we were at when we created them."

Rabeya Yasmin, who is in charge of the Ultra Poor program, has a different view. She has seen the program grow, but she also saw it being replicated in other countries, including Haiti, India, Pakistan, Ethiopia, and Honduras. She has visited most of these countries, spending more time in Haiti than others. Her view is that the basic concepts—asset transfer and immersion training—are the key. Other organizations taking up the challenge do not have the full panoply of BRAC programs in health, education, and income generation, but the core approach seems to be working, and that may be enough. In Bangladesh, however, it may well take 25 years for the approach to have its full effect. There, it has passed its first experimental phase and is now growing. But there will be new issues and new challenges, including urban populations and efforts aimed more specifically at men, and there will have to be experiments in how to bring government into the picture.

Meanwhile, what of Mongli, Fulmala, and Jahanara? Mongli joined the program in 2002. She was put on a weekly stipend of Tk 70 a week and went through BRAC's basic training. She learned how to write her name and understand numbers. She received a slab latrine, and, in due course, she was also given four goats. Her house was upgraded to make it more sanitary and to give her an enclosure for the goats. Within a few months, the goats produced six kids. She sold four of them and used the proceeds to buy a cow.

After her training, Fulmala opted for poultry rearing, and she was given a cage and 36 chickens. She also received three goats. Although she was able to earn money from selling the eggs, her husband wasted some of the income on his own ill-planned income-generation ideas, and Fulmala continued to limp along.

Jahanara used her grant to rent land and go into vegetable farming. She leased 20 decimals (one-fifth of an acre) for planting spinach, cauliflower, and cabbage. On an investment of Tk 1,300, her return was Tk 3,700, enabling her to expand into chilies, potatoes, and *brinjal* (the local name for eggplant or aubergine). With her growing income, she was able to buy 12 chickens and four ducks. She spoke of getting her children into school, buying a cow, and maybe actually owning some land one day.

Notes

1. Mongli's story is taken from BRAC, "CFPR/TUP Progress Report January to June 2003," Dhaka, 2003.

2. The Fulamala and Jahanara stories are taken from BRAC, "CFPR/TUP Progress Report July to December June 2003," Dhaka, 2004.

3. Excerpts from the proposal are taken from BRAC, "Challenging the Frontiers of Poverty Reduction: Overview Proposal," Dhaka, 2000.

4. CFPR Donor Consortium, "Review of the BRAC/CFPR Specially Targeted Ultra Poor Programme: Mission Report," Dhaka, February 2004.

5. CFPR Donor Consortium, "Midterm Review: BRAC, Challenging the Frontiers of Poverty Reduction; Specially Targeted Ultra Poor Programme; Mission Report," Dhaka, March 2005.

CHAPTER 16

University

University: *from the Latin universitas, -tatis: the whole (world)*
Universitas magistrorum et scholarium: community of teachers and scholars

From BRAC's earliest days, training was a major challenge, one that grew as more people joined the organization. The first TARC had been established early, but more space, courses, and trainers were in constant demand as new programs were added and expanded. Training inevitably included a great deal of unlearning and relearning. Relearning was especially challenging for specialists and new management staff coming from the educated middle class, people with preconceived notions about development and poverty. Many carried inappropriate attitudinal baggage; some saw issues through the lens of a privileged university background, and few could be expected to see life from the perspective of an impoverished villager. All of BRAC's earliest staff, including Abed himself, had to unlearn what they thought they knew about poverty and rural life.

Samdani Fakir, BRAC's director of training, said that this process of relearning is an essential part of the orientation process for new staff. He talked about "creating a new kind of learning environment and new ways of information sharing," which, in turn, help to "develop new knowledge, new skills, attitudes, and behavior."[1] This is not just about changing attitudes or building skills; it is as much about subtracting from what is known as it is about adding.

Salehuddin Ahmed, now pro vice-chancellor of BRAC University, recalled his own unlearning experience. When he returned to Bangladesh after completing a PhD in Ukraine, he began looking for a job. As a student, he had participated in a Service Civil International work camp with students from California. They had built toilets for an orphanage in Lalbagh, and the experience piqued his desire to do something useful with his life. He applied for a position in the Planning Commission, but he also applied for a position with an NGO coordinating body. Although he was not offered that job, one of the interviewers was Abed's wife, Bahar, and, before long, Salehuddin was being interviewed for an opening at BRAC. His father, a police fingerprint expert in the criminal investigation division, would have preferred him to join the government, but he didn't discourage Salehuddin. Like many Bangladeshis, Salehuddin remembers the precise date of important moments in his life. April 4, 1979, was the day he started at BRAC.

Soon after he began, he accompanied Abed on a field trip to Sulla, and he was fascinated by what Abed told him about development and the poor. He was surprised, however, when they had to take a dilapidated old bus for part of the journey between Sylhet and Sherpur. This did not fit with Salehuddin's idea of how an executive director should travel. Despite the uncomfortable ride, he was impressed by what he saw in Sulla and decided he wanted to work for this organization. He was given an assignment. Abed said, "You are a fresh PhD, and you have always studied in Dhaka schools and abroad. I want you to understand what is really happening in the villages."

"My parents and grandparents came from the village," Salehuddin recalled, "and we used to go there with our parents to have a good time— good food, good holidays, fun. I had no idea about the poor. I sympathized, but there was no real empathy, no understanding."

He was sent to Jamalpur to set up a food-for-work project in the midst of a terrible drought. It was trial by fire.

> It was my first real exposure. I had a motorcycle. I'll never forget the license—Dhaka HA-338. I used to go to the villages on that motorcycle, and I used to think to myself, "I have a PhD. What the hell am I doing here, riding a motorcycle, trying to mobilize poor people?"

It was a good question, one that each BRAC field employee would have to answer in one way or another as he or she came to grips with the enormity of the challenges BRAC faced, the responsibility he or she had been given, and the inevitable decision about whether to stay with BRAC or leave.

Trials by fire, on-the-job training, and a range of other informal learning opportunities are still required in BRAC, but, early on, more formal processes of training and analysis became an essential and prominent part of the BRAC toolkit. From the earliest days, one objective of its training division was to ensure that a shortage of skills and weak management competencies did not constrain efforts to grow. Indeed, training was (and remains) a strategic instrument in facilitating program development. BRAC long ago decided to set aside 7 percent of its overall salary budget for staff development, a remarkable figure when one considers that, in

1999, BRAC employed 24,700 full-time staff and 34,000 part-time staff, and these numbers have more than doubled since then.

In physical terms, this commitment to training manifested itself in the creation of a dozen TARCs in different locations throughout Bangladesh. Each center employs scores of trainers, offering management, human resource development, and skills-based courses for BRAC employees, villagers, and the staff of other NGOs. In 1998, 45,000 participants, the majority of whom were BRAC staff, attended TARC courses. By 2006, the number had risen to 126,000.

BRAC was conscious, however, that these courses did not fully meet the needs of its more senior staff, so, in 1991, it established a Centre for Management Development. By 1997, the Centre had evolved to the stage where it could offer postgraduate diplomas and a master's degree in NGO management through a collaborative arrangement with the Organization for Rural Associations for Progress (ORAP) in Zimbabwe and the School for International Training in Vermont. In addition, BRAC sent some of its best and brightest for further study abroad. Mushtaque Choudhury, whose story is told in chapter 9, was the first to go overseas for a master's degree and, later, the first to go for a doctorate. Over the years, two dozen others have traveled abroad to do a master's degree, and several have done their PhDs, always posting a bond against their return.

All of this, however, was not enough. By about 1993, Abed was beginning to think about a BRAC University, what he called "an institution of excellence, not just any ordinary university." Like many ideas in BRAC, this one appeared to emerge almost casually, at least according to organizational legend, over lunch. In 1992, Abed had asked an old friend if he would consider joining the organization. Faruq Ahmed Choudhury had known Abed since 1956, when he was a junior diplomat stationed in London where Abed was then studying. They became friends, and their paths crossed many times in the years leading up to, during, and after the liberation struggle.

Faruq went on to a distinguished career, which included stints as ambassador to India and as Bangladesh Foreign Secretary. When he retired from government in 1992, he began looking for new forms of gainful employment. There were offers aplenty from the private sector, but he resisted. After a career like his, he said, "If you join business, you become a tout." So when Abed asked the question, Faruq said yes, joining BRAC as a special adviser and serving for the next 10 years as Abed's counselor, sounding board, and ambassador-at-large.

Whenever they were in Dhaka at the same time, they had lunch together in Abed's office, and they would discuss people, issues, small problems, and big ideas. This is where discussion about a university began. But it was more than a casual lunchtime notion. The university was a logical next step in the chain of educational institutions that BRAC had already created. Abed was concerned that some of Bangladesh's best and brightest were going abroad to study, many never to return. Those who did often brought with them ideas and attitudes that were unsuitable to development work. Higher education in Bangladesh had to be better, Abed thought. More than that, he knew it could be better and it could be made more relevant to the needs of a country with such deep-seated developmental problems.

Abed often referred to something that made a lasting impression on him. A study produced several years ago found that only 33 institutions prominent in the 1600s survive today. Two are churches. One is a parliament, and one is a commercial enterprise, the Hudson's Bay Company. Significantly, 29 are universities. It started him thinking about sustainability, relevance, and the wider importance of education. He asked himself:

> What are the elements of sustainability? First of all, the organization must evolve to meet the needs of its society. Secondly, the purpose or the mission of the institution must be demanded by the society. In other words, the universities created their societies' leaders, so they survived. What universities had to offer seems to have been in demand in all societies.
>
> Why didn't the East India Company survive? They lost their mission. They were set up to make money, but they became involved in conquering land. Businesses often go in the wrong direction. If you look at the Fortune 500 companies, they are always changing. The top companies in the last 20 years have changed dramatically.

There is, of course, no guarantee that a university will do the right thing. He cites the case of Oxford University, which, for years, resisted the idea of a business school. "Business schools are for tradesmen," they said. "That isn't education." Abed laughs and adds, "It was only when a fellow named Wafic Said gave them £20 million that they saw it as a good idea." That is perhaps why Abed did not ask anyone from Oxford to assist in the creation of BRAC University.

For a feasibility study, he turned instead to David Fraser, head of the social welfare department at the Aga Khan Foundation in Geneva. Fraser was an inspired choice. He had the international development background, but he was also an epidemiologist with a particular interest in infectious disease. At the United States Centers for Disease Control, he led a team that, in 1976, identified the strain of bacteria that causes Legionnaires' disease. More importantly from the BRAC point of view, he had been president of Swarthmore College for ten years. Swarthmore was in many ways a model for what Abed had in mind. It was a small, private liberal arts university with fewer than 1,500 students. Located near Philadelphia, it had been founded by the Religious Society of Friends (the Quakers), but it is today a well-endowed, nonsectarian university with a top-notch academic reputation.

Abed drew together a team to assist at different stages of the planning. They included eminent individuals from Harvard and the Ford Foundation, Faruq Choudhury, senior BRAC staff, a retired minister of finance, and prominent Bangladeshi educators. Lincoln Chen, then a professor at Harvard and senior vice president of the Rockefeller Foundation, joined the group. Not unpredictably, after visiting institutions in India, Pakistan, and the Philippines, Fraser recommended a liberal arts university along the lines of Swarthmore, but, according to Salehuddin, an active member of the university planning group, this would not have been saleable to the government nor the University Grants Commission, the gatekeeper for standards and quality in all public and private universities in Bangladesh. BRAC University would have to be more conventional with a wider array of courses and faculties than Swarthmore. It would have to go beyond the soft liberal arts tradition and include hard vocational subjects like architecture, engineering, and computer science. In order to combine the conventional with the best aspects of what Fraser had recommended, BRAC created a hybrid, incorporating new components that were unavailable at other universities into all degree programs.

As with so many things requiring government approval in Bangladesh, the university took three years longer than had been planned, and the holdup was not unrelated to BRAC's parallel struggle to create a chartered bank, described in chapter 17. Faruq Choudhury recalled the day the University Grants Commission came to inspect the premises. "It reminded me of the feeling one used to have in the pit of one's stomach when the inspector of schools in my childhood days visited our school."[2]

On the fateful day, even senior staff members were rushing about dusting and rearranging furniture. They had erected a large, metallic sign on the building, but, because the university had not been approved, it read only "University Building." When the approval was finally received, the word "Building" came down, and the word "BRAC," kept under cover in a back room, was added, changing the sign to "BRAC University."

The university finally opened its doors in 2001, in accommodations not far from BRAC's headquarters, and its first convocation took place in 2006. By then, it had five academic departments: architecture, computer science and engineering, economics and social sciences, English and humanities, and mathematics and natural sciences. It had schools of business, law, and public health. It had two institutes: one for educational development and a second for governance studies.

Abed is particularly proud of the School of Public Health, as is Mushtaque Chowdhury, who became its first dean. The school is named after the late James P. Grant, the legendary head of UNICEF whose child survival and development revolution saved the lives of countless children worldwide. This school aims for the highest international standards, but its feet are firmly connected to terra firma in Bangladesh. It has ties with American and European universities, and it is closely linked with its old partner from the oral rehydration program, the ICDDR,B, the Cholera Lab. International teachers complement local faculty members, and the International Advisory Board includes two doctors from pre-BRAC days on Manupra, Richard Cash and Jon Rohde. In 2006, the first batch of 25 students graduated, and, by then, the reputation of the school had traveled. Of the second batch, half were women, and half were Bangladeshi. More than 270 applications were received from abroad for the 13 positions open to international students, all of them from health-related disciplines. Among them were students from Afghanistan, Ethiopia, India, Kenya, Burma, Nepal, Pakistan, Singapore, Tanzania, Uganda, and the United States.

A discussion in 2008 with a random sample of BRAC University students about their studies and their ambitions would perhaps not be especially surprising to people from countries where the possibility of a university education is taken for granted. But, in Bangladesh, much of what these students say sets them and their generation apart from others. A young woman studying engineering said her parents had discouraged her from architecture because it might be too difficult. One generation back, the idea of a girl studying either architecture or engineering might have been unheard of. A young man said that, when he was a boy, he wanted to be a pilot. Now he is studying commerce. "But," he said, "I may still be a pilot." The ideas of choice and of possibility are something new. They all agreed that a private university is better than a public one because there are no politics here. A degree at a public university, although cheaper, might take a year or two more than planned because of strikes, violence, and student politics. Here, there is none of that. A few complained that a city university with classrooms in office buildings lacked the sports facilities they would like, but they all spoke glowingly of their compulsory residential seminar at one of BRAC's rural training centers. There, they have a chance to get away from home, see BRAC's field programs, and get a completely different perspective on life in Bangladesh. "This is a once-in-a-lifetime thing," one student said, "a pivotal point in my education."

In 2000, Abed remarried. He had known Syeda Sarwat since she was a child because they are cousins. For years, she had worked at Aarong in Chittagong, but life moves on, and so did she, living for a time with her husband and family in the United States. Abed always believed that the English language is a key that can open many doors, and he deplored the state of English language teaching in the schools and colleges of Bangladesh. He asked Sarwat, now widowed, to marry him, and their friends said it was one of his best ideas yet. Never one to miss an opportunity, however, he also asked her to take on the English language program at BRAC University.

At the beginning of 2007, there were 2,560 undergraduate students and 560 in graduate programs. There were academic partnerships with more than two dozen universities in Europe, North America, Australia, and Asia. Expenditure in 2006 was about US$3.8 million, good value by anyone's standards, most of it generated from fees. BRAC provided most of its capital expenditure. Donor funds were limited, representing only 13 percent of the university's income in 2006, but the Ford Foundation provided an endowment of US$700,000 to assist with scholarships for the poorest students. Abed applied a US$1 million award he received from the Gates Foundation to the School of Public Health, and the Rockefeller Foundation kicked in some start-up money. By law, every university in Bangladesh must provide 5 percent of its income from fees for scholarships to the poor. At BRAC University, the figure has been set at 10 percent.

Abed is keen to bring more young people from underprivileged rural areas into national life. Without that, he feels governance and development in Bangladesh will always have an elitist cast. Part of the university's stated mission is:

> [T]o foster the national development process through the creation of a centre of excellence in higher education that is responsive to society's needs, is able to develop creative leaders, and actively contributes to learning and creation of knowledge.

What next? This is always a tricky question where BRAC is concerned because a BRAC idea that might seem little more than a notion today could turn into something very large and concrete within a few short years. BRAC does not see the university growing beyond 5,000 students, but it does intend to build a permanent campus in a Dhaka suburb, away from the traffic jams of Mohakali. Abed believes the university is about knowledge, fresh perspectives, and new understanding. He underlines the need for quality whenever he speaks of the university, but he also speaks about the need for new values in a society where so many are poor and governance has failed.

> Quality, in the final analysis, is embodied in our students, and it is measured not only in terms of their employability, but also in the values they bring to whatever they choose to do in their work life.[3]

Notes

1. Ian Smillie and John Hailey, *Managing for Change: Leadership, Strategy, and Management in Asian NGOs* (London: Earthscan, 2001), 77.

2. Faruq A. Choudhury, "BRAC University: The Attainment of a Goal," *Daily Star,* June 17, 2006.

3. BRAC University, *2006 Annual Report* (Dhaka: BRAC University, 2007).

CHAPTER 17

On Being Ready

Grameen Bank did not begin as a bank. It began as a project developed and managed by Chittagong University professor Muhammad Yunus, who initially obtained funding in the form of loans from the Janata Bank. His first loan was approved in December 1976, and he, in turn, loaned the money on in smaller amounts to poor people he and his colleagues had organized into groups. They worked first in Jobra, a village 20 kilometers north of Chittagong, organizing a savings program and training poor women in the management of money. The mechanism was simple. The Grameen Project borrowed money from the Janata Bank on the good name of Muhammad Yunus. The project organized poor people into borrowing groups, lending the money at a slightly higher rate of interest in order to cover operating costs and bad loans, of which there were very few.

There were problems with the system, however, notably the need for Yunus to sign each and every banking document and having to deal with all of the micromanagement proclivities of Janata Bank officials. In 1978, he was able to organize a new arrangement with the government's Bangladesh Krishi Bank (BKB), a lending institution established to promote agricultural development. The BKB would add to funds borrowed from the Janata Bank. Grameen would henceforth have its own office as a branch of the BKB, using the name Grameen, meaning "of the village." In 1979, Yunus left his post at Chittagong University to expand the Grameen Project to Tangail District near Dhaka, taking a two-year leave of absence that would eventually become permanent.

Grameen expanded, but all financial and managerial decisions still had to be made in monthly meetings convened at the Central Bank in Dhaka, where Grameen and its commercial bankers frequently debated minutiae. Although the expansion to Tangail was successful, the bankers balked at the idea of further expansion. Scaling up, just as in BRAC's case, was greeted with skepticism, anxiety, and procrastination. The Ford Foundation, which had been a key funder at several points in BRAC's development, now stepped in. Yunus asked the Foundation if they could find some sympa-thetic bankers he could talk to in India or the United States. Soon, two American bankers, Ron Grzywinski and Mary Houghton from Chicago's South Shore Bank, arrived and gave the project a thorough assessment. Based on their recommendations, Ford established an US$800,000 guar-antee fund. This enabled Grameen to borrow US$3.4 million at a 2 percent rate of interest from the International Fund for Agricultural Development (IFAD) and a similar amount from the Bangladesh Central Bank. Grameen was on its way.

But Yunus still chafed under the tutelage of the Central Bank, and he lobbied for the transformation of Grameen from a project into an independent bank with its own charter. The opportunity arose not long after the head of the army, General H.M. Ershad, toppled the civilian government in 1982.

"As a military dictator," Yunus later wrote, "the president had no polit-ical legitimacy, and, perhaps in Grameen, he saw a chance to score some political points. Whatever his thinking, it worked in our favor."[1]

In September 1983, the president signed a special proclamation form-ing Grameen Bank, with the government taking 60 percent of the shares. Government ownership was eventually reduced to 25 percent, but it was not until 1987 that the CEO, Yunus, became an appointee of the board rather than the government.

Yunus is a vocal critic of foreign aid. He has rightly pointed out that "donors and consultants tend to become overbearing in their attitudes toward the countries they help."[2] But he goes farther than that, accusing donors of mismanagement and even corruption.

> I have often witnessed the desperation of donor agency officials
> to give away ever-larger sums of money to Bangladesh. They will
> do almost anything to achieve this, including bribing govern-
> ment officials and politicians either directly or indirectly.

Without donors, 15 technical visits from Ron Grzywinski and Mary Houghton, the guarantee fund from the Ford Foundation, and the loan from IFAD, Grameen might never have grown beyond project status. Between 1986 and 1997, Grameen received more than US$57 million in grants from the government of Norway alone. In fact, the donor package for Grameen Bank Phase III totaled US$105.7 million between 1990 and 1995 with funding from the Ford Foundation, IFAD, Canada, Norway, Germany, and Sweden.

"We helped him raise something north of $175 million," says Ron Grzywinski, "probably half of the money raised for microcredit up to that time worldwide."

As Grameen transformed itself from a project into a bank, Abed began to consider how BRAC's multifarious microfinance operations might be formalized, and the idea of a BRAC Bank, not dissimilar to Grameen, began to develop. In 1987, he invited a number of international experts to review the organization's progress over its first 15 years and make suggestions for the future. One of the visitors was George D'Souza from the University Institute for Development in Geneva, who noted that, in the formalization of credit, "the question of creating a BRAC Bank is bound to arise." Many of the BRAC staff he spoke to had reservations about the idea, fearing credit "might come to dominate BRAC's stated priority for the social dimension." D'Souza said, however, that there was a good case for a BRAC bank, one deserving of deep and careful study.[3]

At approximately the same time that Grameen Bank received its approval from General Ershad, Abed spoke to the finance minister about something similar for BRAC. He was told that it was certainly possible, but that the government would have to own 90 percent of the shares and Abed would have to take his marching orders from the Central Bank. Abed weighed the options. Grameen could expand quickly because it was able to get generous donor funding as well as loans at 1 or 2 percent interest guaranteed by the Central Bank. But, as a government appointee, Yunus was constrained in many ways. Most importantly, Grameen was a regulated bank, not a scheduled bank with the ability to undertake a full range of banking functions. Abed had other ambitions.

The idea of a BRAC bank remained alive, but, until the Ershad government was gone, little would change. A popular uprising finally forced Ershad from office at the end of 1990, at about the same time as a team of donor consultants was concluding a voluminous report on BRAC. They observed that BRAC's rural credit programs were "on the track toward financial viability" and consultants should now be engaged to examine the application and approval processes for the establishment of a bank. They said the consultants should make recommendations on shareholder policies, the makeup of a potential board of directors, and investment policies of the bank.[4] The consultants who would eventually make the idea possible had actually been advising BRAC on its credit operations since 1988. This same team had helped to make Grameen Bank happen in 1983, Ron Grzywinski and Mary Houghton.

Grzywinski and Houghton had the right pedigree. With two other partners, they had founded a new type of banking operation in the aftermath of Chicago's devastating civil rights riots, aiming to provide minorities with access to capital. Chicago banks routinely denied loans to low-income individuals and minorities, so the field was wide-open. But Grzywinski, Houghton, and their colleagues had a business proposition that differed from that of most banks. "What if your core business had some purpose other than making money?" asked Houghton.[5] Starting with US$800,000 in equity and a US$2.4 million loan in 1973, they bought the small South Shore Bank, which operated in a part of Chicago beset by urban decay. Their first loans were to people wanting to rehabilitate and rent out dilapidated housing. The lending served several purposes. First, the loans aimed to solve the problem of absentee landlords, whose neglect had led to the decline of the neighborhood. Second, the bank wanted to provide income-generating opportunities for locals. Third, they aimed to improve the overall tone of an inner-city neighborhood that seemed overwhelmed by violence, crime, and the absence of hope.

During the 1980s, when they first visited Grameen and later BRAC, Grzywinski and Houghton were building the South Shore Bank into something of a phenomenon. As it grew beyond Chicago, they changed its name to ShoreBank and provided advice to others interested in microfinance and lending to the poor. One was Arkansas Governor Bill Clinton, who, with his wife, Hillary, strongly supported the efforts of the Winthrop Rockefeller Foundation to create the Southern Development Bancorporation, engaging ShoreBank to raise the capital and hire management. Both Yunus and Abed paid visits to Little Rock in those years, drawn together into a society of mutual interest by Grzywinski and Houghton. By 2007, the assets of ShoreBank would grow to more than US$2.3 billion, its work spreading across the United States and many developing countries. As president, Clinton would go on to establish a new mechanism in the Treasury Department, which funded dozens of similar community development banks and funds in the United States. He would acknowledge that "all these investments were inspired by the ShoreBank model and the leadership of Ron Grzywinski and Mary Houghton."[6]

By the end of 1991, BRAC's cumulative lending had reached Tk 1.47 billion (US$38 million), and the organization was growing very quickly. US$15.6 million of the overall lending had been paid out in 1991 alone.[7] When Ron and Mary* visited BRAC the next year, Abed and his colleagues showed them a full-fledged proposal that aimed to convert BRAC's various rural credit operations into a bank once they had reached a certain level of sustainability. Ron and Mary found no major flaws in the proposal. After considerable discussion, they confirmed Abed's view and recommended that BRAC apply for a scheduled bank charter rather than a special charter like the one given to Grameen. A scheduled charter would allow the BRAC Bank to mobilize savings from a wider clientele than the

---

*In Bangladesh, Grzywinski and Houghton are universally known as "Ron and Mary." Some people who have not met them but know of their work think that "Ronandmary" is one person.

Abed renews an old acquaintance (Photo by Susan Davis)

borrowers alone, and it would give it more flexibility in its operations. They recommended that 70 to 100 percent of the shares should be owned by BRAC, but a smaller number of external institutions, knowledgeable about development finance, might also be invited to purchase shares and sit on the board. And they recommended a number of prohibitions that would protect BRAC and the bank against hijacking by vested interests and human frailty. They examined BRAC's financial projections through 2010 and saw little to criticize. The plan showed sufficient earnings and enough capital retention to support the planned growth, and profit was projected for every year except 1997, when a small loss of US$150,000 was forecast.[8]

Abed sometimes quotes Napoleon's famous line before the Battle of Austerlitz about the qualities he sought in his generals. "Just one," he said, "luck." Where Yunus had been lucky in getting his bank proposal approved by the government, BRAC was to prove decidedly unlucky. The Ershad regime had been replaced by the Bangladesh Nationalist Party (BNP), led by Khaleda Zia, wife of the murdered Ziaur Rahman. This time, the stars seemed better aligned, and, in 1993, five banks, including BRAC, were given preliminary approval by the Central Bank. But when the formal announcement was made, BRAC's name was not there. It was a shock. Abed recalled:

> I talked to the finance minister, and he said he had nothing to do with it. When it went to the prime minister, she had crossed out "BRAC" and written in "Dhaka." So the Dhaka Bank got permission, even though it had been through none of the due diligence procedures of the Central Bank.

It may have been a coincidence (and it certainly would have been impolitic to say so) that most of the shares of the Dhaka Bank were owned by the new BNP public works minister and former mayor of Dhaka, Mirza Abbas. Clearly, however, BRAC had been cheated. But governments change, and so do ministers. By 2007, the Abbas star had fallen so low that the former minister had been jailed on corruption charges related to questionable land deals and his Dhaka Bank. In 1993, however, there was nowhere to file a complaint, and there was nothing BRAC could do but bide its time.

The Awami League, led by the daughter of Sheikh Mujibur Rahman, had reinvented itself, and, eventually, in the elections of June 1996, it had returned to power. Sheikh Hasina Wazed had many old scores to settle, but banking did not seem to be one of them, so Abed applied yet again for a bank charter. He told the new finance minister, "Maybe I'm not Awami League, but at least the BNP considers me anti-BNP." In a highly polarized political environment, that may have given the proposal the cachet it needed. But there would be a condition. Abed would have to join the party and run for parliament. The minister said, "We'll make you a minister in the next government."

Abed knew that, if he joined any party, BRAC would have been "ruined, finished," so he politely declined. At the time, other newly organized banks were lining up for charters, and donations were reported to be tumbling hand over fist into Awami League coffers. Not only was Abed declining high office, he offered no sweetener. Maybe it was his ability to avoid all of these traps that made BRAC attractive or at least acceptable. Whatever it was, in 1999, the government finally gave BRAC its charter.

That, Abed thought, was that. But it was not. Nothing in Bangladesh in those years was ever simple. No political decision ever seemed final until the very last drop of confusion, patronage, and sweat had been wrung from it. Fifteen days before the bank was to open, with staff hired and everything set to roll, they were served with a High Court injunction. They had been hit with a case of public interest litigation, engineered by a Dhaka University professor, Muzaffer Ahmed. Ahmed charged (and the High Court judges eventually agreed) that a charity could not invest in a bank. Whether the litigation was launched in the public interest or as an act of public mischief, this was beside the point. Fifteen years of effort in creating the bank now perched on the edge of an abyss. There was, however, one glimmer of hope. In their decision, the judges did say that a charity could invest money in a commercial enterprise if the profits were wholly devoted to a charitable purpose.

That was the whole point of the BRAC Bank, and it encouraged Abed to continue. He was sure that, in taking the case to the Supreme Court, BRAC could win. It took 13 more months, but, in the end, the decision went in BRAC's favor. The Appellate Division of the Supreme Court held that a charitable organization could invest money in a commercial operation in order to earn more money for its charitable work, whether the funds had been raised locally or internationally. It was, in some ways, a landmark decision because it expanded the definition of what a nonprofit organization could do and it justified all of the income-generation enterprises that BRAC had initiated since the 1970s. But the litigation put the BRAC Bank 24 months behind the other banks that had been approved in the same batch, and the cost had been enormous. Abed estimated that Professor Ahmed's one-man effort to protect the virtue of Bangladesh's nonprofit sector cost almost US$500,000 by the time it was over—for lawyers and bank staff who were sitting idle while the professor argued and lost his case.

The bank had seemed plagued with misfortune as each successive government tried to squeeze benefit from it, and the avenging angel of bad luck dragged it through the court system. But, in several ways, the bad luck served a useful purpose because, in the years between Ron's and Mary's first visits and another one in 1999, the rationale for the bank had changed dramatically. No longer was the bank about formalizing BRAC's existing microfinance operations. It was now about something completely different. Without the delays, Abed might not have had the time to develop a new perspective.

Small Enterprise

Contrary to popular belief, the world's corporate sector, even in the most industrialized countries, is not dominated by large companies. Small- and medium-scale enterprises (SMEs) account for more than 95 percent of all the companies in OECD member countries, which include most of Europe, Japan, and North America. They account for 60 to 70 percent of all employment as well, and they are widely recognized as the engine of much economic growth.

Small is a relative term. A small company in France might seem quite large by Bangladeshi standards. And there are problems with the formal definitions that governments and development organizations use. A small enterprise, however, is generally understood to be one with between five and 10 employees; medium-scale usually refers to something between 50 and 100 workers. Anything under five falls into the category of micro.

In Bangladesh, the SME sector is large and growing. Taken together, in 2003, there were 6 million enterprises employing fewer than 100 people, including medium, small, and micro operations. They employed 31 million people, the equivalent of 40 percent of the adult population.[9] When the numbers are broken down, they are more revealing. Enterprises employing between two and five people contributed more than half of the SME contribution to GDP. And those employing between six and 10 workers contributed a further 10 percent.

The SME sector is important in terms of its contribution to the overall economy, but it is also a major factor in employment. In 2006, there were approximately 16 million Bangladeshi children between the ages of 2 and 14 who would soon join the workforce. At the time, there were also an estimated 10 million inactive people looking for gainful employment. One study examined 47 small industries across the country. They ranged in size from 5 to 29 workers and covered a variety of industries, from *coir* to food processing. The size of investment varied widely, but the average outlay per employee worked out at US$1,250. This is considerably higher than livelihoods created through microfinance, usually less than US$100. But it is significantly less than the cost of a job in the large industry sector. The average cost of job creation in the Chittagong Urea Factory and the Jumuna Fertilizer Factory has been estimated at more than US$200,000 per person.[10]

Where microfinance is concerned, the emphasis is on livelihoods and supplements to family income rather than formal jobs. Clearly, the SME sector is where the largest number of affordable, wage-paying jobs are going to emerge in the years ahead. Small enterprises drive the economy. They grow. It is different with microenterprises. They usually do not grow. Very few of the microfinance clients of BRAC or Grameen Bank or those of the many other microfinance institutions around the world ever graduate from micro to small. In other words, a single microborrower is unlikely to expand a small loan into an enterprise that employs more than one or two people. There are reasons for this. In the case of BRAC, most of the borrowers are women, and few can spend their entire working day on their investment project. The loan supports a part-time effort, and time is often the critical element. The loans and the projects they fund supplement family income. They do not create full-blown formal sector jobs. Microfinance, therefore, can improve individual livelihoods, but it seldom leads to the creation of a formal sector enterprise or further job creation.

A second reason that microloans tend not to create additional jobs is that they are, by their very nature, limited to small, one-off operations.

They rarely exceed a few hundred dollars, which is rarely enough to go beyond a cottage industry or a backyard operation. Third, the poor are no more entrepreneurial than anyone else. In fact, they are probably less so, given the risks they take in making any lifestyle change. The point here is not to denigrate microfinance, but to point out its limitations where wage-paying job creation is concerned.

Abed was beginning to think beyond microfinance and about potential in the small enterprise sector when Ron and Mary returned in 1999. Despite its importance, the SME sector had many problems. Access to modern technology was one. An irregular supply of electricity was another. Raw materials, trained technicians and workers, and a difficult regulatory environment added to the woes of the small entrepreneur. But the top-of-the-list problem for all small industries in every survey of the sector was access to capital. Even when loans were available, often from moneylenders, interest rates were exorbitant.

Ron and Mary did the rounds, visiting several local and international banks. What they found was revealing. "We confirmed that some of the private banks and foreign banks are highly profitable, earning well above worldwide industry benchmarks," they said. But the banks made money by avoiding loan transactions of less than US$20,000, and they steered clear of deposit accounts lower than about US$400. Microfinance had taken care of the very small borrower, and the private banks were taking care of the larger end of the scale. As a result, they said:

> Bangladesh now has an "hourglass" shaped banking market . . . virtually nothing is available from either banks or microfinance providers to the millions in the middle—businesses and individuals—who are severely constrained in their ability to produce and save for lack of access to financial resources and services.[11]

Until modern, competitive financial services were readily available to this sector, including credit in amounts, terms, and conditions that small business could access, they said, "Bangladesh will not be able to create the large middle class that is a prerequisite to social stability."

They recommended that BRAC leave its microfinance operation where it was, as a separate operation from the bank. It wasn't broken, so why fix it? The effective interest rate on microlending was 28 percent, a rate that would be too high in the small enterprise sector, and it would only work against the bank's bottom line. There were other issues as well. The bank regulators would certainly limit the number of branches, complicating matters for the microfinance program that now had more than 1,000 offices across the country. Most important, however, the sole purpose of microfinance was poverty-reduction. In a commercial operation, where at least some of the bank would be owned by investors other than BRAC, there would have to be a combined approach to development and commercial banking.

Drawing on their experience in the United States and on what they had seen in other developing countries, Ron and Mary saw niche markets that could potentially provide excellent returns. Aggressive and innovative savings mobilization was one. For example, no competent bank at the time was raising deposits from rural households. Aggressive and innovative lending to small business was another, with a focus on productive and manufacturing operations underserved by the conventional market. The emphasis would be on small rather than medium. Medium-sized enterprises could get bank financing, even if their role was not well understood. Small operations could not. Here, BRAC envisaged loans that might range from US$1,000 to no more than US$200,000 for working capital and longer-term investment. They also saw a market niche in remittances. Bangladeshis working abroad were sending money home, and people in cities were sending money back to the village. Inefficient state banks had a monopoly on the rural remittance market, and a well-run private bank offering good service and competitive rates would have no problem moving in.

In considering the role of Ron Grzywinski and Mary Houghton, it is worth pausing to take stock of all the foreigners that appear throughout the BRAC story. Many, like Ron and Mary; George D'Souza; Robert Chambers; David Fraser, who prepared the feasibility study for the BRAC University; or David Korten, who, in 1979, described BRAC "as near to a pure learning organization as one is likely to find," came as experts, sometimes at the behest of donors. But if they came twice, it was usually because BRAC invited them back. And although many had a great deal to offer, most came away having taken as much as they gave. The frequent reappearance of Marty and Lincoln Chen, Jon Rohde, Richard Cash, and others from the earliest days of BRAC had something to do with the fact that they were trusted friends, but it had as much to do with the fact that they had grown and learned along with Abed, his colleagues, and the organization. Their continued involvement was not as high-powered technical assistance or as experts from the North coming to inspect or evaluate or push. It was as trusted colleagues who could help BRAC to work through the many challenges that it faced over the years.

Hourglass Banking

The BRAC Bank finally opened its doors on July 4, 2001. The initial stretch of road was bumpy, not least because some of the first managers proved not to be a good fit with the aims and ideals the bank had established for itself. By 2003, however, the bank's vision, systems, and skill sets were better aligned. Imran Rahman, 20 years a banker, became managing director and CEO, and he exuded confidence. With international experience of ANZ Grindlays and Standard Chartered, he joked that BRAC "must have been very desperate to hire me." BRAC's challenge, however, was not to find a top-flight banker for the position, but to convince a top-flight banker of two things. First, that the vision of the bank made sense in the commercial world. Second, that the vision could make money.

"What Abed wanted to do was very unconventional," said Rahman. Certainly, it was not something that any banker in Bangladesh had any experience of, and the concept was relatively unknown to high-flying international bankers as well.

"But he painted a new horizon for me; he opened my eyes. I knew it would be very challenging, but it was also something worth doing."

Abed agreed that Rahman could bring in his own team, and the bank was soon on the move. When Rahman joined, there were fewer than 800 employees. By the beginning of 2008, there were over 3,500. When it began, the BRAC Bank was the smallest in Bangladesh, but, during its first few years, it became the fastest-growing financial institution in the country. In 2007, it was sixteenth in a lineup of 25 or 30 private commercial banks. A year later, it was ninth. On the wall of Rahman's office there was a growth chart. The arrow pointed steadily upward, and across the top of the chart was a slogan that also appeared on pens and calendars throughout the office, "Breaking Barriers 2009."

Rahman spoke of the need for rigorous probity and transparency in a commercial environment populated by sharks, corruption, unsuccessful businesses, and failed banks. The ownership and governance of the BRAC Bank is important in this. BRAC owns just under 32 percent of the shares. The International Finance Corporation, a member of the World Bank, has 9.5 percent, and ShoreCap, which is part of the Shore-Bank Group, has just under 9 percent. The general public has purchased 40 percent of the shares through an IPO that saw share prices skyrocket within weeks of their appearance, an indication of public trust in the BRAC name. Trust is evident as well in the 400,000 depositors the bank attracted in just a few years and in policies that prohibit lending to the tobacco industry, polluters, anyone employing children, and, notably, politicians.

Fate often seems to deal more unkindly with Bangladesh than other countries, and it was certainly cruel to Imran Rahman, who, in midstride at the height of his skills and not yet 45, was struck down by a thrombosis that suddenly and without warning, in 2008, took his life. It did not take the dream, however, or the plans he had set in motion.

And, of course, he had been far from alone. Farzana Chowdhury presides over the bank's lending to small enterprises. She started in BRAC's microfinance program in 1997 and then went to Australia on an MBA scholarship. When she returned, she joined the bank as business development manager and handled the bank's first small enterprise loan in October 2001. Today, not far past 30, she is a vice president. At first, the small enterprise business was slow, partly because the bank had only one loan product and did not know how to assess potential clients. Few of them had land and assets, and most had no track record of commercial borrowing. Many were barely literate. And there were no models for what BRAC was doing, so, at first, it was a case of trial and error. Today, things have changed. There are several loan products specially designed for different types of clientele, including urban, rural, traders, manufacturers, international trading finance, supply and distribution finance, doctors, teachers, and students. There is huge potential in the growing information technology sector, and the bank has created an entire range of commercial services for Bangladeshis living abroad and clients who do not want to earn interest for religious reasons.

Farzana explains the breakdown between credit for manufacturing and trading. In 2007, 70 percent of their small enterprise loans were for trading, but there was a strong push to increase the manufacturing component. "We are not about making loans," she says. "We are about building an entrepreneurial class." She is especially proud of an innovation for women entrepreneurs. By 2006, the bank had made only 200 loans to women, but Farzana says of the unit designed for women, "If you build it, they will come." And they did. In less than two years, the portfolio had grown to more than 1,000 borrowers, although it wasn't easy. "I worked in microfinance," Farzana says, "but small enterprise development is a totally different environment." The bank now provides training on costing, marketing, inventory control, and other basics to help women in start-up situations. "It was very difficult at first," Farzana says. "But if you do it in a focused manner, you get results."

Her excitement is still palpable as she talks about the achievements and all that remains to be done. The bank has almost 100 ATM machines and is now issuing credit and debit cards, all things hitherto unknown to small entrepreneurs. The bank opened with 13 branches and, by the end of 2008, had more than 400 small enterprise unit offices, but that is far from adequate in terms of reaching clients that come from every corner of the country. In order to make disbursements and receive payments, they must still work though a network of corresponding banks, which is costly and very time-consuming. Their own branches are all online, but power failures are a constant headache, and the corresponding banks are totally dependent on paper. Farzana frets about the huge volumes of money making its way ever so slowly through the system, essentially idle, and she worries that, of the country's 3 million potential small enterprise borrowers, the BRAC Bank has reached only 100,000 so far.

The bank soon began to develop another problem, competition. If imitation is the sincerest form of flattery, the flattery is growing. Other banks are now moving into the small enterprise sector, poaching BRAC staff and the experience they have built. This is not a new phenomenon for BRAC. Wherever it has led, others have followed, including hatcheries for day-old chicks, egg and broiler marketing, feed mills, seed production, maize farming, primary education, tuberculosis eradication, milk, yoghurt, and a dozen other innovations pioneered over the years. "It's a new revolution we have created," Farzana says, speaking of the bank. But she might as well be speaking of everything BRAC has done. "People used to think a banker would sit at his desk and the customer would come to him. We say no. We will go to your doorstep. You will get quality service and promptly, and it will be hassle-free." Lessons? "Tolerance and patience," she says. "Lots of tolerance and lots of patience."

Farzana speaks with pride about being invited along with 17 other emerging women leaders to a September 2007 Jamestown conference on the foundations and future of democracy. There, she found herself mingling with people like Hillary Clinton and Condoleezza Rice. Part of the specific invitation to Farzana was a two-week mentorship with Kathleen Murphy, CEO of ING's United States Wealth Management. Farzana says:

> I never know what is going to happen tomorrow. We are growing so quickly. But I was comparing myself with her—she looks after 2,400 people, the same as I do. I come from a developing country, but they face the same problems as me. How do you manage growth? How do you manage business sustainability? How do you manage people?

Farzana was thrilled by the experience, not just because she learned new things and met interesting people, but because she realized she was not just a kid from the sticks. She realized she was part of something that was fast becoming large and important, something that would soon have young people from other countries, perhaps the United States, coming to be mentored by her.

Where Napoleon sought luck in his generals, Texas folklorist Frank J. Dobie gave luck an explanation. "Luck," he said, "is being ready for the chance." Luck is about being ready. The chance to create a meaningful banking institution—that is, the opportunity—had been absent for most of the two decades that Abed had pondered the idea. But, if the bank had been approved in the 1980s when it was first conceived, it would have been nothing like what it is today, and it might never have had anything to do with small and medium enterprise lending.

Entrepreneurs are said to be people who take risks, and Abed himself is nothing if not an entrepreneur. But like most entrepreneurs, he is good at spotting opportunity. And, when the chance comes, he is ready. Many would say that almost every BRAC venture has been laden with risk. Abed does not see it that way. He sees risk only in terms of the damage it might do to BRAC. "I never did anything," he says. "That might damage the organization." So the risk, in his estimation, was never great. He says that damage is one thing, but failure is different. There is no risk and no shame in failure:

> If you fail, you might lose some money. But there is no damage in losing money if you learn from the experience. Learning can cost a bit of money.

And so it should. But, if you learn, you are more likely to perceive an opportunity when it appears—and to be ready.

Notes

1. Muhammad Yunus with Alan Jolis, *Banker to the Poor; Microlending and the Battle against World Poverty* (New York: Public Affairs, 1999), 119.

2. Yunus, *Banker to the Poor,* 145.

3. George d'Souza, "BRAC Strategy for the 1990s," (Geneva: University Institute of Development Studies, November 1987).

4. Donor Review Team Report, misleadingly titled "BRAC 1990 Annual Review," Dhaka, November 1990.

5. "Ron Grzywinski and Mary Houghton: Community Bankers," *US News and World Report,* Nov. 12, 2007.

6. Ibid.

7. BRAC, *Annual Report 1991* (Dhaka: BRAC, 1992).

8. Mary Houghton and Ron Grzywinski, "BRAC Bank Review," October 1992.

9. Abdul Awal Mintoo, "SMEs in Bangladesh," *CACCI Journal,* 1 (2006).

10. Mintoo, "SMEs in Bangladesh."

11. Memo to F.H. Abed from Ronald Grzywinski, Mary Houghton, Lynn Pikholz, and Kaiser Zaman, March 13, 1999, BRAC Files, Dhaka.

CHAPTER 18

The Democratic Deficit

In the general scheme of things, 30 or 40 years of independence is not a long period of time, and it should not be surprising that, in their efforts to create democratic institutions and good governance, many postcolonial countries have faltered, sometimes badly. In its first 50 years of independence, the United States fought a major war against Britain and failed completely to deal with the scourge of slavery. In its next 50 years, it fought genocidal wars against its native people and descended into one of the most murderous civil wars of all time. Its national politics were marred by assassination, graft, and pork barreling. Yet, from this inauspicious start would rise one of the world's great democracies and one of the most powerful economies in recorded history.

Bangladesh came to independence with none of the physical resources of the United States, Canada, Switzerland, France, or any of today's other established democracies. It had no gold, copper, coal, or iron. It had no deep traditions of Magna Carta, *habeas corpus,* or concept of a loyal opposition. Its 24 years as part of Pakistan had conditioned it only to military rule and the corrosive effects of corruption, mismanagement, and dictatorship. That Sheikh Mujibur Rahman proved unequal to the task of achieving the democracy he espoused is hardly surprising. Faced with a broken economy, an oil crisis, runaway inflation, and violent street demonstrations, he retreated into the demagoguery that had informed his politics. In swift succession, the results were political repression, the declaration of a one-party state, assassination, and a military coup.

Where democracy and good government were concerned, the next three decades were little short of disastrous. In the year following Mujib's death, there were coups and counter-coups, resulting finally in the 1976 emergence of Army Chief of Staff General Ziaur Rahman, first as chief martial law administrator and then president. Five years later, he too lay dead, the victim of another coup attempt. Zia's army chief, Hossain Mohammad Ershad, suppressed the coup and supported a return to civilian rule in 1982, but, within weeks of seeing a retired judge become president, he changed his mind and led a coup of his own. Of all Bangladeshi leaders, Ershad would enjoy the longest unbroken spell in office, transforming himself from soldier into a civilian over the eight-year period, creating his own political party, and making sure it won whatever new elections he permitted. Toward the end of the 1980s, however, a new pattern of civil disobedience emerged with opposition parties calling frequent *hartals* (general strikes) in order to paralyze government and commerce.

Forced from office at the end of 1991, Ershad was trounced in the elections that followed by Khaleda Zia, the widow of Ziaur Rahman, now leader of the Bangladesh Nationalist Party. During the late 1980s, Khaleda Zia had worked with Sheikh Mujib's daughter to end the Ershad regime, but, with the 1992 elections, all bets were off. Where Khaleda was set on avenging and vindicating the name of her late husband, Sheikh Hasina sought to avenge the murder of her father. For both, power was the vehicle and an all-consuming passion. Khaleda soon gathered all authority into the office of the prime minister, but elections in 1996, following a year of political turmoil and the appointment of a caretaker government, gave the Awami League and a vengeful Sheikh Hasina their turn at the helm.

Now the tables were turned. Just as Hasina had promoted *hartals* and demonstrations to make it all but impossible for Khaleda to govern, now it was Khaleda's turn to do the same. It became so bad that the final months of the Awami League government were fraught with political turmoil, gangsterism, riots, and strikes, ending with the prime minister's forced resignation, another caretaker government, and, in 2001, the return to power of Khaleda Zia. Khaleda's return was plagued by rising religious militancy, street violence, unprecedented corruption, and a political environment that was fast spinning out of control. She managed to see out her term of office, but the caretaker administration that succeeded her in October 2006 was pushed aside in January 2007 by a much tougher caretaker regime, this one backed by the military.

A firm grasp of the chronology of events is not needed to understand that the constant changes, with accompanying turmoil in the country's laws, policies, and orientation, were not conducive to anything resembling good government. Speaking at the United Nations General Assembly in September 2007, the new acting head of government, known quaintly as the chief adviser, said what most Bangladeshis knew.

"The fabric of our democracy has been torn apart by years of catastrophic corruption," he said. "Politicians, businessmen, and even civil servants are often the perpetrators, secured by their immunity within the system."

Fakhruddin Ahmed, who had by then put both Sheikh Hasina and Khaleda Zia in jail on lengthy indictments of fraud and corruption, was no typical head of government. With a PhD from Princeton, 20 years at the World Bank, and a stint as governor of the Central Bank of Bangladesh, Ahmed knew something about economic management. But he also understood something about political management. Defending the caretaker government's decision to postpone new elections until late in 2008, he said that Bangladesh had learned through harsh experience that:

> [A]n election cannot simply be a once-off casting of votes, but must be part of a dynamic and a continuing process . . . Democracy is not an event; it is an ongoing process. It is not just about casting votes and changing governments; it is about social justice, accountability, and empowerment of the people.

He said that the country's winner-takes-all system had made the stakes of winning so high that even ordinary governance had become polarized and paralyzed.

> If our democratic spirit is to emerge unscathed from this downward spiral and if we are to deliver a free, fair and meaningful election, we must first free our politics from the clutches of corruption and violence.[1]

The Most Corrupt Country in the World

The corruption and violence he spoke of ran deep. In 1996, Mushtaque Chowdhury and Aminul Alam went to some of BRAC's village groups to see what the political chaos meant for the poor. Their report became an article that appeared in the Bangla daily, *Bhorer Kagoj,* and it made sobering reading at a moment when most Bangladeshis wrongly thought that things could not get worse. A woman in Jenidah told them, "Everything has stopped. No vehicles ply the road; no bazaar operates. We are helpless. It is all between Khaleda and Hasina. We have no work. The cost of essentials has spiraled, and we starve." Another said, "These two women are the root of the crisis. They cannot tolerate each other, and we suffer."

A woman in Manikganj said that, in the recent election, "Not more than 20 people went to the polling center here, but thousands were shown to have voted."

Others complained of how much damage the *hartals* were doing to the local economy. Rickshaw drivers would be attacked if they took to the roads during a strike, farmers could not market their vegetables, and the price of basics increased. Mushtaque and Amin conducted their study during a particularly bad period of political unrest, and conditions would eventually improve. But they would worsen off and on again over the coming years. Many of BRAC's programs were seriously affected. Vaccine deliveries stopped, and chickens died. Lending programs withered because banks were often closed. Repayments could not be made on time. Weekly meetings were often impossible. In the countryside, people turned to the BBC and the Voice of America for reliable news about their country, as they had during the 1971 liberation war. As one woman put it, "The news aired by the Bangladesh radio and television says that everything is normal, but no vehicle runs on the roads. People gather to listen to the BBC." Another lamented the future. "Whoever comes to power, the problems will still be there. Peace can prevail, at best, for one or two years, and, afterwards, unrest will start again."[2] She was right. And it would get worse. Partisan politics would come to permeate all aspects of public life, including the police, the judiciary, and the civil service. Accountability ranged from weak to nonexistent, and corruption became the order of the day.

Ideology was not the problem. By the end of the 1980s, there was little to distinguish between the two main parties in their economic programs. Both were pro-business, which, in some ways, helped the economy to grow. In fact, where less than a quarter of the country's parliamentarians had come from the private sector in 1973, the proportion had risen to 60 percent by 2001.[3] It would appear, however, that businessmen were not there to make the system function more effectively. Rather, they had entered politics to join a looting spree. In any case, the parliament they attended was little more than a rubber stamp for whatever policies came down from the prime minister's office. By the mid-1990s, Bangladesh suffered from government by fiat, government by *diktat*, government dominated by cronyism, money, and revenge.

Party *apparatchiks* took key positions throughout the civil service, lowering standards of performance and creating chaos with each change of government as they were swept away by a tide of incoming party faithful. Morale within the civil service, once a source of prestigious employment, plummeted. Judges were now recruited on the basis of party affiliation, and survey after survey found that people believed the police to be the most corrupt of all government departments.[4] The courts and the police, in fact, had become carcinogens in a system that served largely to protect vested interests from the law while doing little to save ordinary citizens from violence and crime. An ordinary citizen would, in fact, have had to be crazy to go to the police for help with anything less than a major crime.

"You would either have to be related to some hot shot within the force," said a young man in Dhaka, "or pay the officials a bribe to speed up the investigation. Otherwise, it's pointless to trust the police."[5]

But look at it from the perspective of a police constable working out of the Shyamoli police station in Dhaka. This is where he lives, eats, and sleeps during the days of the month he is on duty. The living quarters in the middle of the city consist of a shack with walls and roof made of leaky, corrugated tin sheets. The floor is dirt and broken bricks. The beds, which all have to be shared, are jammed together in a single room. The toilet is filthy and dark because the lightbulb has burned out. On monthly salaries of Tk 2,850 (US$42), nobody is willing to spend his own money to replace it. They cook together at night on wood fires in a blackened kitchen, and, during the day, they often go hungry because the police truck that is supposed to bring them lunch on the beat does not arrive. If a constable extorts money from a rickshaw driver or a shopkeeper, there are two reasons. The first is that he can. The second is that he must. One constable explained:

> There is never enough after I send a major portion of my salary back home to my family. In fact, we also put in more shifts than required. The other day, I put in six hours extra while my duty partner had worked for a total of sixteen hours instead of twelve. There is no system of overtime pay.[6]

And then there is the rising spectre of militant Islam. During the 1970s, an NGO called *Gonoshasthaya Kendra* trained young women as paramedics. Unlike BRAC's health workers who stayed close to their own village, the GK paramedics moved from village to village. Traveling on foot was both tiring and time-consuming, but motorized transportation was economically out of the question. A strategy was needed if the program was to expand on a cost-effective basis. The answer was bicycles, an idea so outlandish that its radicalism at the time could hardly be exaggerated. Yet, within a few months, they had overcome the idea, widely held by society in general and even by the paramedics themselves, that women could not and should not ride bicycles. A decade later, BRAC started providing its female field workers with 50cc motorcycles, an equally radical idea, but one that, in fact, met with little scorn from conservative quarters. Of course, over three decades, BRAC and other Bangladeshi NGOs did considerably more for women than provide them with transportation, but the bicycle and motorcycle stories are emblematic of how little resistance there had been to all of the dramatic changes for women over the years since independence.

But then something went wrong. Change can be difficult in any society, especially for those who think of themselves as losers in the equation. In 1994, the fundamentalist parties began to attack NGOs. There had been a prelude to this in 1991 and 1992 when the first democratic government in more than a decade came to power. Ostensibly concerned about the fast-growing foreign funding of NGOs and a growing number of newspaper articles about alleged anti-state and anti-Islamic NGO activities, the Khaleda Zia government instituted draconian new NGO regulations and attempted to shut down an NGO umbrella organization. Following a brief respite, in 1994, there was another flare-up with street demonstrations against NGOs and the creation of something named, remarkably, The Society against Atheists and NGOs.[7] It seemed that NGOs had run afoul of both the right and the left. Left-wing parties accused NGOs of being donor stooges and agents of international capital, while conservative Muslim elements viewed NGOs, especially in their work with women, as the thin edge of encroaching Western modernity and possibly a Christian assault on Islamic values. At the village level, this manifested itself in direct attacks on NGOs, and several BRAC primary schools for girls were burned to the ground.

The lesson some NGOs took from this was that they had gone too far or moved too quickly. At BRAC, the conclusion was different. The problem lay in their assumption that conservative elements were irrelevant and communities had been fully supportive of their work. Even though BRAC would mount new public awareness campaigns about its work, targeting journalists, academics, students, and mainstream politicians, it also reassessed its role in the village, finding new ways to make at least moderate leaders more aware of and more involved in its work.

In fact, the flare-ups would continue over the years. The two mainstream political parties tried to assuage Islamic militants with varying degrees of appeasement, but to little effect. Bangladesh, which has the world's fourth-largest Muslim population, had been spared the extremes of Islamic militancy during the 1970s and 1980s, but things were changing quickly. The first bombs went off in 2003, and there were more in January 2005. Then, in August, hundreds of bombs were detonated across the country, all within hours of one another. Six exploded outside BRAC offices. Journalists were threatened, as were the leaders of several of the country's leading NGOs. More bombs in November and December targeted the legal community, and two judges were killed. This led to a series of arrests, trials, and, in 2007, the execution of six leaders of an ultraconservative organization called *Jamaat ul-Mujahedeen* Bangladesh. But the future was anyone's guess.

As if rotten governance and religious fundamentalism were not enough, Bangladesh looked as if it were competing to win an ugly contest where commerce was concerned. Every year, the World Bank produces a report that compares regulations and the ease of doing business in 178 countries. Singapore, New Zealand, Western European countries, the United States, and Canada always rank among the top dozen performers.

In 2007, Bangladesh slipped from one hundred and two to one hundred and seven, falling well behind countries such as Ethiopia, Pakistan, and Sri Lanka. The report showed that getting a license, registering property, and paying taxes all took extraordinary amounts of time unless the business was willing to go offline with its payments. The average number of days required to start a business was 74, compared with only 13 in Britain. The average license took 252 days to obtain, compared with 40 days in the United States. A total of 425 days was required to register a property, compared with only two days in New Zealand.[8]

In 1997, Transparency International issued its first "Survey on Corruption in Bangladesh," and, for five years running, the organization's international index would rate Bangladesh as the most corrupt country in the world. It was embarrassing, but it made little difference. A sarcastic front-page newspaper headline in 2007 said, "Dhaka improves on its graft image: Climbs up to seventh position from bottom on TI's corruption index."[9] In fact, its overall score had not really changed. It had improved only because new countries had been added while others had slipped to newer depths of iniquity.[10]

But, in all of this, something odd had been happening. The economy had enjoyed impressive growth. During the 1990s, growth rates averaged 4.8 percent, and, in 2007, it was 6.5 percent.[11] The growth rates were impressive, due in part to reasonable macroeconomic management and external pressure from the World Bank and the wider donor community. But growth was lower than the South Asian average, no doubt because of political chaos, corruption, and the cost of doing business. A 2005 UNDP report said that the endless series of *hartals* during the 1990s had cost the economy a staggering 3 to 4 percent of GDP.[12] The *hartal*, a long-standing mechanism for protest, had been developed by Gandhi as a nonviolent form of dissent. But, historically, it was sparingly used. Between 1947 and 1954, there had been six *hartals* in East Pakistan, mainly to protest the country's oppressive language laws. Between 1995 and 2002, however, there were 611. That means there were, on average, more than six crippling general strikes a month, every month, for eight years.

To give Bangladesh its due on the development front, some of the achievements have been enormous. Between 1990 and 2000, there was a 10 percent increase in life expectancy. The infant mortality rate was halved during the same period, and the under-five mortality rate dropped by 45 percent. TB prevalence had been cut by 32 percent, and 84 percent of all cases were being treated with the DOTS approach pioneered by BRAC. The adult literacy rate, which was under 25 percent at independence, had risen to 40 percent, and primary school enrollment, at 87.7 percent, was seven points higher than the regional average. There were more girls in primary school than boys, and almost half were going on to secondary school.[13] Problems notwithstanding, these are impressive achievements, and they beg an obvious question. If governance was so poor, how were such impressive gains realized?

There are several answers to the question. The first is that there was, essentially, nowhere to go but up from the dismal situation that prevailed when Bangladesh became independent. Second, donors had devoted huge resources to improving government services in all of the social sectors. And, finally, government itself was not dedicated to stasis. Regardless of the chaos in the system, politicians understood they had to deliver or face the wrath of the opposition, public rage expressed through *hartals,* and, perhaps always in the back of the political mind, the military. One can only wonder, as with the overall economy, how much better the social indicators might have been and how much lower the poverty had Bangladesh enjoyed more than the most fleeting moments of good governance.

Pour Encourager Les Autres

Donors, government officials, and development experts are sometimes reluctant to see or say what is obvious to many. "The credit for coping so well rests ultimately with NGOs." So said Robert D. Kaplan, a widely traveled and much-published American journalist. "NGOs in Bangladesh represent a whole new organizational life-form. Thousands of them fill the void between village committees and a remote, badly functioning central government."[14] Kaplan noted that NGOs would not have had such influence without the country's moderate, syncretic form of Islam. And he rightly gave full marks to ordinary Bangladeshis "squeezing the last bit of use out of the land." But much of the improvement can be laid squarely at the feet of the NGO community, which is stronger and more vibrant in Bangladesh than almost anywhere else in the world. There are an estimated 20,000 NGOs in the country. Of these, about 2,000 are involved in meaningful development work, many of them receiving considerable support from international NGOs and donor agencies. Most are very small, but many have taken their programming cues from larger organizations. And the large ones are very large.

The positive NGO impact on poverty reduction through microfinance, education, and health programming was made possible by a number of things. First, the government was largely ineffectual in its attempts to harass and control the NGO community. In any case, government was not always or universally hostile to NGOs. It understood that they had lessons to teach and they could provide services where government departments could not. The fine line between support and competition was often misunderstood by both sides, but, in many areas, there was a reasonable compromise.

Second, Bangladeshi NGOs received far more support from bilateral donor agencies than their counterparts almost anywhere else in the world. In 2005, NGOs were programming 20 percent of all bilateral donor assistance to Bangladesh, up from only 6 percent in 1990. Of that, BRAC was probably receiving about half.[15]

There were reasons for this. NGOs could deliver, and government often did not, or at least not without a great deal of leakage. NGOs delivered two things: services and ideas. Even though services are what poor people want and need, and are often what donors count when they are writing checks, in Bangladesh, the ideas have been at least equally important: the idea of social enterprise and the idea of scaling up. NGOs introduced hundreds, if not thousands of important innovations in tackling poverty, in health and education, and in advancing the role of women. They launched and led the global microfinance phenomenon, and they advanced the concept of what an NGO should and can be

But there is a question here about governance. Some argue that donors and NGOs contributed to poor governance in Bangladesh by letting government off the hook for things it should have delivered itself. And what of the much-vaunted role that civil society is reputed to play as advocate and watchdog on human rights, transparency, and democracy? A 2005 study financed by the British government painted an ambivalent picture of a Bangladeshi NGO community overly focused on donor-led service delivery and microfinance. It acknowledged that NGOs were engaged in more advocacy work than in the past and this was having some impact on government policies, but the authors were stingy with their praise, saying that this "does not necessarily indicate that policy advocacy is having an impact on poverty reduction."[16] There was an unspoken implication that an overfed NGO community had not lived up to its billing as defender and proponent of good governance.

Few governments welcome criticism, and bad governments are especially hostile to it. Voltaire's famous line in *Candide* resonates. *"Dans ce pay-ci, il est bon de tuer de temps en temps un amiral pour encourager les autres* (In this country, it is good to kill an admiral from time to time to encourage the others)."* Voltaire was referring to the unfair trial and execution of an exemplary British naval officer. The quote is often used to illustrate overly harsh political punishment that aims, like the mafia, to punish one and teach many. The Bangladesh NGO community received a taste of this in 1999 when the government initiated an inquiry into the financial operations of *Gonoshahajjo Sangstha* (GSS), an outspoken and highly successful NGO working in the field of education. GSS argued that donor funding delays had created a payroll crisis, but the cause of the problem was lost in the ensuing fracas while the government investigated and imposed a caretaker management. In the end, GSS was obliged to fire 6,000 staff and shut down 750 primary schools. More to the point, however, it was also forced to disband a network of 600 lawyers who were providing legal aid to women and the landless poor.

In 2001, another large NGO, *Proshika,* was proscribed from receiving foreign contributions. Its senior managers were arrested and charged with varying degrees of financial mismanagement and fraud, perhaps, as it was widely believed, because it had displayed an ill-considered friendliness toward the recently defeated Awami League government. The harassment of *Proshika,* the arrests and extrajudicial violence continued for years, leaving a once-vibrant organization crippled and bleeding.

Repression notwithstanding, many brave NGOs did speak out during the 1990s and into the new century. Transparency International was one of the most vocal, but many others, often very small, engaged in public awareness campaigns, grassroots mobilization, research, lobbying, and public interest litigation.

A Quiet Revolution

From the early days following its first experiments in Sulla, BRAC understood that development had to be based first and foremost on rights and on an understanding by the poorest of what their rights were. This had been the cornerstone of Paulo Freire's work in Latin America, and it was the foundation of BRAC's functional education programs. People had to understand why they were poor, isolated, and disenfranchised before they could begin to do something about it. Targeting the poor and group formation was as much about creating cohesion and solidarity as it was about anything else. Without that, and without confidence and understanding, funding for economic advancement would have little impact. The focus on women had an even sharper rights focus. BRAC's work with women changed their lives. It transformed their role in the home, their relationships with their parents, their husband, and their children. It changed their role in the village, giving them courage to move about freely and engage people with whom they had never before had the audacity to make eye contact. It gave them the courage to speak out, look up, and look beyond the veil that had constrained them for so long.

In 1983, Marty Chen wrote a book about the time she had spent with BRAC during the 1970s. She called it *A Quiet Revolution.* She noted that, despite the massive development efforts of the 1960s and 1970s, poverty was rising:

> My hypothesis is that women were overlooked, and that if
> women's work had been valued and supported, the tragic
> dilemma of increasing poverty . . . might not have been as
> great. At issue is not only the impact of development on
> women but the potential impact of women on development.[17]

When she wrote, poverty in Bangladesh was still increasing, but a corner had already been turned, and one of the reasons was that BRAC and
others had not overlooked women or their rights.

BRAC's rights orientation took a more formal turn in 1986 when it
started a paralegal program in Manikganj. The basic idea was to help
build legal awareness among villagers about their rights in issues pertain-
ing to land, child marriage, illegal divorce, polygamy, and violence against
women. By the end of the 1990s, human rights and legal education
courses had become a core part of BRAC's program. Ward-level associations were created, drawing elected members from each village organization into regular discussions about social ills in their community,
encouraging the participation of the poor in local arbitration bodies.
Where these traditional mechanisms failed, a more formal option was created. Working with *Ain O Shalish Kendra* (ASK), a leading legal rights
organization, BRAC began to operate legal aid clinics for cases requiring
court adjudication.

But in many ways national political and human rights indicators failed
to improve. BRAC stepped up its human rights and legal services. More
workshops were held for local leaders (1,250 in 2007), and local law
implementation committees were established to act as watchdogs and
arbitrators in minor disputes. The number of legal aid clinics, operated
in conjunction with ASK and the Bangladesh National Women's Lawyers
Association, increased. By 2007, more than 12,000 cases were being handled each year, mostly through traditional dispute mechanisms. BRAC
provided additional support to victims of rape; acid throwing, which is a
common way of seeking revenge or ridding oneself of an unwanted wife;
and other forms of violence against women. For the most serious cases, it
established a panel of lawyers who acted for village members seeking
redress through the formal court system. On average, these lawyers were
nursing about 250 cases through the court system in a year, obtaining
more than US$2 million in compensation for BRAC members.

By the mid-2000s, however, Abed was beginning to see that all of this was
far from enough. The two issues of rights and governance were inextricably
intertwined. On the rights front, he brought in Faustina Pereira from ASK.
Bright, articulate, and determined, Pereira saw her appointment as the
beginning of a repositioning for BRAC in a new rights-meets-development
approach. She believed the velocity of development had outpaced rights

and the balance would have to be improved. Money and technology had created a huge gap between the Bangladeshi underclass and a new kind of super elite, who were heavily influenced by the Internet and videos, and who flaunted their wealth in mansions, cars, and extravagant spending. It is what Pereira called the "peacock syndrome." "BRAC hasn't done enough to change the national mind-set," she says. That, she believes, along with the peacock syndrome, plays directly into the hands of fundamentalists who are set on a return to the traditional values that oppressed women and constrained development.

In 2005, BRAC University established a Centre for Governance Studies. Within two years, the center had been transformed into a full-fledged Institute of Governance Studies, offering postgraduate degrees and conducting research at the intersections of governance and development. The Institute's stated aim is to foster a new generation of researchers, public administrators, and citizens with a critical and analytical perspective on governance. And BRAC brought in Manzoor Hasan, a graduate of LSE and the British legal system, to head it. If Abed wanted to reposition BRAC on issues of governance, he could not have made a better choice. Manzoor had been involved in BRAC's early studies during the 1970s on village power and oppression, helping to write *The Net: Who Gets What and Why*. More recently, he had served as the founding director of Transparency International in Bangladesh.

At the end of 2006, the Institute published the first in what it expected would be a series of annual publications, *The State of Governance in Bangladesh 2006*. The aim of the report was to build on work that others had done and provide a benchmark on issues that could be tracked over time. It was a sober, uncompromising critique of the status quo.

"After fifteen years of democratic rule," Manzoor wrote in the preface, "the system remains unconsolidated, politicized, confrontational, and marred by bad governance."

The report was groundbreaking, but the Institute had plans for considerably more than reports and teaching. Manzoor planned to develop a national integrity strategy with the cabinet division of the caretaker government. He made plans to train a thousand prospective parliamentary candidates, and he planned a gap analysis of Bangladesh's application of the UN anti-corruption convention. He spoke of the need for new thinking about abandoned adolescent boys who were simply cannon fodder for fundamentalists. "Until we do something about them, we fail to take the oxygen out of militant Islam." And Manzoor said that civil society, including BRAC, had failed in its watchdog role. "How could they have become so big and so important and have had so little to say about these things?"

Depending on the success of these new initiatives and who they threaten, there may be backlash. Political life in Bangladesh has a way of taking unexpected turns. By the end of 2008, at the end of the mandate of the caretaker government, Bangladesh had improved dramatically on Transparency International's corruption index. It had improved as well on the World Bank's ease of doing business index, showing what could be achieved in two years. But the two ladies were out of prison, and Bangladesh was returning to the fray of party politics. In December 2008, Sheikh Hasina won a landslide victory in the first general elections in seven years. The elections were peaceful, and a small army of international observers said that they had been free and fair. On New Year's Day 2009, Khaleda Zia conceded defeat—but said, ominously, that the poll had been fraught with vote rigging.

In *The Tempest*, Shakespeare says, "What's past is prologue." The question for Bangladesh is whether the most important aspects of the prologue began in 2009, in 2006 with the advent of the caretaker government, in 1971 with independence, or farther back in time.

As far as BRAC is concerned, Abed said, "We are big enough now to take the flack." He had been listening to Manzoor, and perhaps he had been listening to his son, Shameran, who like his father and older sister had gone to study in Britain. For Shameran, law was the magnet, but returning to Bangladesh at 25 years of age in 2006, he saw other possibilities. One was journalism. While serving as a part-time executive assistant to his father, as his mother once had, he soon carved out a reputation for himself as an incisive commentator on the country's worsening political situation. But the siren's call of politics beckons.

> For me, unless governance changes at the state level, we can only get so far as a country. All the work that BRAC has done . . . we're really not going to move forward unless government becomes much better. Getting into politics would be a means to an end . . . lots of things get worse before they get better, but I have a feeling that things will get better.

He was, in fact, not sure what direction his career would take. Human rights law? Journalism? Politics? BRAC perhaps? He is concerned about compromising BRAC if he does go into politics, and he worries about ever being able to leave BRAC if he were to join on a more formal basis, as Tamara has done. He returns to the discussion about politics, "In the 1980s and 1990s, politics became a playground for the corrupt. There has to be some resistance to that. It will have to come from my generation, not my father's." He looks out of the window in the BRAC office at a slum across the road. "I'm not the only one thinking about this. Lots of others are as well."

Notes

1. Fakhruddin Ahmed quotes taken from the *Daily Star*, Sept. 29, 2007.

2. All quotes from villagers in these two paragraphs are taken from "Bangladesh: Politics, Development, and Perspectives of the Poor" by Mushtaque Chowdhury and Aminul Alam (Dhaka: BRAC, October 1996).

3. Institute of Governance Studies, *The State of Governance in Bangladesh 2006* (Dhaka: BRAC University, 2006), 14.

4. Institute of Governance Studies, *The State of Governance in Bangladesh 2006*, 68.

5. "Making the Police People Friendly," *Star Weekend Magazine*, Sept. 27, 2007.

6. Ibid.

7. Richard Holloway, *Supporting Citizens' Initiatives: Bangladesh, NGOs, and Society* (London: IT Publications, 1998), 155.

8. World Bank, *Doing Business 2008* (Washington: World Bank, 2007).

9. *Daily Star*, Sept. 27, 2007.

10. Transparency International's Corruption Perception Index for various years can be found at http://www.transparency.org/.

11. Asian Development Bank: http://www.adb.org/Documents/Economic_Updates/BAN/2007/QEU-Sept-2007.pdf.

12. http://www.undp.org.bd/publications/Beyond percent20Hartals.pdf.

13. UNDP, *Asia-Pacific Human Development Report 2006*, (Dhaka: UNDP, 2007).

14. Robert D. Kaplan, "Waterworld," *Atlantic*, January/February 2008.

15. Verulam Associates, "The Impact of Big NGOs on Poverty and Democratic Governance in Bangladesh," (Dhaka: DFID, 2005), 6–7.

16. Ibid.

17. Martha Alter Chen, *A Quiet Revolution: Women in Transition in Rural Bangladesh* (Cambridge: Schenkman Publishing, 1983), 241.

CHAPTER 19

Afghanistan

A large white Emirates Boeing 777 from Dubai landed at Dhaka's Zia International Airport a little after 10:30 on a cool December evening in 2007. When the doors opened, a small, bearded man emerged to face a bewildering crowd of reporters, family members, and BRAC officials. Noor Islam, who had been posted by BRAC to Afghanistan two years earlier and spent almost twelve weeks as a captive, living in caves and surviving on little more than gruel, stale bread, and water, was home.

Noor Islam's ordeal began three months earlier in Afghanistan's Logar Province, where he served as manager of BRAC's microfinance project. One September morning, he was in the office, sitting alone at his computer, when he heard a loud pounding on the door. He opened it to find six men with AK-47 automatic rifles pointed at him. Four were in police uniform, but, as they bundled him into what looked like a police vehicle, he saw that the jeep's olive green paint had been badly applied. After a 10-minute ride, he was transferred to another vehicle and driven over bad roads into the mountains. A series of forced night marches, with daylight halts in caves, led him to his final place of incarceration, a large mountain cavern where the only way of telling night from day was by listening to the prayers of his captors.

Noor had learned Dari, but his captors spoke Pashto, so communication was almost impossible. He was bound and blindfolded much of the time, certain he would soon be killed. From time to time, he heard helicopters in the distance. He thought of his wife and young son Arian, and he prayed. On one occasion, he was taken to meet his captors' commander, a man named Abdullah. They took off his blindfold so he could navigate the rocky terrain beyond the cave, but they replaced it with a pot so he could only look down at his feet. He told Abdullah, "I am a Muslim, and I am in Afghanistan not to fight, but to promote microfinance for the development of the people." He told them, "My father's name is Abdul Gaffer Mollah." They replied, "Oh, you are a *mullah* . . . Good!" But more weeks would pass in the dark cave.

I used to get very nervous in the evenings. At night they held
meetings, but I could never understand what they were discussing. I was very afraid. Every night I thought they would kill
me. Sometimes I felt like a chicken in a coop. Whenever they
left the cave at night, I would pray.[1]

Over 82 days of captivity, he was allowed only one opportunity to bathe.
Normally clean-shaven, his beard grew.

The kidnapping of Western aid workers and journalists was widely
reported in the international press: two Germans in 2007, a Danish
reporter, an Italian journalist in Helmand, a Canadian reporter abducted
near Kabul in 2008, two French aid workers in the southwestern province
of Nimroz. When 23 foolhardy South Korean missionaries were kidnapped from their bus in 2007, it made global headlines. In the first half
of 2008, there were 84 incidents involving aid workers. In August, three
more (two Canadians and a Trinidadian American) were murdered.
Ransoms paid by the Italian and Korean governments made life that
much more dangerous for every other outsider in the country, and it was
undoubtedly a factor in Noor Islam's ordeal. His story was big news in
Dhaka, but, like the wider story of BRAC in Afghanistan, it was of little
interest to the world's media. His kidnapping and return to his family in
Jamdi, a village in Jessore District, was almost completely unreported outside of Afghanistan and Bangladesh.

In recent years, the history of Afghanistan has been rehearsed countless times by journalists, historians, and political scientists, including the
Anglo-Afghan Wars between 1839 and 1880, the country's formal independence in 1919, and the long period of stability under King Zahir Shah
between 1933 and 1973. A bloodless coup in 1973 was followed by a much
bloodier communist takeover in 1978 and then the Soviet invasion on
Christmas Eve a year later. More than 100,000 Soviet troops were involved
in the occupation, and estimates of the death toll in Afghanistan during
the next decade range between 600,000 and 2 million. As many as 5 million
Afghans, out of a total population of 30 million, fled to Pakistan, Iran,
and beyond.

Funded covertly by the United States and Pakistan, anti-Soviet
Mujahidin forces fought a 10-year insurgency that led finally to the Soviet
withdrawal in 1989. A rump pro-Soviet government in Afghanistan outlived the Soviet Union, but, by the mid-1990s, the country had fallen into
anarchy and warlordism as various factions vied for control. With the
Soviets gone from both Afghanistan and the world, the West lost interest,
and aid fell to a trickle. In 1996, one of the factions, the Taliban, an ultraconservative group driven by a strict, antimodern interpretation of Islamic
law, captured Kabul, and, by 2000, it controlled 95 percent of the country.

The Taliban grip on Afghanistan was cruel and uncompromising, and its leadership welcomed like-minded Al-Qaeda operatives and their leader, Osama bin Laden. When Al-Qaeda was directly implicated in the 1998 bombings of American embassies in Kenya and Tanzania, Afghanistan once again appeared on Western radar. And, with the Al-Qaeda attacks on the United States on September 11, 2001, the Taliban's days as a government were numbered. The bombing began on October 7, and the Taliban were driven from power by November 15. A new era had begun.

As in Bangladesh, many cultural influences have shaped Afghanistan. It has known Buddhism, and it was an outpost of the Mughal Empire for many years. Like Bangladesh, its sovereignty was compromised for centuries, and, like Bangladesh in 1971, the new Afghanistan was emerging from a great ordeal. Life expectancy was only 43 years, child mortality was astronomical, and per capita income was only US$230 a year. Afghanistan was among the poorest half-dozen countries on earth. Its economy shattered and its people traumatized, it bore many of the same scars as Bangladesh. Both are Muslim countries, sharing some of the same cultural roots. But the similarities end there. Where Bangladesh is flat, Afghanistan is mountainous. Water is to Bangladesh what drought is to Afghanistan. Heavy population density created both problems and opportunities in Bangladesh that had few parallels in the sparsely populated Afghanistan. Where Bangladesh is ethnically and linguistically homogenous, Afghanistan is a polyglot of large and small ethnic groups, held together by geography, shared history, and perhaps religion, more than by any idea of nationhood.

Foreign Aid from Bangladesh

Today, BRAC is by far the largest NGO in Afghanistan. Within five years of the Taliban's departure, it was working in 22 of the country's 34 provinces, including some of the most difficult areas in Helmand and Kandahar. At the end of 2008, 84,000 students—84 percent of them girls—were enrolled in more than 2,600 BRAC schools. It had more than 3,500 community health workers, and its clinics and health posts treated more than 170,000 people that year. More than 180,000 people had joined its village organizations, and its outstanding loan portfolio in November 2008 was US$28 million against cumulative lending of US$142.3 million.

But this had not been a case of "I came, I saw, I conquered." Far from it. First, BRAC had to reach people, no easy task in an ultraconservative country beset by political psychoses and living a security nightmare. BRAC did have advantages over other newcomers. Most of its staff was Muslim. They were Asian, and the Afghan government had invited them. The first visit to Afghanistan in January 2002, however, was tough. Amin led a team of four, and they concentrated their time on Kabul and Mazar provinces. The needs were obvious, and they believed they had a lot to offer, but, as they started to develop plans, they met with a frigid donor response. After much thought and consultation, they devised a program that would have cost US$1.2 million, but everyone, including NOVIB, one of their most stalwart donors in Bangladesh, turned them down. Part of the problem was that, while donors knew and respected BRAC in Bangladesh, in Kabul, they did not. Here, BRAC was little more than an oddity.

Abed decided they would begin with their own money. Persuading the Central Bank of Bangladesh to allow the transfer of US$200,000 in hard currency out of the country was no easy task, and Bangladesh providing foreign aid was certainly something of a first. Gradually, however, donors in Afghanistan began to realize that BRAC was a contender. Sweden supported an education project, and the Oxfams in Canada and Hong Kong gave assistance for health efforts. BRAC used its own money for microfinance, however, counting on the Consultative Group to Assist the Poor (CGAP) for more substantial inputs. CGAP is a consortium of 33 public and private funding organizations (bilateral and multilateral development agencies, private foundations, and international financial institutions) working together to fund microfinance programs around the world.

But they were slow. Very slow. BRAC had made commitments based on projections of CGAP support, and its own credibility was now on the line. Amin recalls how desperate he was when he went to see Britain's DFID representative. "I need money now," he told her, requesting US$200,000.

"She was like a God-sent angel," he said. They had discussed US$200,000, but, to his pleasant surprise when the money came six weeks later, which was record time for a bilateral donor, it was in sterling rather than dollars. The CGAP money also arrived in due course, as did support from a who's who of donor agencies, all soon realizing that BRAC could be effective and efficient in what was an increasingly difficult situation. They also realized that, because BRAC was less threatening than others were to armed factions and militants, it was less constrained in its movement than most other international organizations. In fact, BRAC essentially made Afghanistan safe for microfinance. Over the first few years, when others were wondering how and whether to become involved, BRAC geared up quickly, representing 82 percent of the country's entire microfinance portfolio. This gave others the confidence to start, and, while BRAC has continued to grow, it now has only half of the market share.

In education as in other fields, BRAC was able to build on what it had learned in Bangladesh. There, primary enrollment rates had been low and dropouts high. If they went to school at all, girls left long before boys, rarely reaching secondary school. Distance, combined with bad teaching and parent apathy, made the two concepts of education and schooling contradictory and mutually exclusive. BRAC's educational approach in Bangladesh had been based on four fundamentals. First, BRAC reduced the distance between children and schools. It created village-based schools where parents could become involved. Second, quality was emphasized with smaller classes, better teachers, and more appropriate learning materials. Third, there was an emphasis on girls from poorer families. Fourth, there were rescue programs for children who had never entered the old system and those who had dropped out early.

Under the monarchy, Afghanistan did have a relatively good educational system. Half of primary-age children were enrolled, and most provincial towns had secondary schools. With the Soviet invasion, however, all that changed. Teachers were regarded as subversive, and schools were seen as centers of anti-Soviet resistance. Under the Taliban, things became worse. Education for boys was a low priority, and it was forbidden for girls. When they were driven out in 2001, the adult male literacy rate hovered around 50 percent, and, for women, it was less than 15 percent. Overall, it was the lowest in Asia.

BRAC started slowly. In 2004, it established 83 experimental primary schools. Some were for older children who had dropped out or never started, a three-year program covering four years of primary education that was geared at making children eligible for high school. A course for younger students covered the same ground, and a third stream of feeder schools provided a one-year crash course to prepare children for the second year of existing government primary schools. More than 80 percent of the students were girls. They also developed an accelerated three-month program for older girls, using established school facilities during vacation periods. They formed school management committees and set up a materials development unit, just as they had in Bangladesh 20 years before. They produced and translated teachers' guides, learning materials, and supplementary reading for children. Adolescent reading centers were supplied with newspapers, magazines, and books in order for girls to keep up with what they had learned in school.

The teacher situation was just like Bangladesh in the 1970s. There were no female teachers available for rural schools anywhere. As in Bangladesh, BRAC had to recruit and train its own teachers while simultaneously overcoming tremendous prejudicial attitudes in almost every village where it set foot. It began with a basic 12-day preservice training program, a one-day refresher course every month, and a longer six-day refresher once a year, along with constant monitoring and a lot of hand-holding from program organizers and master trainers. It worked. BRAC's

83 experimental schools became 2,600 in less than four years, its 2,753 students became 84,000, and its 83 teachers became thousands—all of them women.

Why Not?

Little of Afghanistan's health system, such as it was, survived the wars. The infrastructure was broken, its medical staff was poorly trained, community awareness was low, and drugs and equipment were in short supply. Historically, almost all health services had been institution-based, which meant that people had to first find a health facility if they wanted treatment, and these were invariably kilometers, if not hundreds of kilometers away from where they lived. Even where facilities did exist, they covered less than one-third of the population. Fewer than 15 percent of deliveries had a trained health worker present. One out of five children died before the age of five, and there was only one doctor for every 50,000 people, a figure that pales in comparison with Bangladesh's 40 or Norway's 826.

BRAC began its health programs in 2003, and, within five years, they were operating seven district hospitals, 66 basic health centers, 20 comprehensive health centers, and more than 500 satellite clinics. The foundation of the program was similar to what had been established in Bangladesh, and some of the hard-won lessons of three decades there could be transposed without great difficulty. Community health workers, for example, became the lynchpin of the effort. These are women recruited in the village. They know the village, and they take health messages and basic treatment to their clients rather than the other way around. They work only two hours a day, but they are able to visit each household at least once a month to discuss health, hygiene, family planning, and prenatal care. If someone needs more specialized treatment, he or she will be referred to a health center or a hospital. As in Bangladesh, the community health workers earn their keep through the sale of basic fixed price nonprescription pharmaceuticals and family planning supplies. In what looks like an anomaly, they also sell iodized salt. Treated salt, common in many Western countries for decades, helps to prevent iodine deficiency disorders and thyroid problems. Iodine deficiency, the greatest single cause of preventable mental retardation, can also cause stillbirth and miscarriage. Until UNICEF introduced the idea, iodized salt was unknown in Afghanistan, but, like so many simple interventions, it soon began to make an enormous difference.

The health workers also take BRAC's oral rehydration message to mothers, and they identify TB victims. The long periods required in Bangladesh for testing and adapting the ORS and DOTS approach could be dispensed with in Afghanistan because, by 2003, these BRAC-pioneered methods had become accepted worldwide. BRAC also started mobile clinics, taking diagnostic teams with basic curative capacities to remote areas, offering pre- and postnatal care, family planning services, and pharmaceuticals beyond the competency of the village health worker.

As in Bangladesh, the heart of BRAC's microfinance program in Afghanistan is the village organization, which is comprised of the specific target group BRAC seeks to assist, those with less than a half-acre of land, day laborers, and women, especially widows. Village organizations are made up of several smaller groups of five women. Each selects a leader who becomes part of the overall village management committee. Each organization meets once a week to deposit savings, consider loan applications, and receive repayments. A compulsory levy of 5 percent is attached to each loan for savings, and members can add whatever else they want to that amount, knowing that higher levels of saving will entitle a member to a larger loan on the second round. Conditions being what they are in Afghanistan, new members initially asked what would happen should a borrower die. BRAC instituted a death benefit, a kind of life insurance policy that pays 5,000 Afg (about US$100) to each member's nominated beneficiary, whether there is a loan outstanding or not.

A large proportion of the loans in Afghanistan are for traditional home-based activities, including tailoring, carpet weaving, small shops, and fruit and vegetable sales. The ultimate solution to impoverishment, however, is not a rearrangement of the limited economy in a given village, although that can help if it changes perceptions and the economic balance. The larger challenge is the same one BRAC faced in Bangladesh in the 1970s: production. The challenge is to produce new things and more things, and to connect the village economy with the world beyond. In Bangladesh, the BRAC Bank had become the vehicle for small enterprise loans, but, in Afghanistan, this higher level of lending began as part of the microfinance program. Here, loans ranged between US$1,000 and US$10,000 for the renovation of small bakeries, shoemakers, garment businesses, and delivery operations.

Agriculture is the backbone of the economy, but Afghanistan is a dry, mountainous country. Only 12 percent of the land is arable, and less than 6 percent is actually cultivated. Virtually all of it is hostage to unpredictable winter snows and early spring rains. Here was a new challenge for people from a land where the traditional problem is too much water. Modern equipment, seeds, fertilizer, and pesticides are virtually unknown in Afghanistan. And because everything is done manually, agricultural workers, who are unemployed during much of the year, are in very high demand during the peak periods of sowing, harvesting, and threshing. The labor problem, along with all of the other factors, results in low productivity and a heavy dependence upon Iran and Pakistan for food imports.

By the beginning of 2008, BRAC's agricultural program was operating in 46 districts across 12 of Afghanistan's 34 provinces. There were three basic elements. The first was vegetable cultivation for home use and sale, including tomatoes, turnips, radishes, cauliflower, spinach, beans, onions, and potatoes. BRAC provided seeds, training, technical support, and loans, and, by the end of 2006, 1,200 acres of land was devoted to new production. The second element was cereal crops: maize, rice, and the staple, wheat. Here the aim is not just more production, but significantly higher yields through the use of better seeds and fertilizer. In 2006, 4,700 farmers were engaged in a pilot project that BRAC had initiated with assistance from the UN's Food and Agriculture Organization (FAO). Farmers were given a one-day training program, and extension workers who would stay with them through the pilot were given 12 days of training and access to more intensive trials at BRAC demonstration plots. Some 240 tons of seed were distributed during that first season.

The third element of the agriculture program is orchard gardening and horticulture nurseries. There are 600,000 farmers engaged in some level of fruit production in Afghanistan, but productivity has traditionally been low. BRAC established central nurseries in Mazar and Balk provinces, and then it created more than 400 small-scale nurseries around the country. Apart from the income that flows to the owners of these nurseries, the saplings serve two purposes: they supply others with guava, apricot, jardalu, and peach plants, and they supply a government environmental reforestation project. In 2006, a million seedlings were produced in BRAC nurseries.

Livestock development, an integral part of Afghanistan's farming systems, was a priority. Cattle, sheep, and poultry are all critical elements of the farming economy, producing meat and dairy products, wool, hides, fat, and other products. The survival of existing animals has precedence over everything else, so BRAC established three veterinarian-staffed livestock clinics. It operates mobile clinics. It runs basic three-day training programs on cattle, sheep, goats, and poultry rearing. It runs a 21-day artificial insemination training program, aimed at improving dairy production in seven provinces. Where chickens were concerned, vaccination was largely unknown, and mortality rates were high. By the end of 2006, BRAC had trained 775 poultry development workers, supporting them with extension workers, refresher courses, the supplies they needed, and the credit to finance their newfound livelihoods.

Small amounts of information and money, along with access to supplies and markets, can make a huge difference in the lives of very poor people. Mohammed Ayub and his wife, Saleha, for example, scratched out a meager living for themselves and their four children in Qalai Rashid village. When she was 42, Saleha joined the BRAC organization in her village. She took a course on cattle rearing, learning about the health of animals, deworming, and nutrition. Then she took a loan of 10,000 Afg (about US$200) and bought a single cow. When the time came, her husband took the cow to a BRAC artificial insemination center, and, with a second loan supported by the proceeds of milk sales, Saleha bought another cow. In less than two years, she had two cows and two calves. She was producing seven liters of milk a day and earning US$20 a week, enough to repay the loan, send the children to school, and still have money left over for other family needs.

Or take Jannab Gul, a 37-year-old woman who, along with her children, had depended for the family's survival entirely on her husband's meager efforts at vegetable farming in North Kordak. Her first BRAC loan allowed her to buy three sheep. She took the three-day course on sheep rearing. She had them vaccinated, and she fed them as best she could. BRAC extension workers visited and helped her with advice. At the end of a year, she sold two of them and used the proceeds to buy 10 younger sheep. By the end of the second year, she had 13 sheep, and she was making plans for 100. Jannab Gul could now add sheep farmer to the list of her abilities.

In Bangladesh, BRAC learned early that, if its programs were going to succeed, it had to invest heavily in training as well as research and evaluation. Its three training centers in Afghanistan, staffed by 42 full-time trainers, offer day classes and residential courses to its own staff, government departments, other NGOs, and community leaders in everything from basic primary health care to policy advocacy and financial management. A heavy emphasis is placed on training of trainers in order to develop local capacities in local languages and reduce the dependence on Bangladeshis. And, as it had in Bangladesh, BRAC established a research and evaluation unit to look for new endeavors and evaluate existing ones.

All of this looks rather straightforward—bring in some experts, get money, start programs, learn, adapt, and go to scale. But, of course, there are huge obstacles to accomplishing anything in Afghanistan. Western NGOs have been stymied by security problems, and large international organizations have been criticized for moving at a snail's pace, running up incredible bills, and kowtowing to the Western military agenda. BRAC had several advantages over others. First, its confidence in itself, its early determination to go to scale, and the systems it brought set it apart from every other aid operation in the country.

Second, its cost structures were vastly lower than any other international operation, which made it appealing to the Afghan government and donors alike. It had no large white Pajeros or Land Rovers, and it had no large white people. There are no Bangladeshi troops in the coalition forces to confuse the political equation. BRAC's staff lives modestly, and while about 170 Bangladeshis work in the program, they represent less than 5 percent of the total BRAC workforce. Most of its staff, including many of its professionals and senior managers, are Afghans. And BRAC's *modus operandi* is very different from that of most Western NGOs. It is not part of the standard expatriate community, and its Bangladeshi staff tends to socialize among themselves. Few of its staff hole up in walled compounds. BRAC's Kabul office is not in the best part of town. Beyond Kabul, most staff live at or near one of BRAC's 429 offices. One result of all this is that the organization is not well known or understood among other international aid workers. But, if they were going to succeed, this is the way it had to be done. They had to be in the village and of the village. They had to be able to go to the homes of the people they wanted to reach.

At first, it was extremely difficult. Jalaluddin Ahmed, BRAC's first country director in Afghanistan, knew development and knew BRAC, having worked in a wide variety of assignments since 1980. But he was not ready for what happened at first in Afghanistan. He needed staff who could conduct standard community surveys, so they advertised in a variety of ways. But nobody turned up. Those few who eventually appeared did not come back the next day. When two brave women eventually agreed to work for BRAC, they came with conditions. They would only work in their own village, and they would work together or not at all. There were language issues, and BRAC soon made it compulsory for all Bangladeshi staff to learn basic Farsi. "If you have to go through an interpreter, you lose a lot," Jalaluddin said. "You need uninterrupted communication."

Sultan Mohammed had worked with BRAC for 11 years when he was posted to Afghanistan to set up a regional microfinance program. Like others, he found it extremely difficult at first while learning the language and trying to gain the trust of the locals.

"The Imam is very important," he said. "You have to be sure to go to mosque every Friday or more often. They are not learned, and you have to explain everything."

BRAC people were accused of being American agents, an issue that became much more prominent after the invasion of Iraq. They had to explain why they were taking interest payments from women when Islam forbids interest. They had to spend time with a variety of village leaders, the *sura,* and the local commander. They had to spend time in the village holding weekly meetings, gaining the confidence of women and especially their husbands.

Security is certainly a concern. "At the beginning, there was no problem," Jalal said, "but I have seen a calm country become volatile." But BRAC has advantages. BRAC's Bangladeshi staff are socially and culturally similar to their Muslim brothers, and that helps. And the locals usually assist in solving security problems. "If the community is convinced about you, you will be a lot safer." They have rarely been forced to stop working. BRAC, however, is not immune from violence. Mohammed Wahidullah, an Afghan microfinance manager in Bhaglan province, was shot and killed in June 2007. And Abdul Alim, who had joined BRAC in Bangladesh in 1997, was shot and killed in September 2007. Alim, area manager for the Badakshan microfinance program, left a wife and two young children, who will now grow up without their father.

When Noor Islam was kidnapped a few days after the second killing, BRAC had to reconsider its position. Were these events politically motivated and the beginning of a trend? Had they miscalculated the security risk and the things they believed had shielded them? Following the kidnap, Amin flew to Afghanistan, where he met with government officials, Bangladeshi diplomats, and his own staff. They concluded that the events, while tragic, were not politically motivated and BRAC had not been targeted in any special way. The incidents may have been about robbery, ransom, or a grudge, but they did not constitute a reason for panic or flight. The violence in Afghanistan had certainly escalated in 2007, however, and it was anybody's guess what the future might hold. Sultan Mohammed, back in Bangladesh now, mourned the loss of Alim, his friend and colleague. "He was a brilliant student, and he did excellent work in Bangladesh and Afghanistan. He was our colleague, our brother." The tragedy has not daunted Sultan, however. Would he go back to Afghanistan? "Sure," he said, almost casually. "Why not?"

As the insurgency in Afghanistan gained strength in 2007 and 2008, wide cracks began to appear between the military and development communities. ISAF forces understood the need for development in Afghanistan's rural areas, but, too often, they saw it in terms of what are sometimes called "quick impact projects," including school reconstruction, roads, wells, footballs, and backpacks. Too often, they wanted to implement projects themselves as a visible gesture of goodwill by forces competing with the Taliban for hearts and minds. The problem is that genuine long-term development is not only about infrastructure and smiling kids waving at a passing jeep. It is not quick, and attribution may be as difficult as it is irrelevant to those who benefit. Literacy, good health, and jobs cannot be created overnight, and they certainly cannot be delivered by soldiers out of the back of a Humvee.

The debate between the military and its development counterparts is sterile. In fact, from a military point of view, there is undoubtedly a need in insurgencies for a degree of hearts-and-minds assistance and emergency aid in areas where the military alone can work. But that is not development, and, if the military is effective in its core competency, hearts-and-minds operations will not be long-term in their nature or their impact. The problem, as a 2007 study explained, is more fundamental:

> The international community has spent only eight percent of the total funds it committed to Afghanistan between 2002 and 2006 on development and poverty relief. The conventional wisdom is diametrically opposed: eighty percent of spending should go to economic, political, and social development. The question of how much development assistance Afghanistan can absorb in a relatively short time is very real, but the current balance is clearly badly off.[2]

Afghanistan in 2008 was not the Afghanistan of 2002. In many ways, the war in Iraq had compromised the bright hopes for a new order. Corruption had become endemic, the security situation had deteriorated, governmental capacity at all levels was weak, and people were tired beyond exhaustion from war and unrequited promises. Underscoring the growing insecurity, two more of BRAC's Bangladeshi staff were abducted in October 2008. BRAC, along with many other international and local organizations, had demonstrated what could be accomplished and had done so quickly, effectively, and against great odds. With peace, order, and good government, the potential in Afghanistan could be boundless. But few among the legion of Afghan-watching international political scientists, journalists, and aid officials were willing to risk a positive prognosis five years hence.

In 2006, Abed started looking for funds to establish the BRAC Bank in Afghanistan. He felt the time had come to institutionalize small enterprise lending, as had been done in Bangladesh. At the time, fewer than 2 percent of the country's small and medium enterprises had access to institutional credit at reasonable rates of interest, but they were the backbone of the country's commercial economy.[3] He spoke to Ron and Mary at ShoreBank. He spoke to the International Finance Corporation and the World Bank's Multilateral Investment Guarantee Agency (MIGA). All were wary. The general security situation had worsened considerably since the military intervention began, and there seemed no end in sight to the fighting. "Are you sure we should invest in this situation?" they asked him.

Abed knew there was risk,

> But we cannot write off a country of 30 million people to nothingness. We have to show confidence, otherwise who else will come in? I know Afghanistan is going to survive. Thirty million people are not going to be washed away. We will have problems;

it is a risk. But we need courage for the long haul.

In trying to persuade investors, he recalled a time 35 years earlier:

> Afghanistan is like Bangladesh in the seventies. People wrote it
> off. But where were 140 million people going to go? If we had
> all written it off, what would have happened? People in
> Afghanistan are living in abject poverty and there is all kinds
> of horrendous barbarity going on. But even then, we can help.
> No country should be written off; no people are beyond
> redemption.

Abed got his equity investment from ShoreCap, the Dutch Triodos Bank, and IFC, with investment guarantees from MIGA. And, on November 9, 2006, he presided at the opening ceremony in Kabul of the full-service BRAC Afghanistan Bank, the fourteenth bank in Afghanistan and the first to emphasize small-scale enterprise development. Back home, in the one hundred and ninety-sixth issue of BRAC's internal newsletter, news about the opening of the bank and Abed's subsequent meeting with Afghanistan's President Hamid Karzai was just one of many items, including one about International Women's Day, a visit from famed financier and philanthropist George Soros, and a new road safety awareness program that was being launched in Bangladesh. It was not that the editors of *BRAC News Brief* missed the significance of the event in Kabul. It was more a case of seeing exactly what its significance was, one of many events in the day-to-day life of an organization where the extraordinary has become ordinary to those who were making it happen.

Notes

1. Noor Islam's story is told in the *New Nation* (Dec. 14, 2007), *Daily Star* (Dec. 15, 2007), and *South Asian Media Net* (Dec. 25, 2007).

2. Janice Gross Stein and Eugene Lang, *The Unexpected War: Canada in Kandahar* (Toronto: Viking Canada, 2007), 266.

3. ShoreBank International, "Providing SME Credit in Afghanistan" (2006).

CHAPTER 20

The Source of the Nile

Tanzania

In June 2004, BRAC received the $1 million Gates Award for Global Health, which recognizes extraordinary achievement in improving health in the developing world. Melinda Gates, the award's co-founder, explained its purpose.

> Bill and I established the Gates Award to shine a spotlight on the heroes of global health—the individuals and organizations whose pioneering work is transforming health in the developing world . . . Fazle Hasan Abed and his colleagues at BRAC are true heroes, whose tireless commitment has been saving and improving the lives of millions for more than three decades.[1]

The award, however, was only the beginning of what would become a much larger and deeper relationship between BRAC and Gates. Eighteen months later, the Foundation would provide money that would take BRAC to Tanzania, specifically US$15 million over five years.

Tanzania is an island of relative stability in a volatile part of Africa. Despite its economic and democratic progress, however, the quality of life for the average Tanzanian has not greatly improved in recent years. Life expectancy is 44 years and falling, and the infant mortality rate is rising. Both trends are due largely to the country's high HIV/AIDS infection rate. Roughly half of the population subsists on less than US$1 a day, and two out of every five Tanzanians are unable to meet their basic daily needs.

Hold that picture for a moment. Imagine visiting an aircraft factory where four or five large planes are under construction. The factory is alive with activity, noise, and the urgency of enterprise. One aircraft is almost fully formed, its unpainted body gleaming in the brightly lit factory. Technicians are swarming inside and out, fitting equipment and testing joints and seals. Other planes are in various stages of construction. Parts of a fuselage and tail are surrounded by scaffolding. In another part of the factory, a fuselage section with wings attached is being lowered into position by a series of cranes. A visit to BRAC in Tanzania is a bit like this. The program has been scoped out, and large parts of it are under construction. There is ferment and activity everywhere.

Abed, Amin, and Imran Matin visited the country in 2006 and discussed the potential with government officials. They traveled through the countryside, and they marveled at the wide-open spaces and the absence of people. How could there be so much poverty, they wondered, when there was so much land? By mid-2007, the factory is in full swing. Thirteen Bangladeshis have come from BRAC, headed by Mohammed Bari Chowdhury, a BRAC veteran who has recently worked on a fledgling BRAC effort in Pakistan. In the long run, agriculture will be the key, and BRAC has sent one of its best agronomists, Mohammed Abu Bakar, to develop a plan. Abu Bakar looks more like a Muslim cleric than an agronomist. He has a beard, but there is no moustache. He wears a long *kurta* and a white Islamic cap. He speaks about farming with the fervor of a missionary. He speaks of his Danish postgraduate degree in seed technology, his studies in the Philippines, and his work in developing BRAC's seed multiplication operations in Bangladesh. He speaks about the Asia Pacific Seed Association, where nobody was interested in NGOs until he arrived, and the joint venture projects that BRAC worked out with Australia's Pacific Seeds and Hefei Fengle, China's second-largest seed production company. He is a missionary, and agronomy is his message.

He explains that virtually all farming in Tanzania is rain-fed. There is no irrigation, and water is a perennial problem. He is thinking about maize and the three varieties that are common here. In Bangladesh, BRAC experimented with maize for its poultry feed mills, and now gets yields of 10 tons per hectare. In Tanzania, where maize is grown for human consumption, the yield is only 1.5 tons per hectare. Abu Bakar has visited Tanseeds and the government research farm, but these are underperforming. Tanzania has seven agroecological zones, and he is now focusing his attention on two of them: the coastal zone and one in the north. He has leased some land for trials, and the government has provided some space at one of its research farms. He will start with maize, cassava, and perhaps some rice. He also plans to experiment with vegetables, including tomato, cucumber, and others. Traders import seeds into Tanzania, but neither they nor the farmers have the technical capacity to use them to best advantage. There is no organized seed multiplication in Tanzania, and that will be the next step once BRAC has some crops that work. Government extension services are weak or nonexistent, so the scope here is huge as well. But there are issues. If they can identify a crop for potential growth, labor may become a problem. And, if they are able to increase production beyond subsistence farming, transportation to market may be difficult as well. Abu Bakar is thinking ahead and calculating the possibilities and the potential pitfalls, but he is optimistic.

Six months later, the first crops on his experimental farms have been harvested, and the results are good. He has doubled the yield, and, in some cases, he has achieved better results than in Bangladesh. "Water is the issue," he says. "Water." Maybe in a year they will have the beginnings of a plan that can eventually be taken to scale.

Mohammed Mizanur Rahman is establishing BRAC's poultry and livestock program. He is focusing on chickens, and he has an idea of something that might eventually look like BRAC's integrated poultry operation in Bangladesh. There is a large unmet demand for chickens in Tanzania, and there are hatcheries, a step ahead of where Bangladesh was when BRAC began. In the rural areas of Tanzania, however, weak extension services are the drawback, and there is a high mortality rate among chickens. That will be the first target in the four regions where BRAC is starting to experiment. As in Bangladesh, they are recruiting poultry volunteers who will earn money from the services they provide to their neighbors. A baseline survey has been done with 500 rearers, and a training program has started. The plan is to have 20 volunteers in each of the four area offices, each serving 300 women farmers working at different trial stages in the chain: day-old chicks, vaccinators, and model rearers. There are major problems with fowl cholera, Gambaro, and Newcastle disease, but better knowledge and a vaccination program that can be taken directly to the farmer's doorstep will start to make a difference.

They are also working on plans for 100 model cow rearers and 100 model goat rearers in each of the four branches. All of this is experimental, designed to build confidence among farmers and learn what works and what does not. Like Abu Bakar, Rahman is thinking ahead. Knowledge of the small producer will be key, and it may take five years, but the potential in Tanzania is huge. Rahman has visited some of the hatcheries in Tanzania, and he has learned that the parent stock all come from South Africa and the Netherlands, which adds significantly to the cost of day-old chicks. He can see other inefficiencies in the current system, including transportation and the way vaccine is distributed and used. The first step, however, is to reduce mortality and increase farmer confidence. Then they can begin to think about the infrastructure that will be required to get inputs to more farmers and products to market.

Mohammed Abdus Salaam has come to Tanzania as BRAC's country health manager after 20 years of designing and managing health programs in Bangladesh. BRAC has supplemented his master's degree in economics with advanced courses at the Asian Institute of Management and Swansea University, and he did a master's in primary health care management at Mahidol University in Thailand. He has been in Tanzania less than six months, but he realizes already that BRAC will have to adjust the plan that was proposed to the Gates Foundation. Government here is not going to roll over and agree to just anything suggested by an untested newcomer. BRAC is going to have to move judiciously, and it will have to prove itself.

The health program will piggyback on the microfinance program, starting in four areas (Dar es Salaam, Zanzibar, Tanga, and Arusha), each with five branches. There are two medical officers in charge of the program, one Tanzanian and one Bangladeshi. Each branch office has an area specialist, a trainer, and 20 health volunteers drawn from the microfinance groups. Training has already been given, and the volunteers have conducted simple surveys on basic health information, family planning, water, sanitation, and toilet facilities. The health volunteers will have a limited mandate at the beginning, focusing mainly on basics such as mosquito nets and repellant, water purification tablets, condoms, and nonprescription drugs. In due course, BRAC will introduce a rapid diagnostic test for malaria that can detect the disease in as little as 15 minutes. Water and sanitation are major problems. Knowledge of HIV/AIDS is quite good in Tanzania, and Salaam plans to introduce a voluntary counseling and testing program. Prenatal care is not bad in Tanzania either, but postnatal care and child mortality are serious problems, so this will become an area of focus. Immunization rates are high (as much as 80 percent), but Salaam thinks BRAC can get it to 100 percent.

Tanzania ranks fourteenth among countries with the largest TB burdens, and the detection rate is low. Here is an area where BRAC could make a significant difference, but there is a problem. BRAC's success with TB in Bangladesh was based on two things. The first was health volunteers who could apply the directly observed therapy, actually watching each patient take the medicine. The second was the bond system. In Bangladesh, the patient pays a Tk 200 bond at the beginning of treatment. At the end, when tests come back negative, Tk 50 goes to the health worker and Tk 150 is returned to the patient. There is little doubt that the health workers and monetary incentive are major parts of what has made the system so successful in Bangladesh. In Tanzania, they have the health workers, but the government has so far disallowed the bond. And officials are skeptical about the health volunteers as well. They have seen a lot of NGO games, and they are concerned that all of this might become some sort of scam. There is an additional problem. In Tanzania, NGO activity has been component-based, so the Ministry of Health sees only health NGOs and health projects, and the link between health and microfinance is not immediately obvious.

But it is still early days. Salaam speaks highly of the organizers they have hired. There are 300 now, and all of them are women.* A few have come from a background in health and some from social development work, but, because they are all young and all speak English, there are not as many communications problems as had been expected. Almost all came to the program with a better education than is available to BRAC in Bangladesh, and all are considerably more outgoing than Bangladeshi women.

The same is true among the microfinance staff, which is where the Tanzania program has placed its greatest initial emphasis. Money makes the world go round, and group formation for savings and credit has worked well. Several other organizations have already introduced microfinance in Tanzania, so the concept is not new. There are women ready, willing, and able to join groups in areas where other NGOs have not appeared. By May 2007, BRAC had organized 630 groups in seven regions with a total membership of 17,000. Eighteen months later, there were more than 80,000 members and 3,000 groups. BRAC had opened 30 branch offices, and, by the beginning of 2009, it had disbursed US$22.3 million in loans. Most of the early lending was to women wanting to add to an existing enterprise of some sort, for example, more chickens, a better shop, or a new sewing machine. This was not high-risk lending to the very poorest. This was a cautious start-up program while the organizers felt their way in other areas, learning about communities and gaining the confidence of villagers and the government.

BRAC is new in Tanzania, and its reputation has not preceded it. The government and donors worry about NGO games and untried ideas. Tanzanians have a deep suspicion of "Indians" and worry about anything that smacks of commercialism, hence, perhaps, the concern about a TB bond. But BRAC comes with powerful assets. Its 13 Bangladeshi staff do not fit the standard generalist NGO mold. All are experienced, top-notch professionals in their field. BRAC's overheads are minuscule in comparison with other international NGOs because all of their staff lives together in shared accommodation, and they do not bring their families with them. They receive a generous salary supplement and get home leave every six months, but they are still paid on the basis of their Bangladeshi salaries, so BRAC's staff costs are tiny in comparison with other agencies. And they have brought BRAC's phobia for vehicle fleets with them. BRAC has purchased low-horsepower motorcycles and many bicycles for staff,

---

*This chapter describes a moment in mid 2007 during BRAC's startup in Tanzania. By the beginning of 2009, the 300 health workers had become 735 and growing.

but the entire operation in 2007 had only one vehicle with more than two wheels. There may not be any fully built planes in this factory yet, but there soon will be.

Uganda and Beyond

BRAC's start-up in Uganda was a little different in the sense that there was no large institutional donor like the Gates Foundation to salt the clouds. And getting approvals from the Ugandan government proved difficult. Officials were skeptical and demanded a reference from the Ugandan ambassador to Bangladesh. There was only one problem with this. Uganda did not have a diplomatic mission in Dhaka. Finally, a notarized copy of BRAC's rather impressive financial statements was accepted as proof that BRAC was a legitimate entity.

Seed money this time was provided by NOVIB, BRAC's old friend from Holland, and, as things developed, they went to UNICEF for support with the education program and a variety of foundations and banks for assistance with microfinance.

"We have no money to bring from Bangladesh," said Khondoker Ariful Islam (Arif), the country manager. "But we have the skills to do things, and, in time, we can mobilize the money."

He spoke highly of BRAC's fund-raising offices in the United States and Britain, which were able to mobilize support for early interventions, such as the establishment of a 25-bed training center in Kampala. Training has been the key to BRAC success in all of its programming, and the establishment of this training center to serve BRAC's own needs and those of other NGOs was something completely new in Uganda.

The microfinance program was launched in June 2006, and Abed was there to hand over the first loan. In little more than a year, they had opened 34 branch offices, and they were already one of the largest NGOs in the country. But Uganda is not Tanzania. Its history has been turbulent, and, despite growing prosperity in the south, its northern districts have been wracked by war, poverty, and refugees. In 2006, when BRAC began, there were 2.8 million people in camps for the displaced, and the security situation was abysmal. This is where BRAC began its schools. Arif is proud of what they were able to do in a short space of time. Many children in the camps had enrolled in the formal education system, but many more had been bypassed. "All of the NGOs work from the district headquarters. Most travel with a police escort to the camp and return to their base by sunset." BRAC was the first NGO to set up branch offices inside the camps.

There are challenges in adapting the BRAC model to Africa. In Uganda alone, there are 26 different ethnic groups, which means there must be a great deal of adaptation. Microfinance was easy enough to initiate, but, as Arif put it, "borrowing money doesn't get your chickens vaccinated or properly fed." Making the connections between borrowers, the suppliers of inputs, and buyers, the keys to BRAC success in Bangladesh, would take time. BRAC knew something about maize, a staple in Uganda, but it would have to learn about cassava and other crops. The common culture, religion, and language that helped to facilitate replication in Bangladesh did not exist here. But, like Tanzania, in Uganda, women were far more self-confident than in Bangladesh, and they were ready, willing, and able to become involved as participants, trainees, and staff members. There was a moment of hesitation in the early days, however, when BRAC set up its first staff training program. Here was a group of Asians, mainly men, who had hired two dozen young Ugandan women to manage an unknown NGO, and now it was asking them to attend a residential training program. If the government had been skeptical, the parents of these young women must also have had doubts.

In southern Sudan, the experience goes back farther than in Uganda, to a period between 2001 and 2004 when UNICEF brought in some of BRAC's field people as consultants. Here, the situation is much worse than in Uganda. The country is emerging from a 50-year civil war, and, in the south, the entire infrastructure has been destroyed. Here, the human suffering is worse than anything Arif has ever seen, and he talked of BRAC's plans for education, health, livestock, and agriculture. He expects to have 50 branch offices within two or three years, but the donor bureaucracy is slow, and, as elsewhere, BRAC still needs to prove itself.

Abed visited Sudan with Amin after the 2005 peace agreement, and Arif met them at Entebbe airport when they returned to Uganda. "I think we will do something in Sudan," Abed told him. Arif mumbled something about how difficult logistics and communications were in southern Sudan, and Abed recalled the British experience of East Bengal.

> Three hundred years ago, they came by ship. It took them six months, and when they arrived, there were no roads. Still, they reached Sylhet and they planted tea gardens and built schools and towns. If they could do that, coming from Britain, we should not have any serious problems in Southern Sudan.

Arif had another opportunity to express his reservations, saying how little he knew in comparison to Abed who, after all, had created a huge organization with money, systems, people, and experience. Here in East Africa, they had very little but their wit and their own personal experience to fall back on. The conversation moved on to other things, and Arif, who had read books about the Nile, told Abed how he had recently made a trek to visit the source of the great river.

> I was surprised. I told Abed *bhai* that it was nothing but a tiny canal—nothing. And he told me, "Arif, all great things in the world start small. All rivers are nothing more than small streams at their source, but as they travel, and as time passes, some are joined by other rivers, and over time a small river can become great.

Will the BRAC experience travel? One theory about BRAC's success in Bangladesh revolves around the homogeneity of Bangladesh society, culture, language, and religion. The problems in one part of what is, after all, a small country, are very similar to those in most other places. Once a cost-effective formula was developed, whether it was in microfinance, health, or livestock, it could be widely replicated without a great deal of variation. Although BRAC is the largest, it is not the only large Bangladeshi NGO, so, if it is not something in the water, the ability to grow must be fostered by more observable factors. That then, begs the question as to whether BRAC models can be applied elsewhere and taken to scale. The jury is still out where Africa is concerned because the experience is so new, but BRAC brings something to Africa that it did not have when it started back in Sulla in the 1970s. It has a solid understanding of what creates and nurtures poverty and what is needed to change the status quo. It experiments, it listens, and it goes straight to those it wants to work with. It innovates, and it learns. The cultural homogeneity that may have been essential to early success in Bangladesh is no longer so important. It has not been a limiting factor in Afghanistan, and BRAC is unfazed by teething pains in Tanzania, Uganda, and Southern Sudan. The problems there, in fact, are nothing compared to the failures of some of its first experiments in Sulla and Manikganj. Teams have visited Malawi and postwar Liberia and Sierra Leone, and BRAC has fledgling operations in Haiti, Pakistan, Sri Lanka, India, and China. The question is not so much whether it can travel because it has. It will be like Abed's river, and its success will depend for its breadth and depth on what other streams flow into it as it makes its way toward the sea.

Notes

1. http://www.gatesfoundation.org/GlobalHealth/Announcements/Announce-040603.htm.

CHAPTER 21

In Larger Freedom

The House that Jack Built

Unlike the nursery rhyme, which tells us a lot about the house that Jack built but nothing about Jack, this book has tried to describe the building of the house and something about its builders. It has described many of BRAC's achievements, delving into some in more detail than others. Many, however, have been left out for reasons of space, while the description of others has been compressed. The chapters on BRAC's microfinance and small-scale enterprise lending, for example, do scant justice to the variety and detail of the organization's overall savings and loan operation. The book does not describe BRAC's work with the urban poor, and it has only sampled BRAC's rural development work. There is no discussion, for example, of its fish and prawn hatcheries, nor of its 178,000 ponds, which generate livelihoods in fish cultivation and freshwater prawns. The surface area of these ponds and oxbow lakes is more than 23,000 hectares, roughly the size of 9,600 football fields. Horticulture has been mentioned in connection with mulberry trees, but BRAC's wider agroforestry programs, its 8,000 village nurseries, and the 15 or 16 million seedlings it produces every year have been bypassed. BRAC's work with urban schools, indigenous children, and kids with special needs is not here.

Description of the health programs has focused mainly on oral rehydration, TB, and the work of the *shasthya shebikas,* barely mentioning BRAC's family planning efforts, water and sanitation, malaria control, or its work on HIV/AIDS. A limb and brace fitting center provides artificial arms and legs for 1,200 people annually, and 37 *shushasthyas* (health centers) provide out- and inpatient services for thousands of people every year, along with low-cost lab facilities and essential medicines. BRAC's human rights and legal aid programs are supported by 400 theater troupes that stage 58,000 plays a year, educating as they entertain. BRAC's research, evaluation, and training divisions are mentioned throughout the book, but only in passing. Many of BRAC's multifaceted enterprises have been described, but others have been left out, again for reasons of economy, including a cold storage operation for potatoes, four tea gardens, and the Delta BRAC Housing Finance Corporation. Each of these operations has a story to tell about social enterprise and its relation to poverty alleviation, innovative management, and long-term sustainability.

BRAC went to Sri Lanka immediately after the Asian tsunami to provide relief assistance, as it has done many times in Bangladesh. In due course, its work in Sri Lanka turned to reconstruction and then to longer-term development. BRAC is working in Haiti and Pakistan, and it is exploring the potential for operations in India, China, Sierra Leone, and Liberia. In order to help finance it global expansion, it has established two nonprofit fundraising arms, each with its own board of trustees, one in London and one in New York. In the United States, BRAC had put together a fund of almost US$70 million for microfinance operations in Africa by the beginning of 2009.

BRAC has had its share of failures. The deep tubewell project described in chapter 12 is one of the larger disappointments because its potential seemed so great. There have been others. BRAC experimented with the use of power tillers as a kind of halfway technology between bullock power and tractors. It did not work. It also experimented for a long time with health insurance for the poor, but it could not make that work either. The idea of health insurance has been revived in recent years, however, and it may yet bear fruit. Most of the early Sulla work was a failure in the sense that few of BRAC's immediate objectives there were achieved. But Sulla gave BRAC the lessons it needed to learn, adapt, and grow, so, in that sense, it was far from a failure.

The overall BRAC enterprise with 3,000 offices and 57,000 employees, not counting the teachers and health workers who would triple that figure, requires a significant degree of administration and financial management. The scale of the personnel operation, for example, is staggering. BRAC may hire as many as 1,000 people in a single recruitment drive. After the jobs are advertised, 3,000 to 4,000 individuals will be called for an interview. Of these, about half will be given a written test, and, of them, 60 or 70 percent may pass. Perhaps 80 percent of the ones who pass will be given a five-day preservice training program, an examination, and a further interview, and, from that number, 1,000 will be hired. The starting salary for a program organizer with a master's degree is about Tk 10,000 (US$150) a month. The very highest salary in BRAC, with all allowances for health, travel, and housing included and attainable only after 10 years of service, is approximately Tk 110,000 (a little under US$20,000) a year.

Where financial management is concerned, BRAC has an Audit Directorate that manages the organization's external audit function. In

2006, there were 46 external auditing missions, some conducted as a matter of course on behalf of BRAC. Others were to meet donor and governmental requirements. An internal audit department, staffed by 137 professionals, audits the head office, all commercial projects, and each area office at least once a year, and, more frequently, where problems have been identified. A department called Procurement, Estate, and Management Services handles the management of land, offices, and procurement. It has to balance a variety of needs and demands, some of them from inflexible donors. The European Union, for example, a major supporter of BRAC's education programs, requires international tendering on all procurement, so BRAC has been obliged to place ads as far afield as the *New York Times,* even though there is little chance that an American supplier could meet its terms and conditions. BRAC's own procurement manual is 116 pages long with sample technical specifications, tender information, tender preparation forms, and details of tender security requirements.

The movement of people was a challenge almost from the beginning, and, as BRAC grew, the transportation problem grew as well. BRAC solved part of it some years ago by supplying 50–80cc motorcycles to any employee who needed one. The employee purchases the motorcycle on an installment plan over seven or eight years, and the employee handles the maintenance, not BRAC. Simple. But, as always, there were problems. When they started using an open bidding system, they were offered 50cc bikes from an unknown company in China at less than one-third the cost of Hondas assembled in Pakistan. BRAC is not a small purchaser, and the savings on 1,000 bikes was significant. The Chinese motorcycles, however, did not last. Today, hundreds of them are rusting behind the Aarong shop in Niketon, testimony to the old adage of "penny-wise, pound-foolish."

Over the years, outsiders have often suggested that BRAC could not run without Abed. Asian deference to authority, they say, is the glue that holds the whole thing together. It is certainly true that Abed is the guiding light, a font of ideas, drive, and enterprise. But he has not been able— nor has he tried—to micromanage the organization for a very long time. Abed's great strength where personnel is concerned is his ability to recognize, delegate, motivate, and retain good people. A core team of senior managers, many of whom joined in the 1970s, assists him, including Amin, the student Marxist; Mushtaque, who liked statistics; and the heads of training, microfinance, education, administration, and accounts. Of these, Amin has perhaps been the most vital. One longtime observer put it this way, "Without Amin, there would have been no BRAC." Amin has been at the forefront of all of BRAC's initiatives, from microfinance, health, and enterprise development to the new operations in Afghanistan and Africa. He is the operations genius, the man who could take Abed's ideas and operationalize them. Abed concurs:

> Amin is not loved by slackers, but people respect his ability to work beyond endurance. He is the most entrepreneurial man, an exceptional person with an exceptional commitment to rural development. BRAC would not be what it is without him.

Abed himself is not a workaholic, at least not in the sense that he works until 10 at night. He may work until 7 or 8, but he does not go to work early, and he does not take work home with him. He relaxes on the weekend, and, except for when he travels, he does not carry a cell phone. And then it is only used for emergencies. He does not use a computer, odd for someone running such a huge enterprise and odd for someone who studied computer technology for a full year as far back as 1966 and introduced WiMAX technology to Bangladesh. His explanation? "I never learned to type." One of Abed's strengths as a manager is his ability to know what is important, such as typing perhaps, and another is his ability to change hats and focus.

> Whenever I work at anything, even when I was at Shell Oil, I was totally dedicated to what I did. I do the same when I am thinking about educating children, or when I am at BRAC Bank. When I am at the bank, I am a banker.

Abed understands money and numbers, perhaps the most important skills he took from his education and Shell Oil. But he is also an exceptionally clear thinker. He has a quiet tenacity, and he will not give up on an idea until it has been fully tested and retested. He is seemingly unflappable in a crisis, an important quality in an excitable country. Bangladeshi leaders, whether in business, politics, or labor, are much given to fiery speechifying. Abed is the antithesis of this. He is calm and contemplative but assertive when it matters, and there are things he will not tolerate. He has instilled in BRAC a zero-tolerance attitude towards insubordination, sexual harassment, and theft. "He can avoid fools with a smile," said his old friend Faruq Choudhury, "but he is at his best when he is thinking."

In an organization as large as BRAC, there have to be regular injections of newcomers, and this has been going on from the start. Many have reached midlevel and even senior management levels within a few years, handling much more responsibility than Amin and the others had at the same age. Some of them have been described in this book: Farzana Chowdhury, in charge of small enterprise development at the BRAC

Bank; Tamara Abed at Aarong; Imran Matin, head of research and evaluation; Rabeya Yasmin, head of the Ultra Poor Program.

While most people grow up in BRAC, some senior managers have been brought in laterally. Mahabub Hossain, the executive director, came from a career at the Bangladesh Institute of Development Studies and the International Rice Research Institute in the Philippines. He brings an agenda. He wants to rebuild a family feeling in BRAC, improving the work environment, creating a mentoring arrangement for newcomers, and building more quality checks into systems that have been strained by expansion. He wants to build greater synergies between programs, and he wants to equip BRAC with a longer-term vision than the budget span of its existing programs. And he brings with him a passion for agriculture and a desire to see BRAC do more to tackle the country's still-unsolved food problems.

Rumee Ali has come in to oversee all of BRAC's enterprises and build more. Rumee brings 25 years of banking experience, including stints as the general manager in Bangladesh of Grindlays Bank and CEO of the Standard Chartered Group. He also served as deputy governor of the Bangladesh Bank before joining BRAC. He saw BRAC at a distance before he joined, but he had not grasped the extent of BRAC's commercial operations or the philosophy behind them, something he had to try to understand himself before he could explain it to others. BRAC enterprises represent a social business model that redefine the concept of corporate social responsibility. He gives the example of the dairy operation, which was established to provide poor farmers with an outlet for expanded production and a fair price.

When Rumee started at BRAC, he did a strategic review of all of the business operations and discovered that 16 of the 60 chilling stations at the time were not only losing money, "they were not even marginal in my estimate, unlikely to turn around in the next two or three years." His obvious recommendation was to close the stations or move them to more viable locations. To him, this was a no-brainer, but he was told that the stations would have to stay where they were because they were in ultra poor areas. Removing them would deprive many of a fair price and their livelihoods.

BRAC's enterprises "are not run as truly commercial enterprises, but to implement BRAC's mission of working with the poor to bring about real and significant change."[1]

Rumee draws a semicircle on a sheet of paper, with a line under it. At one edge of the circle, he writes "exploitative." At the other, he writes "idealistic." The one extreme represents the worst of the commercial world; the other represents the most naïve aspects of NGO income-generation efforts. Neither is sustainable, for obvious reasons. He draws a hand on the clock between 10 and 11. Here we are moving toward a more sustainable commercial business, one that understands corporate social responsibility as something more than donations to orphanages, one that is in tune with the society in which it operates.

On the other side of noon, he draws a hand on the clock between two and three. Here is where he locates social business, a commercially viable operation organically linked to poverty alleviation and one whose surplus benefits the organization rather than shareholders.

BRAC enterprises have evolved into this kind of model, creating hundreds of thousands of livelihoods for the poor, but Rumee's latter point is as important. In poor countries, philanthropy is weak, and there is no tradition of charitable giving for development. Homegrown civil society must rely, therefore, on foreign NGOs and donor agencies for their sustenance unless they can find an alternative. Few alternatives have been identified. They will always be dependant on charity and the kindness of strangers, that is, on outsiders who come and go. Their understanding of local needs and conditions is imperfect, and their priorities shift. BRAC has changed this paradigm entirely.

Connections and Alliances

Like the cat that killed the rat that ate the malt that lay in the house that Jack built, the story of BRAC is one of connections and linkages and the need to create them where they did not exist. The need to find an outlet for village handicrafts first led to improved designs and quality and then to the creation of a retail outlet. One Aarong shop became two, and two became six. The idea of better poultry required a comprehensive set of linkages on both the supply and the marketing sides of the actual chicken, including hatcheries, chicken feed and the introduction of maize, the need for better maize seed and the creation of a tissue culture laboratory, and a seed multiplication operation and seed testing lab. Downstream connections led to a factory that produces bags, sachets, and containers for seeds, milk, and salt, along with a system for marketing eggs and chickens beyond the village. The same was true of the dairy operation and silk production and a dozen other enterprises.

Abed remarked:

> I think the first linkages began with Paolo Freire's idea of teaching literacy and conscientizing people at the same time. We had the idea that teaching meant an instructor imparting knowledge, instructing people. Some people know and others don't know. Freire gave us the idea that knowledge can be

created through discussion, through action and reflection, and so BRAC's whole idea of training changed. That was the first connection, from training to conscientization.

A next logical connection was made between education and the need for educational textbooks, charts, and other teaching material. Abed said:

> The printing press came in on two counts. First, we were expanding our education program, and we needed a printing facility. And second, Mrs. Gandhi had declared an emergency at that time in India, and she was trying to control NGOs by restricting their donor funds. I thought, "My God, if it's happening there, it's bound to come here, and our donor funding will stop if we don't toe the government line." We needed an income to survive, and so the printing press had two goals.

Today, the press is one of the three largest in Bangladesh, turning out several million textbooks a year, all of BRAC's stationery, leaflets, posters, checks, and other forms of security printing. Its clients include other NGOs, donors, universities, and a range of private sector companies. Where the second goal is concerned, BRAC Printers and Printing Pack together contributed over US$600,000 to BRAC's health, education, and development programs in 2006. This connection, the idea of earning money, was questionable when BRAC Printers began. But Abed had watched closely as Oxford University Press (OUP), a nonprofit enterprise owned by Oxford University, was taken to court by another publisher on the grounds of unfair competition. As a nonprofit, OUP was not paying taxes, and it was therefore said to be competing unfairly. OUP contributes 30 percent of its annual surplus to the university, but the court supported its nonprofit status for another reason.

"The purpose of the university is to generate knowledge," Abed recalled, "and publishing books is directly related to that."

BRAC Printers and all of the other BRAC enterprises have the same social purpose. The OUP story was an arrow he would keep in his quiver, drawing it several times over the years to defend BRAC's surplus-generating enterprises.*

---

*BRAC does, however, make a strong point in its annual reports about taxes. It may be a nonprofit organization, but it contributes directly to the national exchequer through employee income tax deductions, import duties, a value-added tax applied to the sale of the products it produces, and tax deductions at source from third parties. In 2007, BRAC's tax bill was the equivalent of almost US$4 million.

The BRAC story is also about innovation and drive. Some innovations were small but pivotal, for example, the results-based payments to health workers giving ORS training. If trainees remembered the message, the trainer earned. Or the bonus payment for TB workers if their patients tested negative after six months of treatment. Or the idea of using liquid nitrogen in a cold chain to preserve bull semen. Or the idea that, if the maize required for chicken feed wasn't being grown in Bangladesh, then it should be. And, if the yields were low, they should be improved. And, if the seeds were not appropriate to Bangladesh, better seeds would be developed. And, if there were no packaging for seeds, then BRAC would build the factory and make the packaging.

One might say that BRAC has been lucky with its donors, but it is worth recalling our earlier definition of luck. Luck is about being ready. BRAC was consistently ready for what donors had to offer, and donors were lucky in the sense that they were ready for what BRAC offered, including new lessons about the drivers of poverty when standard ideas about integrated rural development were failing, programs for women as gender rose on the international agenda, and sustainable lending when the idea of give-aways was falling from favor. BRAC offered intelligent, well-documented programs when government services were near collapse. It admitted error, and it acknowledged failure, but it could explain them, and it demonstrated that it could learn from error and apply the lessons. All of these were refreshing traits in a failure-prone donor universe.

BRAC has also been able to manage another donor-related issue, getting the best from short-term donor thinking and funding in support of an organization that is all about the long term. Managing this interface is often the key to success, and BRAC has had to work hard to get it right. The challenge is especially difficult in a country like Afghanistan, where political needs drive the development process and generous funding now may turn into sharp reductions later as the political priorities of donor countries change. Managing front-end generosity in support of a program that can sustain a donor downturn is no easy feat, especially in situations where real development achievements take 10 or 15 years or more.

Today, BRAC is 80 percent self-sufficient. In other words, donors provide only 20 percent of its annual income, but donors remain an important source, not just of funding for innovation, but of ideas and strategic linkages. One of BRAC's first and best donors was the German NGO, Bread for the World (*Brot für die Welt*), which Abed first encountered on Manpura a year before the creation of BRAC. Bread for the World, willing to take a chance on an untested organization, gave BRAC some of its first support in Sulla, Jamalpur, and Manikganj. Oxfam, which included Oxfam GB, Oxfam Canada, Oxfam USA, and Oxfam Hong Kong, was another early supporter and risk-taker. The Dutch NGO, NOVIB, which would later join the Oxfam family, was and remains a stout sponsor of new initiatives and ventures too risky for others. The Gates, Rockefeller, Nike, MasterCard and NoVo Foundations have all been important supporters, as have the Aga Khan Foundation and the Soros Economic Development Fund. Virtually all of BRAC's start-ups—from the first microfinance programs in the early 1970s to its work in Uganda and Sudan—were funded by NGOs and foundations. Larger donors like DFID, the European Union, UNICEF, Canada, Norway, Sweden, Denmark, the Netherlands, and Australia came in later, allowing the experiments to go to scale.

The Ford Foundation, never a large donor, was consistent in the innovative support it was able to provide, including funding for key BRAC staff to study abroad, the first introduction to ShoreBank, seed money for the library at the new BRAC university, and assistance with the creation of a streamlining donor consortium when BRAC was weighed down by 100 grants and dozens of different reporting requirements. Susan Davis, who spearheaded the creation of the donor consortium when she was with the Ford Foundation in Bangladesh during the 1980s, has returned to BRAC, as so many do, this time as president and CEO of BRAC USA. BRAC USA's mission is to increase BRAC's visibility in the United States, harness the power of its friends, and mobilize support for new BRAC operations in Africa and Asia. Davis brings a long career in development, microfinance, and advocacy to the task, and she is supported by an impressive board of directors that includes Adrienne Germain and Ray Offenheiser, other Ford Bangladesh alumnae, and Richard Cash, whose knowledge of Bangladesh goes back to the relief effort on Manpura. Lincoln Chen (another Manpura alumnus) chairs the board, and Ron Grzywinski— chairman and co-founder of ShoreBank—is the treasurer.

The Ford connection illustrates another BRAC strength, the formation of alliances and lasting friendships. When he returned to Bangladesh from England in 1969, Abed became friendly with the small circle of expatriate doctors and scientists at the Pakistan-SEATO Cholera Research Laboratory. This connection carried Lincoln and Marty Chen, Richard Cash, Jon and Candy Rhode, and others to Abed's house in Chittagong after the 1970 cyclone. Those friendships led to the creation of HELP, and they were renewed personally and professionally many times over the following years. One of the first renewals was the 1973 return to Bangladesh of Lincoln and Marty Chen. Within two years, Marty had joined BRAC as one of Abed's two executive assistants. Lincoln, this time employed by the Ford Foundation, was again based at the Cholera Research Lab, where there were new synergies to be developed. Abed recalled:

> The Cholera Lab was a science organization. They had created oral rehydration therapy by 1968, but in 1979, eleven years

later, Bangladeshis still knew nothing about it, and the news-papers were asking why the Cholera Lab had achieved so little. When we started experimenting with ORT, the Cholera Lab loved it . . . at last their science was going to the people. They loved our work and we exploited their science.

The same kind of thing would happen repeatedly over the years, with small interventions often leading to something much larger. Abed said:

I think most human beings want to be successful in whatever they do, and when they find an opportunity to work with an organization that can give them some satisfaction, they want to team up. It's not that we have to find these people; they find us.

In Larger Freedom

One who found BRAC was Bill Clinton. Abed first met the future president when he was the little-known governor of a small southern state, interested in how microfinance might be applied in Arkansas. Years later, President Clinton paid a state visit to Bangladesh. "Picturesque" is not a word that many would use to describe Dhaka, but, for this occasion, it was swept, cleaned, and painted. Bunting and banners were hoisted everywhere, and people began to refer to the much anticipated visitor as "Bill Clean-town."

Part of the itinerary was a visit to a BRAC school, but the Secret Service nixed the plan at the last moment. The presidential helicopter would have to pass over rice fields that could not be secured. So the children and teachers were bused to the American embassy in Dhaka, where the students missed their arithmetic lesson and met the President of the United States instead.

In a private moment, the president told Abed, "When I leave the presidency, I want to do what you do." In 2007, they met again in New York when Clinton honored Abed with an inaugural Clinton Global Citizenship Award. Wangari Maathai, the Kenyan Nobel Peace Prize laureate, had been asked to introduce Abed, perhaps because she had spent some time at BRAC a few years earlier. In her introduction, she said she had learned more from BRAC than any organization she had ever encountered. It was certainly an occasion to remember, but, for Abed, the high point was a leatherbound book the former president gave him. Published in London in 1811, it was *The Whole Historical Dramas of William Shakespeare.*

When Clinton spoke, he said that people like Abed "are proving without a doubt that one person can change the world." Abed might have argued that it was not one, but 57,000 people. One person had been at the helm, however, and BRAC has certainly changed much in the world.

On top of the world: Abed and Nobel Laureate Wangari Maathai at the Clinton Global Initiative Awards in 2007 (Photo by Susan Davis)

The award was given on the occasion of the second Annual Meeting of the Clinton Global Initiative, which brings together leaders from business, NGOs, and government to devise solutions to the world's most pressing development challenges in education, health, and poverty alleviation. Here was the forty-second President of the United States, now retired, taking up a challenge articulated by the thirty-second president, almost seven decades earlier.

In January 1941, 11 months before the United States entered the Second Word War, Franklin D. Roosevelt addressed the United States Congress and spoke of a future world founded on what he called "four essential human freedoms."[2]

> The first is freedom of speech and expression—everywhere in the world. The second is freedom of every person to worship God in his own way—everywhere in the world. The third is freedom from want—which, translated into world terms, means economic understandings which will secure to every nation a healthy peacetime life for its inhabitants—everywhere in the world. The fourth is freedom from fear—which, translated into world terms, means a worldwide

reduction of armaments to such a point and in such a thorough fashion that no nation will be in a position to commit an act of physical aggression against any neighbor—anywhere in the world.

He concluded by saying that this was "no vision of a distant millennium." Rather, it was "a kind of world attainable in our own time and generation."

Roosevelt's vision of a future world went far beyond any previous political articulation of the preconditions for sustainable peace. It went beyond anything contained in the Covenant of the League of Nations, which had set out to prevent war for all time, but which spoke hesitatingly about anything that might be required to meet this objective, beyond treaties, investigations, and munitions.

Roosevelt may have had his timing wrong, but he was not wrong about the need for a fundamentally different appreciation of the essential ingredients for a peaceful world. A year later, he and Winston Churchill would create the concept of a United Nations joining together "to defend life, liberty, independence, and religious freedom and to preserve human justice in their own lands as well as in other lands."[3] Less than four years after that, the representatives of 50 nations would gather in San Francisco to sign the Charter of the United Nations "to save succeeding generations from the scourge of war." The Charter spoke of "fundamental human rights . . . of the equal rights of men and women and of nations large and small." And it spoke of the need "to promote social progress and better standards of life in larger freedom."[4]

"In larger freedom" is almost a throwaway line, but one that would be recalled 60 years later by UN Secretary-General Kofi Annan. He wrote:

> When the UN Charter speaks of "larger freedom," it includes the basic political freedoms to which all human beings are entitled. But it goes far beyond them, encompassing what President Franklin Roosevelt called "freedom from want" and "freedom from fear." Both our security and our principles have long demanded that we push forward all these frontiers of freedom, conscious that progress on one depends on and reinforces progress on the others.[5]

Much of this has been forgotten in a world that seems determined to cast security into a purely military context with high-visibility aid projects aimed more at winning hearts and minds (and perhaps some contracts down the road) than anything else. One might have thought that kind of thinking had passed or that it should have. Today's threats do include war, civil unrest, organized crime, and terrorism. But these do not spring wholly formed from virgin soil. Nor do they stop as they once did at national borders. Similarly, borders are no defense against infectious disease, environmental degradation, mass migration, and poverty. All of these threats travel easily in today's globalized world. The price of our inattention to the four freedoms is the ever-increasing emergency action required to quell uprisings and war, to save people whose poverty makes them vulnerable to an earthquake or a tsunami, or to halt an avian flu pandemic in places where local capacities to do so are close to zero. We spend between US$4 and 5 billion a year on UN peacekeepers to end wars in countries like Sierra Leone, Liberia, and the Congo, but a tenth of that to prevent their recurrence. In Afghanistan, we spend a king's ransom trying to defeat those who thrive on the absence of things we treat as an afterthought.

Abed and his colleagues understood, after their first bruising in Sulla, that the importance of living in dignity was paramount. Rights, including legal rights, children's rights, and rights for women and for men, were cornerstones of long-term development, and they were keys that would open the door to other rights, including education, health, shelter, and income. Kofi Annan said it well:

> A world in which every year eleven million children die before their fifth birthday, almost all from preventable causes, and three million people of all ages die from AIDS, is not a world of larger freedom.

Abed and his colleagues understood the importance of individual initiative, but they also understood the need to create the conditions that would allow initiative to grow. They understood that the market could generate an untold number of livelihoods, but they also understood there is no such thing as a free market in the rural areas of Bangladesh, Afghanistan, and Africa. If enterprise was to work, supply chains and opportunities had to be created for inputs and marketing to go along with the training and finance required. They also understood that, if they could get the mix right (education, health, and enterprise), they could take it to scale. Or rather they understood that, where tens of millions live in abject poverty and governments are weak, small demonstrations of what can be done are not enough. They have to be taken to scale, or they have little value.

"Small is beautiful," Abed said, "but big is necessary."

E.F. Schumacher, who wrote *Small Is Beautiful*, generated the appropriate technology movement in the 1970s. The subtitle of Schumacher's book was "Economics As If People Mattered," a good tagline for everything BRAC has accomplished. Abed's gift lies in taking many small things and putting them together into a whole that is much larger than the sum of the parts, always remembering that people matter.

A newcomer, someone with degrees from Oxford and LSE and a PhD in development studies from the University of Sussex, arrived at BRAC recently, expecting to find genius around every corner. What struck her instead was the ordinariness of everything. The component parts were ordinary, and they were all based on ordinary common sense. She discovered that the magic lies in how it all fits together, making ordinary things happen in extraordinarily difficult situations and turning the whole into something quite amazing.

In a 2006 interview, Abed said something about his son Shameran thinking his father had not accomplished very much. Confronted with this, Abed talked about a discussion he has obviously had with Shameran more than once.

> Shameran believes that politics are the only way to change society. That's why I said he thinks I haven't accomplished very much. It's one way of thinking—that in order to change society, you need to have power. But when you think about it, real change in society comes not so much through politics; it is through ideas. Ideas change thinking and ways of doing things. Politicians don't do very much of that.

But he is wrong about Shameran's view of his accomplishments. The son is immensely proud of what the father has accomplished. Perhaps seeing firsthand what is possible, however, he is as impatient for change as his father has become in recent years. Abed says:

> My only regret is that I didn't move faster; that I didn't take on more, earlier. It took thirty years for us to really begin to expand. Steve Jobs' wife, Lorraine, asked me why it had taken BRAC thirty years to come out of Bangladesh—to begin to work in Africa. I said, "Lorraine, you live in the first world; you think globally. We didn't think globally in those days. We thought only about our own country and its problems. It took me thirty years to think that maybe we were ready to go global."

He recognizes that fate works in odd ways, and he knows very well that his ambitions were once limited. When he lived in England, he campaigned for the communist candidate in Hampstead, developed an appreciation of great art and architecture, and mused about someday retiring to Tuscany.

If the cyclone and the liberation war hadn't happened, I might still be working for an oil company, or retired like all my friends in Shell Oil. One is in Maryland, another is in Texas, another in California. They're all abroad and their children are all industrial bankers.

He laughs, perhaps thinking of his own son and daughter and the ways in which they have chosen to work for change in Bangladesh.

He recalls the personal tragedies in his life:

These things are part of human existence, but I suppose having BRAC helped me to get over the tragedies more easily than if I didn't have a permanent preoccupation. There is only one life to live, and if you can leave something behind in terms of improving other people's lives—improving the world in whatever small way you can—that is what I look for. That is what drives me.

Notes

1. Rumee Ali, "BRAC Enterprises and How They Relate to Development," (Dhaka: BRAC, December 2007).

2. http://www.americanrhetoric.com/speeches/fdrthefourfreedoms.htm.

3. "Joint Declaration of the United Nations on Cooperation for Victory, January 1st, 1942," http://www.presidency.ucsb.edu/ws/index.php?pid=16169

4. Charter of the United Nations, San Francisco, June 26, 1945.

5. Kofi Annan, "In Larger Freedom: Decision Time at the UN," *Foreign Affairs,* May/June 2005, http://www.foreignaffairs.org/20050501faessay84307/kofi-annan/in-larger-freedom-decision-time-at-the-un.html.

Glossary

Many words used in English have their origins in Indian languages: *curry, toddy, cheroot, loot, chintz, calico, shawl, typhoon, monsoon, catamaran, nabob, buggy, veranda*. A *bungalow* was a style of house common in Bengal. A *dam* was a small Indian copper coin; hence, *to give a dam*. Several *Bangla* words are used in this book, and their meaning will be clear enough with the first usage. This glossary explains some of them further.

bhai	brother
bundh	an artificial embankment; a dam, dyke, or causeway
coir	fiber from the outer husk of the coconut, used for making matting, ropes, and twine
deshi	Bangla, meaning "of the country"; a *deshi* chicken is a local variety
dheki	a wooden device for husking paddy to make rice
factory	a trading establishment at a foreign port; the manager was known as the *factor*
gonokendra	*gono* means center; *kendra* means people or public; *gonokendra* is BRAC's term for a community center
gur	homemade sugar
hartal	a general strike
khal	a drainage canal
khas	land held by the government
lungi	a floor-length sarong-like cloth tied around the waist; the most common garment of male apparel in Bangladesh
nakshi kantha	traditional embroidered quilt

nawab	a title of rank, like a peerage, without necessarily having any office attached; sometimes corrupted as *nabob.*
purdah	literally, *curtain;* the Muslim practice of keeping men from seeing women
samity	committee or group
Sharia law	Islamic religious law, derived from the Koran as the word of God, the example of the life of the prophet Muhammad, and fatwas (the rulings of Islamic scholars)
shebika	female volunteer worker
shebok	male volunteer worker
sonar Bangla	golden Bengal
thana	a political jurisdiction with its own police station; Bangladesh is divided into six administrative divisions. Divisions are subdivided into 64 districts (*zila*). These are further subdivided into *upazila* (subdistricts) and *thana* ("police stations"). Each thana, except those in metropolitan areas, is divided into *unions,* each union comprising several villages.
upazila	see *thana*
zamindar	a landholder paying revenue directly to the government

Acronyms

BRAC	Bangladesh Rehabilitation Assistance Committee; Bangladesh Rural Advancement Committee; Building Resources Across Communities
CFPR	Challenging the Frontiers of Poverty Reduction
CIDA	Canadian International Development Agency
DFID	Department for International Development (UK)
DOTS	Directly Observed Therapy (Short course)
GSS	Gonoshahajjo Sangstha (a Bangladeshi NGO)
ICDDR,B	International Centre for Diarrheal Disease Research, Bangladesh (known locally as "the Cholera Lab")
ICT	information and communication technologies
IGVGD	Income Generation for Vulnerable Group Development
IRDP	Integrated Rural Development Program
MDG	Millennium Development Goals
NFPE	Non Formal Primary Education
ORS	Oral Rehydration Solution
ORT	Oral Rehydration Therapy
ORW	Oral Replacement Worker
OTEP	Oral Therapy Extension Program
Oxfam GB	Oxfam Great Britain
PEDP	Primary Education Development Program

SIDA	Swedish International Development Agency
SME	small and medium enterprise
SWAp	Sector-Wide Approach
TARC	Training and Resource Centre
UNDP	United Nations Development Program
UNICEF	United Nations Children's Fund
USAID	Unites States Agency for International Development
WHO	World Health Organization

Selected Bibliography

This bibliography contains the principal works that have been used. Details of books, studies, reports, and articles that have been cited only once are contained in individual endnotes. In 1983, the spelling of the name of Bangladesh's capital city was changed from Dacca to Dhaka, hence the different spellings in the bibliography and endnotes.

Abdullah, Tahrunessa A., and Sondra A. Zeidenstein. *Village Women of Bangladesh: Prospects for Change.* Oxford: Pergamon Press, 1982.

Ahmad, Kamruddin. *The Social History of East Pakistan.* Dacca: Amina Khatun, 1967.

Ali, Tariq. *Military Rule or People's Power.* New York: Morrow, 1970.

———. *A Sociopolitical History of Bengal and the Birth of Bangladesh.* Dacca: Zahiruddin Mahmud Inside Library, 1975.

Ashoka. *Achieving the Millennium Development Goals: Strategies from F.H. Abed.* Arlington, Va.: DVD, 2005.

———. *Innovator for the Poor: The Story of Fazle H. Abed and the Founding of BRAC.* Arlington, Va.: DVD, 2005.

———. *Thinking Big and Scaling Up: Insights from F.H. Abed.* Arlington, Va.: DVD, 2005.

Bornstein, David. *The Price of a Dream.* New York: Simon and Schuster, 1996.

BRAC. *The Net: Power Structure in Ten Villages.* Dhaka: BRAC, 1983.

———. *Peasant Perceptions: Famine, Credit Needs, and Sanitation.* Dhaka: BRAC, 1984.

———. *The State of Governance in Bangladesh 2006.* Dhaka: Institute of Governance Studies, BRAC University, 2006.

———. *A Tale of Two Wings: Health and Family Planning Programmes in a Upazila in Northern Bangladesh.* Dhaka: BRAC, 1990.

————. *Who Gets What and Why: Resource Allocation in a Bangladesh Village.* Dhaka: BRAC, 1984.

Carr, Marilyn, Martha Chen, and Renana Jhabvala, eds. *Speaking Out: Women's Economic Empowerment in South Asia.* London: IT Publications, 1996.

Chambers, Robert. *Rural Development: Putting the Last First.* Burnt Mill, Essex: Longman Scientific & Technical, 1983.

Chen, Martha Alter. *A Quiet Revolution: Women in Transition in Rural Bangladesh.* Cambridge Mass.: Schenkman Publishing, 1983.

Chowdhury, Mushtaque, and Richard Cash. *A Simple Solutions: Teaching Millions to Treat Diarrhoea at Home.* Dhaka: University Press, 1996.

Dani, Ahmad Hasan. *Dacca.* Dacca: Asiatic Press, 1962.

Dichter, Thomas, and Malcolm Harper. *What's Wrong with Microfinance?* Rugby: Practical Action, 2007.

Dignard, Louise, and José Havet, eds. *Women in Micro- and Small-Scale Enterprise Development.* Boulder, Col.: Westview, 1995.

Edwards, Michael, and David Hulme, eds. *Making a Difference: NGOs and Development in a Changing World.* London: Earthscan, 1992.

Faaland, Just, and J.R.Parkinson. *Bangladesh: The Test Case for Development.* London: Hurst & Co., 1976.

Gustavsson, Styrbjorn. *Primary Education in Bangladesh: For Whom?* Dhaka: University Press, 1990.

Harper, Malcolm. *Credit for the Poor: Cases in Microfinance.* London: IT Publications, 1998.

Hartmann, Betsy, and James Boyce. *A Quiet Violence: View from a Bangladesh Village.* London: Zed, 1983.

Holloway, Richard. *Supporting Citizens' Initiatives: Bangladesh, NGOs, and Society.* London: IT Publications, 1998.

Hye, Hasnat Abdul. *Below the Line: Rural Poverty in Bangladesh.* Dhaka: University Press, 1996.

Khan, Azizur Rahman. *The Economy of Bangladesh.* London: Macmillan Press, 1972.

Khan, Azizur Rahman, and Mahabub Hossain. *The Strategy of Development in Bangladesh.* London: Macmillan, 1989.

Lifschultz, Lawrence. *Bangladesh: The Unfinished Revolution.* London: Zed, 1979.

Lovell, Catherine H. *Breaking the Cycle of Poverty: The BRAC Strategy.* West Hartford, Conn.: Kumarian, 1992.

Mascarenhas, Anthony. *The Rape of Bangla Desh.* Delhi: Vikas Publications, 1972.

Muhith, A.M.A. *Bangladesh: Emergence of a Nation.* Dacca: Bangladesh Books International, 1978.

Olsen, Viggo. *Daktar: Diplomat in Bangladesh.* Old Tappan N.J.: Spire Books, 1973.

Rondinelli, Dennis A. *Development Projects as Policy Experiments.* London: Routledge, 1993.

Sachs, Jeffrey D. *The End of Poverty: Economic Possibilities for Our Time.* New York: Penguin, 2005.

Smillie, Ian, and John Hailey. *Managing for Change: Leadership, Strategy, and Management in Asian NGOs.* London: Earthscan, 2001.

Stevens, Robert D., Hamza Alavi, and Peter J. Bertocci. *Rural Development in Bangladesh and Pakistan.* Honolulu: University Press of Hawaii, 1976.

Timm, Richard W. *Forty Years in Bangladesh: Memoirs of Father Timm.* Dhaka: Caritas, 1995.

Van Schendel, Willem. *Reviving a Rural Industry: Silk Producers and Officials in India and Bangladesh; 1880s to 1980s.* Dhaka: University Press, 1995.

Yunus, Muhammad, with Alan Jolis. *Banker to the Poor; Microlending and the Battle against World Poverty.* New York: Public Affairs, 1999.

———. *Creating a World without Poverty: Social Business and the Future of Capitalism.* New York: Public Affairs, 2007.

Index

About the Author

Ian Smillie has lived and worked in Africa and Asia. He was a founder of the Canadian development organization, Inter Pares, and was executive director of CUSO from 1979 to 1983. He was an adjunct professor at Tulane University in New Orleans from 1998 to 2001. During 2000, he served on a UN Security Council expert panel investigating the links between illicit weapons and the diamond trade in Sierra Leone. He is an associate of the Feinstein Center at Tufts University.

His latest books are *Patronage or Partnership: Local Capacity Building in Humanitarian Crises* (Kumarian, 2001); *Managing for Change: Leadership, Strategy, and Management in Asian NGOs* (with John Hailey, Earthscan, 2001); and *The Charity of Nations: Humanitarian Action in a Calculating World* (with Larry Minear, Kumarian, 2004).

He serves as research coordinator on Partnership Africa Canada's Diamonds and Human Security Project and is an NGO participant in the intergovernmental Kimberley Process, which has developed a global certification system for rough diamonds. He is chairman of the Diamond Development Initiative, a new international NGO working with Africa's 1.3 million artisanal diamond miners.

He was appointed to the Order of Canada in 2003.

Also From Kumarian Press . . .

Microcredit and Microfinance:

The Poor Always Pay Back: the Grameen II Story
Asif Dowla and Dipal Barua

More Pathways Out of Poverty
Edited by Sam Daley-Harris and Anna Awimbo

Savings Services for the Poor
Edited by Madeline Hirschland

The Commercialization of Microfinance: Balancing Business and Development
Edited by Deborah Drake and Elisabeth Rhyne

New and Forthcoming:

How the Aid Industry Works: An Introduction to Development Studies
Arjan de Haan

The Myth of the Free Market: The Role of the State in a Capitalist Economy
Mark Martinez

Reluctant Bedfellows: Feminism, Activism and Prostitution in the Philippines
Meredith Ralston and Edna Keeble

Coping With Facts: A Skeptic's Guide to the Problem of Development
Adam Fforde

Visit Kumarian Press at **www.kpbooks.com** or
call **toll-free 800.232.0223** for a complete catalog.

green press
INITIATIVE

Kumarian Press is committed to preserving ancient forests and natural resources. We elected to print this title on 30% post consumer recycled paper, processed chlorine free. As a result, for this printing, we have saved:

3 Trees (40' tall and 6-8" diameter)
1,544 Gallons of Wastewater
1 million BTU's of Total Energy
94 Pounds of Solid Waste
321 Pounds of Greenhouse Gases

Kumarian Press made this paper choice because our printer, Thomson-Shore, Inc., is a member of Green Press Initiative, a nonprofit program dedicated to supporting authors, publishers, and suppliers in their efforts to reduce their use of fiber obtained from endangered forests.

For more information, visit www.greenpressinitiative.org

Environmental impact estimates were made using the Environmental Defense Paper Calculator. For more information visit: www.papercalculator.org.

 Kumarian Press, located in Sterling, Virginia, is a forward-looking, scholarly press that promotes active international engagement and an awareness of global connectedness.